The Spy Who Changed the World

Mike Rossiter

headline

First published in 2014 by
HEADLINE PUBLISHING GROUP

First published in paperback in 2015 by
HEADLINE PUBLISHING GROUP

1

Cataloguing in Publication Data is available from the British Library

Paperback ISBN 978 0 7553 6566 1

Typeset in Miller by Palimpsest Book Production Limited,
Falkirk, Stirlingshire

Printed and bound in Great Britain by
Clays Ltd, St Ives plc

Headline's policy is to use papers that are natural, renewable and recyclable
products and made from wood grown in sustainable forests. The logging and
manufacturing processes are expected to conform to the environmental
regulations of the country of origin.

HEADLINE PUBLISHING GROUP
An Hachette UK Company
338 Euston Road
London NW1 3BH

www.headline.co.uk
www.hachette.co.uk

ACKNOWLEDGEMENTS

I could not have written this book without the significant assistance of several people. The archive research was not limited to the United Kingdom, and I would like to thank Christina Overmeyer for the help she gave me researching material in Germany. She spent many hours negotiating with the BStU, the archive of files maintained by the East German Secret Police in Berlin, and several days translating the findings of the archivist assigned to the case, Frau Gudrun Wenzel. Christina also met me in Berlin for a search through the records of the Bundesarchiv and then translated the results. This was a reversal of roles for us, because I first met Christina as a young au pair looking after my sons and trying to improve her English, and she has now just completed her Masters at Beyreuth University.

A successful search of several archives in Moscow for material on Klaus Fuchs and Grete Keilson was carried out for me with great enthusiasm and initiative by Margarita Bolytcheva, a young journalism student at Moscow University, who has a great future ahead of her I am sure. The results of this, and a variety of other Russian source material gathered from various libraries, was translated for me by Angela

Spindler-Brown, with whom I have worked over the years on many Russian adventures as a translator, archive researcher and producer. My original visit to the Kurchatov Institute would have been impossible without her, and we went on subsequently to visit chemical warfare camps and other KGB archives for further documentaries. I am very lucky to be able to call on the assistance of all three people.

The book would not have been published without the help and advice of my agent Luigi Bonomi, whom I once saw referred to in print as "cuddly". I am not sure of that, and I value more his honesty and optimism. Simon Thorogood, at Headline, commissioned me to write *The Spy Who Changed the World* and has not only guided it through the publishing process, but sat and listened over coffee when I thought the project was getting out of hand. The copy editor Brenda Updegraff has gone over my text, made it readable, pointed out my mistakes, explained why some sections were not really working and struggled under a very tight deadline to get the book into decent shape. I am lucky to be able to work with these three people as well.

I finally have to thank my wife Anne, and my two sons Max and Alex, who are by now immune to the problems of living with a writer. I'm lucky to have them in my life.

This is a story that contains some difficult scientific concepts and I have tried to simplify them as much as possible to help the flow of the narrative. I am not a nuclear physicist and I have probably made some mistakes; these and any other errors that may be noticed are my responsibility, as of course are the opinions and interpretations contained in the book.

Mike Rossiter, March 2014

Contents

Acknowledgements v
Introduction: A Trip to Moscow 1

ONE. Trinity 13

TWO. The Interview 21

THREE. The Commitment 32

FOUR. We'll Always Have Paris 44

FIVE. Asylum 54

SIX. Interned 67

SEVEN. The Biggest Secret 77

EIGHT. A Lady from Banbury 92

NINE. Allies in Name 109

TEN. Mission to New York 120

ELEVEN. Camp Y 134

TWELVE. The End Result 147

THIRTEEN. After the Bomb 162

FOURTEEN. Dangerous Days   178

FIFTEEN. Pillar of the Establishment   190

SIXTEEN. The Third Contact   204

SEVENTEEN. The Next Big Thing   216

EIGHTEEN. A Family Affair   233

NINETEEN. The Hunt   240

TWENTY. Hey Joe   255

TWENTY-ONE. Trailing Mr. Fuchs   268

TWENTY-TWO. The First Encounter   277

TWENTY-THREE. One Step Forward, Two Steps Back   290

TWENTY-FOUR. Confession   300

TWENTY-FIVE. Trial   318

TWENTY-SIX. A Visit from the FBI   335

TWENTY-SEVEN. Legacy   347

Epilogue: Fuchs: the Final Chapter?   363
Bibliography   373
Index   379

Introduction:
A Trip to Moscow

Just how big a spy was Klaus Fuchs? Fuchs was arrested and jailed in Britain in 1950 for passing secrets about atomic research to the Soviet Union. At the time, Fleet Street claimed that he was a traitor who had sold the secrets of the atom bomb to the Russians. But as the initial storm of hysteria passed on to other crises and other spies, hard facts about the Fuchs case seemed elusive, despite investigation by writers more serious and authoritative than journalists in the popular press. The well-known author Rebecca West wrote a lengthy exposé of Fuchs's treachery in *The Meaning of Treason*. Two years after the trial a book about the "atom spies", *The Traitors* by Alan Moorhead, was published and it turned out that the author had been selected and provided with enormous help by the British Security Service, MI5. Then a few years later the eminent historian Margaret Gowing turned her attention to Fuchs as a small part of her exhaustive volumes on the history of Britain's nuclear programme.

Despite all this work, facts seemed thin on the ground. True, Fuchs was a German scientist who had been a refugee from Nazi Germany, he had worked on atomic research, and his sentence of fourteen years' imprisonment had been based on his own confession. The rest seemed contradictory. Was he, as the official history of Britain's nuclear programme implies, a second-rate scientist merely handing over the work of others? Did he have any secrets to sell? Some academics suggested that the Russians would have built their bomb anyway, whether Fuchs had given them a few pointers or not. What sort of a person was he? Was he an evil conspirator or a slightly repressed man, naïve, divorced from reality, who gradually came to see the error of his ways? Was it true, as the MI5-sponsored book claimed, that their chief interrogator, William "Jim" Skardon, skilfully probed the psychology of Fuchs and persuaded him to confess?

I thought that I would get to the bottom of some of these questions several years ago, when I went to Moscow to interview someone who was intimately connected to Fuchs's work as an atomic scientist. My appointment was with Academician Georgi Flerov, a man who had played a significant role in the first Soviet atomic bomb. It was Flerov who had written a letter to the Soviet chiefs of staff in 1942 suggesting that a nuclear weapon was possible, that it was likely that scientists in the United States, Britain and Germany were already working on this question, and that the Soviet Union should start its own programme urgently.

Flerov had later travelled to Berlin, in May 1945, shortly after the defeat of Nazi Germany, dressed in the uniform of a colonel in the NKGB,[1] the Soviet State Security organization. He was hunting for German scientists who had worked

---

[1] Soviet intelligence changed its organization and its name several times over the period covered by this book. To avoid complications and unnecessary sets of initials, I will call them the OGPU before 1934 and the NKGB after that date. Soviet Military Intelligence, the GRU, was and remained a separate organization.

on the Nazi atomic programme during the war and arranging for them to go to the Soviet Union. It was not an easy invitation to refuse. Later, he had been the last scientist to leave the test tower when the first Soviet nuclear weapon was detonated.

It wasn't easy to get to see Flerov. I had first written to the Soviet Academy of Sciences, without any response. But change was in the air of the Soviet Union: Mikhail Gorbachev was in charge and the policy of openness had been announced. Towards the end of 1988, I received a telephone call from a woman at the French Embassy in London, in the scientific attaché's office. She told me that she had a message from Academician Flerov. He would be staying at a hotel and spa in Granville, on the Normandy coast, recuperating from a hip operation. Apart from the telephone number of the hotel, there was nothing more she would tell me.

In January 1989 I took a ferry from Portsmouth to St.-Malo. Despite the talk about reform in Moscow, the Cold War was not yet over. Leaving Portsmouth, the ferry passed close to a Russian "trawler", moored just outside the 3-mile limit. Its upper works supported a huge array of aerials and satellite receivers, monitoring the naval base at Portsmouth. It was evening, and the ferry's navigation lights reflected brightly off the dark sea, which was already showing signs of an expected storm. It became so rough that we could not complete the journey and docked instead at Cherbourg. At five in the morning I was on a coach that took the long coast road to St.-Malo.

Georgi Flerov was a short, bald man in his seventies, with bushy, prominent eyebrows. He had a penetrating glance, accompanied by a slightly humorous expression. We talked for about four hours, about his experiments with plutonium, his letter to the chiefs of staff and, more importantly, about arrangements to film him at the Kurchatov Institute in Moscow, which had been the first Soviet centre established for research into atomic weapons. It was named after Igor Kurchatov, the young and energetic scientist who had headed the Soviet bomb programme, and who had directed Flerov's work leading up to the first explosion. He also mentioned that he would like us to film at his Joint Nuclear Research Institute in Dubna, where he was the emeritus professor, but he would have to negotiate separate permission for this.

I asked Flerov about the role of spies like Klaus Fuchs. He said that the information that they had supplied had saved some time, maybe one or two years at most. But everything had to be worked out, and the conventional explosives, the reactors and the plutonium had to be made in the Soviet Union by Russian scientists.

Flerov was still recuperating from his operation, and after four hours of conversation he became tired. He confirmed that he would make the arrangements for my visit to Moscow, and I left.

On the ferry back to Portsmouth I thought more about what Flerov had said. He seemed not to want to talk about the role of espionage, or the contribution of the German scientists towards the work of their Soviet counterparts. But if the information they supplied had really saved two years, then that was a long time. After all, it had taken the US only three years to build a bomb. Two years of money and labour saved was not something to be easily dismissed.

Four months later, I was on an Aeroflot flight to Moscow. The arrangements had been impossibly complicated, and permission to interview Flerov at the Kurchatov Institute had been granted only on the condition that I would use a Soviet film crew, something that I had been reluctant to accept. As it turned out, the compromise was a mistake, but that's another story.

It was my first visit to Moscow and what I discovered came as a profound shock. A British diplomat I once interviewed told me that the Soviet Union was just Upper Volta with rockets. This was a judgement I found harsh. As a young boy I had been excited by Yuri Gagarin, the first man in space, a Russian as well, and thought the diplomat was arrogant and patronizing.

Ironically, I had been given a room in the Hotel Cosmos, on the outskirts of Moscow, past the outer ring road near to the Science Park and Kosmonaut Museum that celebrates the successes of the Russian space programme. The hotel is a massive building in the shape of a huge curved wall, with a broad spread of steps leading down to the road and, incongruously, a statue of Charles de Gaulle looking towards the heroic arch at the entrance to the park. The Cosmos was built to house foreign visitors to the 1980 Moscow Olympics and had 1,700 rooms. It was now being used by Intourist to corral visiting Western businessmen, invited to Moscow by various government departments in the first flush of Gorbachev's effort at liberalization. The lobby and bars were full of Russian women and their pimps; they seemed to have no trouble getting past the security men at the doors, who were there to stop ordinary Russians from entering. Our Russian coordinator, who met me at the airport, explained that this was because the hotel was a hard-currency area, and that ordinary Russians would not be able to buy anything anyway. She seemed oblivious to the transactions going on at the tables around us in the bar, although it was true that the Russians were selling, not buying.

Reports in the British press about the moribund Soviet economy had not prepared me for the truth. Outside the hotel, boys of ten or eleven would rush up to any foreigner, offering Red Army cap badges or a variety of Party lapel pins in return for dollars or cigarettes. I took the metro to Red Square and went to the famous GUM store, which everybody referred to as the Soviet Harrods. There was nothing on the shelves. I found one or two bakers, which were crowded with aggressive shoppers who seemed resentful at my presence. Returning to the hotel, I stopped at a small corner shop. It was grimy, the bare floorboards caked in dirt, and all that was on display was a crate of shrivelled potatoes. The hotel restaurant seemed to be as short of food as the Moscow shops. Breakfasts were a chaotic affair, with crowds of suited foreigners chasing trays of bread rolls, or hardboiled eggs, with never enough to go round. At night the only meal available was pickled fish and deep-fried chicken Kiev.

One businessman I met was the director of an English company producing heavy-duty laptop computers. He'd been invited to Moscow by the Ministry of Heavy Industry, a euphemism for the state-owned arms manufacturers, lured by a teaching deal and an offer to purchase five thousand of his expensive laptops. This would have netted his company £1 million, a decent sum in 1989. His first day had been as he expected. His driver picked him up promptly and took him to an office to address a classroom of middle-ranking bureaucrats on networks and the values of mobile computing. After three days, his driver was picking him up at eleven o'clock and half the members of his seminar didn't turn up. At the start of the second week, he had stopped going altogether because his driver had vanished. One day he was driven instead to a government office where he was asked if he would consider a barter deal: his five thousand laptops for several million pairs of shoes. He had taken this offer seriously, but his company in the UK had told him no one was prepared to buy Russian shoes at any price. He remained in the Cosmos, in limbo.

What, I wondered, would Fuchs have made of this society? Was this what he had spied for?

On my second day, Flerov arranged to pay me a visit. In my naïvety, I did not think that he would be able to negotiate the strict security and the hordes of touts in the lobby. But I saw him walking with a slight limp down the corridor towards me. He was calm and unruffled. He had arrived in a huge black ZiL, a limousine used by high-ranking officials and Party leaders, and he had walked unobstructed into the hotel. He stayed with me for an hour, and said that he was sorry that the visit to Dubna had not been authorized; however, he would be able to tell us everything we wanted to know when we came to the Kurchatov Institute the next day.

What he went on to say revealed more about his motives for talking to me. He knew that the US work on the atomic bomb, the Manhattan Project, had been the subject of any number of books and documentaries, and he felt that it was time for his own comrades' efforts to be recognized. In particular, too much attention was being given to the spies. Here I detected a real passion. Flerov thought that the NKGB were now claiming far too much credit for the success of the bomb project. The scientists were now fighting back to rescue their reputation.

The next day both the Soviet camera crew and the driver of the crew bus seemed reluctant to go to the Kurchatov Institute. They spoke of it as something that was secret, and they didn't know anything about it. When we finally arrived I couldn't understand their attitude. The ochre-walled entrance was at the end of a street called Akademik Kurchatov and there was an enormous black marble bust of the scientist, at least 20 feet high, in front of its main gate, which had a large, two-storey building as a gatehouse. At the start of the work on the Soviet atomic bomb, at the height of the war against Nazi Germany, Kurchatov had vowed never to shave his beard until the project had succeeded. The black statue reproduced the long beard that developed, but it didn't show the sharp brain and quick-witted humour that he was reputed to possess. We drove in and were guided through extensive forested grounds to an old wooden dacha.

Entering, I was greeted warmly by Flerov, and was surprised to see that there were about twenty people assembled in a large room. Several tables were laid out with an enormous spread of bread, caviar, cold meat, pickles and salads. As I started to talk to some of the people in the room I realized there were several present who had also worked with Kurchatov, and they too expected to be interviewed. One woman, Zinaida Ershova, had travelled to Paris in 1937 to study under Irène Curie, Marie Curie's daughter. Ms. Ershova had worked with Kurchatov in Moscow from the very beginning.

The film crew had set up the camera and lights in an alcove separated by some folding doors from the main room where the buffet was laid out. I noticed that the old atomic veterans had arranged their chairs in a circle so that they could observe the interview. I thought that this wouldn't help if Flerov wanted to say anything indiscreet, but I was running out of time.

As we started filming, Flerov began to describe his impressions of Kurchatov and to tell his by now fairly well-worn story of his own letter to the High Command. His account changed little from what he had said in the spa in Granville several months before. He was not going to give away any secrets.

Then Flerov started to describe how Lavrenty Beria, head of the NKGB, had taken control of the project. This was the reason that he himself had gone to Berlin in 1945 in the uniform of an NKGB colonel. Surprisingly, he was extremely outspoken about Beria, describing him as uneducated and a thug, who understood nothing of the project. He talked about one incident when Beria asked a scientist, menacingly, if he was familiar with the inside of the Lubyanka, the NKGB's headquarters and prison. As they got closer to the first test explosion, Beria became more and more anxious about the outcome, and all the scientists knew that their lives would be forfeit if it was a failure. I had not expected Flerov to talk about this, and during a pause to begin a new roll of film I turned around to see the reaction of the other members of the institute. We were alone. The folding doors had been quietly closed behind me and the old scientists, who had been keenly observing until then, had been hidden, safely distanced from Flerov's attack on the head of the NKGB.

Flerov repeated his remarks that perhaps eighteen months or two years might have been saved by espionage, but how, and with what information exactly, he could not say. He personally had never seen any information from the NKGB; everything he did and worked on had been the result of discussions with other Soviet scientists. Kurchatov might have seen material from the spies, but it was a deep secret, a deadly secret, as anything to do with Beria was. And Kurchatov never talked about it.

Academician Flerov decided that the interview was over. He indicated politely that he had nothing more to say and rose from his chair. Ms. Ershova took his place. She was short and slim and must have been in her eighties. She started, with remarkable composure and apparent eloquence, an unbroken narrative that I found impossible to interrupt. She described the work that she did on the crucial problem of refining uranium, which she had begun in 1942. She talked about various accidents and explosions in the Moscow facility, and the scientists' complete lack of understanding about the dangers of radiation. It was astounding that she was still alive. She spoke of the changes in direction and facilities when the NKGB started to fund the research in 1943, and outlined the things that the German scientists helped with, as well as the things that they knew nothing about. She too had almost nothing to say about espionage, or any other material help from the NKGB. These things, she said, had never been talked about, nobody ever knew anything about them. The German scientists, on the other hand, had been in Moscow, and later in Sukhumi on the Black Sea; they were known, and anyway their knowledge was limited to specific things.

I left the Kurchatov Institute, and Moscow, knowing nothing more about Klaus Fuchs. A few months later the Berlin Wall collapsed and the Soviet bloc went into its final economic and political meltdown. Former officers in the NKGB—or the KGB as it became after the war—started writing their biographies, or gave highly coloured interviews to Western journalists. Some of the Soviet archives were also suddenly made available to journalists and researchers, but their files were hard to decipher and the secrets of the catalogues remained in the heads of elderly ladies who seemed to be their sole guardians.

Gradually, over the years, more and more information surfaced, in the United States and in Britain. In addition, shortly before he died in 1988, Fuchs had given an interview to an East German film crew—the first time in his life that he had talked about his work as a scientist, and as a spy. This also became available with the reunification of Germany. Some MI5 files were finally released to the National Archives, although they remain heavily censored. All this means that it is now possible to piece together more fragments of the hidden history, to put some meat on the previously skeletal story of hackneyed anecdote and disinformation that passed for so many years as the account of Klaus Fuchs and his espionage. What does this new information now reveal?

For over forty years, the world was in the grip of the Cold War, and at times Armageddon seemed frighteningly close. In 1940 nuclear warfare was science fiction. Five years later it was reality. Five years after that a nuclear arms race was under way, and five years after that, by 1955, giant thermonuclear explosions were poisoning the world's atmosphere and there seemed no limit to the destructive power that scientists could conjure out of the atom. Klaus Fuchs was connected to all of this. He played a key role in the creation of atomic weapons for each of the three wartime allies who later became the chief enemies in the Cold War, and he assisted them all in their creation of even more powerful H-bombs.

It wasn't only his own work as a mathematician and physicist that contributed to the nuclear standoff. It was his politics and his belief in the need for political action that became a catalyst for the birth of the nuclear age. An age which, of course, has not ended, merely changed its form. Klaus Fuchs was the most important spy of the twentieth century—a spy who changed the world.

ONE

Trinity

K laus Fuchs stood in a crowd of scientists and guest visitors on the crest of some high ground known as Compania Hill. It was 4.30 on a dark and cold morning in New Mexico on 16 July 1945. The disparate group on the hill had been building up since two o'clock, climbing out of army buses, stiff-limbed and shivery after the night drive from Los Alamos. As they did so, they looked east towards a faraway tower illuminated by the white beams of searchlights. The weather had been foul that night, with strong, buffeting winds of 30 miles an hour, rain and lightning adding to the drama and tense uncertainty of the occasion.

Fuchs was a boyish-looking man of thirty-four, slim, with a full bottom lip and a quizzical way of staring through his spectacles that seemed calculated to disarm. He lit a cigarette and glanced around, picking faces out of the darkness. There was his nominal boss, Hans Bethe, head of the Theoretical Division, a brilliant physicist, a fellow German and, like Fuchs, a refugee from the Nazis. Fuchs had great respect for Bethe, not just for his intellect but also for his patience and strength of character. Fuchs recognized several others. There was his friend and colleague Rudolf Peierls, head of the British scientists at Los Alamos, a German Jew from Berlin with whom Fuchs had worked since joining him at Birmingham University in 1941. There was the Hungarian Edward Teller, another theoretical physicist whom Fuchs knew had a powerful intellect, but who was also stubborn, with a giant ego. Impatient with Bethe, Teller had walked out of the Theoretical Division, ironically making space for Fuchs and Peierls to take over his work.

James Chadwick had travelled all the way from Washington to be there. A Nobel prizewinner, he was in charge of the British Scientific Mission to the United States, and therefore in charge of Fuchs and Peierls. Chadwick was part of that British nuclear physics aristocracy who had studied under the early giants like Hans Geiger and Ernest Rutherford, and whose discovery of the subatomic particle called the neutron had paved the way for the event that they had all assembled here to watch.

On top of the tower, barely visible 15 miles away across the valley floor, was a small corrugated-iron hut. In it was an assembly of curiously shaped blocks of high explosive, formed to make a sphere about 1.5 metres in diameter. Inside this globe sat two pieces of a rare and exotic metal called plutonium. They too were joined in the shape of a sphere, but much smaller, about 15 centimetres in diameter. The two halves of the sphere of plutonium were plated in a thin coat of shiny nickel and gold. Plutonium was so radioactive that it was warm to the touch; one scientist described it as like holding a baby rabbit. Its very existence was highly secret, and its formation into the small, finely machined artefact that nestled in this cradle of high explosive was what the group of young scientists on the hill, and the hundreds more in the base camp and in the instrument bunkers closer to the tower, had all been striving for.

Fuchs had no precise idea of the size of the effort

involved, but he knew that in fact the intricate assembly of explosive and metal represented the culmination of the work of thousands of scientists and engineers, from more or less the complete range of professions and disciplines that a modern society supported. The speed at which things happened in the United States constantly surprised him. Fuchs had come from bombed and blacked-out Britain, where everything was scarce or rationed and it was hard to do anything. Here in the United States the food was plentiful, the energy and resources seemed limitless.

The workers in huge mines, factories and laboratories across the whole of North America, and the scientific elites of two continents, had worked with unremitting energy to produce the object that sheltered from the winds and rain in the corrugated-iron hut on top of the tower. The whole effort had been so secret that President Harry Truman, taking office after the death of President Franklin D. Roosevelt in May, had only recently learned of it. Now here they were, after all the frustrations, delays and mistakes of an unprecedented scientific and engineering programme, with just one question remaining. Would it work?

The scientists around Fuchs and the others in the base camp knew that they bore a special responsibility for the answer. The assembly on the tower was the final expression of the science of nuclear physics, a science that was barely fifty years old. The early pioneering work on radiation by Ernest Rutherford and Marie Curie had started a process of experimentation that revealed the structure of atoms and the particles that composed them. This work also showed the possibility that the nucleus of atoms contained enormous energy, and that the atoms of some radioactive metals could release this very quickly. In precisely what form, and how quickly, were the basic questions that had occupied Fuchs, Bethe and scores of the other scientists now on Compania Hill. The assembly on the tower was the size and shape that it was not because an engineer had told them that was the easiest way to make it. Rather it was because Fuchs and his colleagues in the Theoretical Division had calculated the exact shape and size it needed to be to release the energy in the atoms of the plutonium, and release them so quickly that a huge explosion would be the result.

The small ball of plutonium would be instantly compressed when the surrounding explosives detonated and the existing radiation in the form of neutrons would enter the nucleus of other atoms and split them. This would release more neutrons to repeat the process, and it would do so at a speed that would quickly encompass all the atoms, releasing their energy simultaneously. It should create, they calculated, an enormous explosion—so big that for safety even the base camp had to be 10 kilometres away from the tower.

Already there had been some alarming questions raised about the outcome. Two days earlier a trial test of the sphere of explosives, which must detonate in perfect synchronization and create a uniform shock wave, had failed.

Bethe and others in the Theoretical Division who had been responsible for the original calculations had spent hours going over their work and looking at the trial test results. They finally concluded that they had been correct, and it was the trial test results that were wrongly recorded. So the test with the real thing was going ahead. But there was no escaping the anxiety. If any one of the mathematicians or scientists had it wrong and this highly expensive and secret sample of plutonium was wasted, then General Leslie Groves, head of the US atom bomb programme, the Manhattan Project, would be relentless in his pursuit of the culprit. Crucifixion might be a preferable option.

Many of the scientists knew that there was more than one way to get it wrong, and in the last few days there had been a lot of discussion about whether the whole project had transformed into something that they had not originally bargained for. People like Peierls, Bethe, Fuchs and other key scientists had fled the fascist regimes that spread across Europe like the Black Death in the 1920s and early 1930s. German universities were home to some of the most creative centres of theoretical physics, and everyone knew that there were German scientists prepared to carry on their work under the Nazis. The dreadful possibility that Hitler would have a nuclear weapon in his hands before the Allies had been the constant spur for everyone working on the Manhattan Project. Now things had changed. Hitler was dead. Nazi Germany had surrendered unconditionally in May. War in Europe was over, and fascism had been defeated. The war against Japan was still raging in the Pacific, but Japanese cities were being razed to the ground by raids from long-distance Boeing B-29s and everyone knew it was only a matter of time before the Japanese would also be defeated. Why was work on the atomic weapon still being relentlessly prosecuted?

Leó Szilárd, a Hungarian now naturalized as a US citizen, had first imagined the possibility of a chain reaction of nuclear fission back in 1933. He had, with the Italian Enrico Fermi, dreamed up the idea of a nuclear reactor and in 1939 had sent a letter, signed jointly with Albert Einstein, to President Roosevelt urging him to authorize work on some form of nuclear weapon.

Now he was actively lobbying against using the weapon. He arranged meetings with Robert Oppenheimer, scientific leader of the vast Manhattan Project, and General Groves. He sought out Jimmy Byrnes, who had been one of President Roosevelt's closest personal advisers. Szilárd believed simply that using the weapon—even showing the world that it existed—would start an uncontrollable arms race. He was horrified to learn that the US government's thinking was that using it against Japan would be a useful tool in negotiating with the Soviet Union about the shape of the post-war world.

Other scientists thought that, rather than being used against Japan, the bomb should be exploded somewhere remote, in a demonstration that would encourage the Japanese government to surrender.

The protests of Szilárd and others met swift rebuttal. How can we not use the bomb if it would shorten the war against Japan by several months? How many lives, of both American soldiers and Japanese civilians, would that save? The nation had invested the vast sum of $2 billion in the Manhattan Project. There had to be a visible result for that. As the arguments went back and forth, the truth gradually sank in. Scientists had created a new source of energy, whose power still had to be fully tested, but they did not control it. Politicians and the military would decide how and where it was used.

As they stood in the cold, grey dawn of the New Mexican desert, however, most of those questions had receded to the backs of their minds. There was only the one really urgent issue now: would it work?

As the time for the test drew near, conversations grew quieter. Tension rose. This had to work. A day ago, when Bethe and the others had gone through the calculations to find out why the explosives test had failed, there was the odd doubt that they had missed something, or that there had been an unforgivable mistake in an equation. Fuchs was now certain that it would work. The only question was how big an explosion, measured in tonnes of TNT equivalent, would the device produce.

Ten minutes before the scheduled detonation, a green signal rocket was fired into the air and a siren sounded at base camp, heard by the men on the mountain some seconds later. There was an expectant shifting. They had been told not to look directly at the blast for fear of being blinded.

They were to turn their backs, and welders' goggles had been offered to protect their eyesight. Now, though, as the test shot became imminent, the urge to see was overwhelming, and people made sudden last-minute decisions not to wear their goggles, or to get out of their cars and brave the ultraviolet radiation. A second rocket fired, then another blast of the siren, lonely and mournful. Five minutes to go, and men who were used to calculating in nanoseconds were gripped by a stomach-churning combination of anxiety and excitement. Would it work? Five minutes seemed endless.

Then a final rocket to mark a minute's countdown. Edward Teller, who had abandoned work on the plutonium bomb because he wanted to work on the potentially more powerful hydrogen bomb, started to cover his face with thick suntan lotion and put on heavy gloves to protect his hands from the flash. A shortwave radio squawked into life, and they heard the last seconds of the countdown.

Almost 20 miles away a bright flash appeared, and grew, filling the dark pre-dawn with a penetrating daylight, like the sun at high noon. A strange globe rose in the sky. Fuchs later remembered that it seemed alien, and magnificent, with weird flashes of blue and green pulsating on its surface. Then it expanded and was eclipsed by a huge shock wave. Fuchs and the others on Compania Hill continued to watch as the fireball seemed to subside and a great purplish column rose up into the sky. Then they heard the blast, like the crack of a gun, then duller thunder, as echoes crossed the desert and rebounded from the hills to the east.

Everyone was shocked into silence by the sight. It had worked.

As they looked up at the giant cloud that rose into the sky, it dawned on them that it was over 20,000 feet high. They had been almost blinded by an explosion that was 20 miles away. Fuchs knew that the blast had been far bigger than most of the estimates produced at Los Alamos. The men whose brainchild this had been were stunned by what they had witnessed. The results of their work had exceeded the imagination. They returned to Los Alamos, quieter, and pensive, still trying to absorb the experience of being eyewitnesses to the explosion of the first atomic weapon in the history of mankind.

Fuchs said that, as he walked away, someone asked him, "Now what will happen? How will we use this?" He replied, "It's too late to ask that."

Five days later the British physicist William Penney, who had set up experiments to study the blast effects of the explosion, held a seminar at Los Alamos. His preliminary calculations based on the first test results suggested that an equivalent bomb would destroy a city of around four hundred thousand people. Not a building left undamaged. Not a person left unharmed.

TWO

The Interview

Four and a half years later, on 19 December 1949, Klaus Fuchs was working at his desk in his office at Harwell, a former Royal Air Force base in Oxfordshire, now the home of Britain's Atomic Energy Research Establishment. Since the first nuclear explosion in New Mexico, Fuchs had become an important part of Britain's nuclear hierarchy. He was now the deputy head of the Theoretical Division of the establishment at Harwell, which was at the centre of the British government's effort to build an independent nuclear industry. There was the promise of economic benefits from nuclear energy, but more important was the development of nuclear weapons, considered vital to maintain Britain's status as a world power.

Harwell had expanded greatly since its former life as an airbase. The security perimeter was stronger, a small village of prefabricated houses had been built on surrounding land to accommodate the influx of scientific and administrative staff, and the offices and workshops had multiplied. Some of the old aircraft hangars survived, however, and now they housed Europe's first nuclear reactor, known as GLEEP, a small experimental atomic pile that had gone critical—in other words, a nuclear reaction had started—in 1947. Harwell also ran a cyclotron for research into subatomic particles, and a new electronic computer, which had started operations early that year. Fuchs sat on the various committees and working parties that managed all these facilities, as well as others around the country. A full-size nuclear reactor to produce plutonium was under construction at Windscale in Cumberland, and other sites at Capenhurst in Cheshire and Springfields in Lancashire were producing enriched uranium and plutonium for weapons research at Fort Halstead in Kent. Fuchs was busy. His experience of the first very early atomic research in Britain and later at Los Alamos, as well as his theoretical brilliance, meant that he was consulted about everything in the British nuclear programme.

Fuchs was working with many colleagues who had become friends in the years since 1933 when he had landed in the UK as a refugee student. His immediate superior was Herbert Skinner, whom he had first met when they were both studying at Bristol University shortly after Fuchs's arrival in the country. Egon Bretscher, a colleague from Los Alamos, was head of the Nuclear Physics Division at Harwell. Fuchs remained close friends with Rudolf Peierls, who had gone back to Birmingham to continue his academic career after the war but was still a consultant to the Department of Atomic Energy.

Fuchs had also become quite friendly with Harwell's head of security, a former Royal Air Force wing commander, Henry Arnold. Fuchs never complained about the strict checks on movements in and out of Harwell, or Arnold's sometimes persistent questions about visitors. In fact, he had met with Arnold a few weeks earlier to talk about a problem that was concerning him. His father Emil, a Quaker, had continued to live in Germany throughout the war. He had been imprisoned and tried by the Nazis in the 1930s, but had been treated leniently because of intense lobbying about his case from the international Quaker movement and the American Friends Service Committee.

Emil had been an active socialist, a member of the German Social Democratic Party and a pacifist. He had visited his son earlier that year, bringing with him Fuchs's nephew, Klaus Kittowski, and they had both been introduced to many of Fuchs's associates and colleagues. The problem now was that Emil had been offered a lecturing post at the University of Leipzig in the Soviet zone of Germany and he was eager to take it up.

Fuchs had kept much of his role in the bomb project at Los Alamos from his father, who was of course a pacifist. Harwell was ostensibly an establishment for research into the peaceful uses of energy, but Fuchs was in close touch with the British atom bomb project and knew that any connection with the Soviet Union would be a threat to his security clearance. He had told Arnold that his father, even at the age of seventy, was determined to take up the job in Leipzig and that he could not persuade him to do otherwise. Fuchs thought it right for Arnold to know about this and to discuss it with his superiors and the Security Service. Fuchs was not surprised, then, when Arnold knocked on his office door and told him that there was someone from MI5 who wanted to talk to him about his father.

As he went into Arnold's office Fuchs saw a stranger, tall, slim, looking older than his forty-five years, with a thick moustache. Arnold introduced them, then left them alone.

William James Skardon, or Jim as he was universally known, had driven up from London that morning. He was a former Special Branch officer who had been brought into the Security Service, or MI5, in 1942. He had questioned several former communist agents, one of whom had been an MI5 secretary who had revealed to the Communist Party of Great Britain the names of MI5 informants in its headquarters. He had gone on to interrogate Lord Haw-Haw, William Joyce, the Nazi collaborator who had broadcast German propaganda during the war and been executed for treason in 1946. Skardon was now the leading interrogator in B Branch, MI5's counter-espionage section. Opinions about him amongst his colleagues differed greatly. Peter Wright, of *Spycatcher* fame, thought he had the comforting, solid manner of a trade-union shop steward, an odd comparison for a member of MI5 to make, while Dick White, director of B Branch and later to become head of MI5 and then MI6, considered him all image and style, a friendly confessor rather than a bone-crushing interrogator.

As he sat at Arnold's desk in Harwell that day, cradling his pipe in his hand, Skardon was looking for the first time at a man about whom he had heard a great deal. Fuchs's hair was brushed back, accentuating his prominent forehead, and his round spectacles gave him an owlish appearance, adding to the image of an unworldly intellectual. Skardon kicked off the discussion by saying that the presence of his father in the Russian zone of Germany was a considerable security risk. He would have to ask Fuchs some questions, some of which might be impertinent but which would help the department to make a fair assessment of the risks involved.

Fuchs understood this. After all, it was he who had brought the whole matter of his father to the attention of the Security Service.

Skardon then started to ask Fuchs about his early background and his family. Fuchs filled in the details as best he could, and Skardon, sitting with a file in front of him, helped him with some of the dates. The Security Service had not previously known some of the things that Fuchs told Skardon. He had been politically active while a student, he explained, and had joined a national student organization that had communist affiliations. He had moved to Berlin, then, with the Nazis in power, he had been asked to take part in an international conference in Paris, organized by a well-known French communist, Henri Barbusse. The conference was part of an anti-war and anti-fascist campaign that would probably now be described as a communist front. Then he had sought asylum in the UK, where he had studied at Bristol University, and afterwards had gone on to do research at Edinburgh University. He might, he said tentatively, have gone to Switzerland in 1934 to see his brother Gerhard. Skardon didn't respond to this, so Fuchs moved on.

After Germany invaded France in May 1940 Fuchs had been interned as an enemy alien, along with many other German refugees, and sent to a camp in Canada. He had been politically active in the camp, along with two other internees, Hans Kahle and another whose surname was Abrahamson. Fuchs described some of the issues over which they had agitated. The most important had been a campaign to prevent the son of the former crown prince of Germany from becoming the camp leader, and resistance to the registration of Jews in the camp, because it was feared that these internees might be sent to Germany in exchange for Canadian prisoners of war.

Skardon had no reason to question anything that he was saying. Fuchs continued, talking about the time when he returned to Britain from Canada and started to work on the complexities of building an atomic weapon. He was probably coming to the conclusion that this interview really was about nothing more than the problem that might be caused by his father becoming a professor in the Russian zone of Germany. He continued to play his hand, describing his move to New York as part of the British Scientific Mission to the US bomb programme—the Manhattan Engineering District, as it was known. He was working flat out during that period, he said, and had little spare time for social activities.

This was the point for which Skardon had been waiting. He now revealed the one piece of information that he possessed. He looked at Fuchs and stated that in New York Fuchs had been in touch with a Soviet official or representative of the Soviet government and had passed to him information about his work.

Fuchs's mouth opened, then he smiled and said, "I don't think so."

Skardon went on to say that he was in possession of precise information which showed that Fuchs had been guilty of passing secrets to the Soviet Union. Again, he mentioned New York. Fuchs repeated, "I don't think so."

Skardon observed that this was an ambiguous reply, and Fuchs pressed him, going on the offensive, saying, "I don't understand. Perhaps you will tell me what the evidence is. I have not done any such thing."

Skardon was not prepared to reveal anything more. He had in reality very little hard information, and the fact that its source, a Soviet coded message, had been decrypted was itself so secret it could not be mentioned. So he contented himself with telling Fuchs that he was not prepared to discuss the matter; he was stating a fact.

Fuchs stepped up his denials, saying that he was unable to assist Skardon. He was not responsible for a leak, and had been doing all he could to win the war.

Skardon now shifted his ground slightly, to some information that had been supplied by the Royal Canadian Mounted Police and the FBI in the United States. The defection in 1945 of an employee of the Soviet Embassy in Ottawa had led, a year later, to the arrest of Israel Halperin, a mathematician at Queen's University in Toronto and a member of the Communist Party of Canada. Halperin had been investigated, arrested and tried for espionage, but at the end of his trial the jury had found him not guilty. However, his address book, which had been found by the RCMP, contained Fuchs's name and address in the internment camp in Canada. Curiously, it also listed Fuchs's sister, with an address in Cambridge, Massachusetts. What, Skardon wanted to know, was the reason for this? Fuchs appeared puzzled and denied all knowledge of Halperin. Then he recalled, as if suddenly remembering, that Halperin was the name of a professor to whom his sister had written, and who had sent scientific journals to Fuchs in the internment camp. However, he had, as far he knew, never met him.

"Is this typical of the evidence against me?" asked Fuchs, pressing Skardon in an attempt to find out what else had prompted this interview and what lay behind the blunt accusation that had just been levelled against him.

Skardon replied that he could not reveal his sources, in the same way that if Fuchs chose to confess, he would not break faith with him—although what that promise was really worth Skardon didn't elaborate and Fuchs didn't question.

Skardon then asked about the work that Fuchs did in New York as part of the British Mission and what the security arrangements had been. Fuchs mentioned the names of the other leading scientists: Rudolf Peierls was there, of course; Nicholas Kurti had arrived shortly before Fuchs went to Los Alamos; and there were others like Tony Skyrme and Frank Kearton. Fuchs didn't think any of those people were involved in spying. He could not remember the names of the junior staff, or recall how they were recruited. But it was unlikely that any of those people would be spies either.

Skardon had suggested by his line of questioning that any evidence he had was to do with a leak in the New York Mission. He confirmed this by continuing to ask about the arrangements that had been in place to ensure the security of the scientific papers produced there. They were duplicated and numbered, said Fuchs, but he couldn't remember any more precise details. Some were duplicated in the Mission's offices on Wall Street, and then later it was done in the offices of the Kellex Corporation, in the Woolworth Building on Broadway. The New York Mission was working on particular ways of enriching uranium to make it more radioactive for an atom bomb. Most of this work was writing theoretical papers to give to the US corporations working on the project. Kellex was a subsidiary company set up by the engineering firm M. W. Kellogg, which had a contract to build the plant for uranium enrichment at Oak Ridge in Tennessee.

Fuchs still kept all his papers in a safe in his office, he said, and a quick look at them would reveal the date when Kellex took over duplication of the reports. Fuchs phoned his secretary, who did not reply, so he took the opportunity of going to his office to bring copies of the scientific papers from the British Mission that he still had. There were ten of them, all of which Fuchs had written.

This was the first time that Skardon saw the type of work in which Fuchs was involved. He was extremely impressed. In his report of this meeting he pointed out that Fuchs was the sole author of ten out of the seventeen papers produced in New York between January and July 1944. Skardon could not, of course, understand them. They were, he wrote later, "wholly abstruse mathematical calculations, and to my unpractised eye represent extremely solid work throughout the period. He must have worked from dawn to dusk."

The interview continued, with Fuchs saying that he did sometimes take papers away from the office, and that it was possible that he had taken some of them when he visited his sister Kristel in Cambridge, Massachusetts, although he couldn't believe that either she or her husband would have used this opportunity to pass any information on. He recalled that he had made only one visit to Canada, to Montreal, in the time that he was in New York. Anyway, he had already said that he had never met Halperin.

Fuchs and Skardon stopped for lunch at 1.30 p.m. The MI5 investigator decided to let Fuchs eat on his own, to give him the chance to mull things over. Fuchs obviously had a lot to think about, but when they met again after lunch his position hadn't changed: there was nothing that he could do to help. Skardon now returned to the question of Fuchs's father, saying that the Ministry of Supply—the government department with responsibility for atomic energy development—was actively considering what to do about Fuchs and whether it would be possible for him to remain in his present position.

Skardon then made a clumsy suggestion that, if Fuchs were to cooperate with the questioning about his activities in New York, a recommendation from MI5 might make it possible for him to stay at Harwell. Fuchs for his part made it clear that, without any evidence being shown to him, it was impossible for him to help in the inquiry at all.

In fact, Fuchs continued, it was the obvious inability of Skardon to come up with any evidence at all that had stopped him from becoming angry and demanding to know why he was being accused in this way. He then went on to say that, if there was this sort of suspicion hanging over him, then it might be best for him to resign anyway. Fuchs knew how important he was to British nuclear research and he may have thought that this was the best way to remind Skardon of this fact, but it's probable that the implied threat went over Skardon's head. Even Wing Commander Arnold had been kept in the dark about Fuchs's other activities for the British government outside Harwell, and there is no evidence that Skardon, or his masters in MI5, were aware of them either.

After four hours, Skardon called it a day and prepared to head back to London. The interview with Fuchs had got him nowhere. His report sits firmly on the fence:

> I find it extremely difficult to give a conclusive view qua the guilt or innocence of Fuchs. His demeanour during our interview could have been indicative of either condition. If he is innocent, it is surprising that he should receive allegations of this kind so coolly but perhaps this squares with his mathematical approach to life. It could also be argued that he is a spy of old standing and was prepared for such an interrogation.

In case his superiors in MI5 thought that he was backsliding, however, he continued that in the light of the evidence, it was difficult to find any candidate for the suspect other than Fuchs himself.

Fuchs went back to his office in Harwell. There is no record of precisely what his thoughts were. At this time, to be accused of any connection with the Soviet Union was extremely serious. Guilty or not, it was a fatal threat to any career in nuclear research. Two years previously another British scientist, Allan Nunn May, had been arrested for handing over secrets to the Russians. Fuchs himself had seen scientists removed from Harwell because of mere suspicions, and increases in Cold War tensions meant the atmosphere was now even worse. The Russians had only recently ended their blockade of Berlin, and just four months ago it seemed that they had managed to explode their own nuclear weapon. There was much alarm in the corridors of Whitehall. After Skardon's accusation, Fuchs might have immediately moved to discuss what to do next to defend himself. He might have contacted his superiors at Harwell. Lord Cockcroft, head of the Atomic Research Establishment at Harwell, might have listened sympathetically, and would

certainly have understood more than Skardon did how
valuable Fuchs was. Or he might have spoken to a close
friend like Rudolf Peierls, who was well connected, or he
might even have sought legal advice. He did none of these
things. On returning to his office he telephoned his dentist.
His plate was hurting and he wondered if he could make
an appointment to come and have it repaired.

Fuchs was actually in a very good position after his long
conversation with William Skardon. He now knew that
there were some suspicions about him, and he knew where
they were centred. Nothing had been mentioned other than
his work in New York, and Fuchs's narrative of his life,
including his early student days in Germany, had been
listened to without question. It was a great comfort, because
it revealed how little MI5 knew about him. If he kept calm
and stuck to his story, he was safe. The only thing that could
destroy him was the truth.

THREE

The Commitment

By the time that Klaus Fuchs became a refugee in 1933, he was a committed member of the German Communist Party, an experienced activist already accustomed to living a clandestine life. He was the product of a family with a strong sense of moral principles, and of a country that had experienced a long descent into fascism.

Klaus was born on 29 December 1911, in the last golden days of peace before the start of war in Europe and the beginning of half a century of violence and terror. Eight years later, the young Klaus was living in a country that was akin to a living corpse. Two million people had died and another five million had been wounded in the First World War. By the time the armistice was signed, food rations in Germany provided about half the minimum calories needed by an active adult. Coal and fuel were scarce. People were demoralized and desperate. Blind and limbless veterans of the army joined the ranks of the unemployed and begged on the streets.

In the aftermath of the First World War, a wave of revolutions swept through the remnants of the old imperial powers. The Russian royal family had been overthrown in

1917, and the Bolsheviks had seized power and set about establishing a communist society. In most other European countries the uprisings failed. In Germany a movement of popular rebellion began in Kiel on 3 November 1918 when sailors of the German High Seas Fleet mutinied and seized their ships. After the removal of Kaiser Wilhelm on 9 November local insurrections spread throughout the country and by January 1919 there were workers' councils in Munich, Hanover, Frankfurt and Hamburg. The slogan of the sailors in Kiel, "Peace and bread", was frighteningly similar to the slogan of the Bolsheviks, and it seemed that Germany would go the way of revolutionary Russia.

There were some significant differences, however, between the chaos of Germany and the overthrow of the Russian tsar, and they profoundly affected the course of events. Most of the workers' councils in Germany were created by spontaneous movements of trade unionists, not by the German Communist Party, which barely existed as the war ended. The fundamental factor was that the German Social Democrats (SPD) were the largest and most solidly established reformist party in Europe. When the SPD had voted for war in 1915, the leaders of one of its left factions, Karl Liebknecht and Rosa Luxemburg, had themselves split from that party to form the Spartacists, a group that led many of the 1919 insurrections. Liebknecht and Luxemburg then called a conference in Berlin to establish the Communist Party of Germany, or KPD, in 1919, but its formation was too late. It was permanently overshadowed by the Social Democratic Party.

The Social Democrats were not revolutionaries. As the guardians of the parliamentary republic established at Weimar, their leader, Friedrich Ebert, moved against the threats to the new German state. He sent in troops against the sailors' councils in Kiel, and bands of armed veterans, known as Freikorps, were mobilized and provided with material support by Gustav Noske, the minister of defence. Over the next few months the various insurrections were crushed. In Berlin a workers' and soldiers' council was overthrown, and in January Liebknecht and Luxemburg were captured and murdered. In May a Freikorps stormed Munich, the centre of the self-proclaimed Bavarian dictatorship of the proletariat. A wave of killings ensued as armoured cars, flamethrowers and artillery were used to crush resistance. So the post-war Weimar Republic was established.

This was the society in which Klaus Fuchs was to grow up, but despite the privation and bloodshed around him he said that his childhood was a happy one. He shared it with an older brother and sister, Gerhard and Elisabeth, and a younger sister, Kristel. His father, Emil, was a pastor in a Lutheran church in Eisenach, in Thuringia; he was a man of great principle, a pacifist and Quaker who also joined the Social Democrats, the first pastor ever to do so. He apparently paid dearly for this decision, because the church removed him from his post and he had to move with his family to Kiel, where he took a job in the university.

Emil Fuchs had an extremely strong influence on his children, emphasizing that behaviour had to have a moral imperative, and his presence in their lives was profound and long-lasting. In later life, when Kristel realized that Klaus had worked on the atomic bomb, one of her first thoughts was how her father would be so upset—despite the fact that she was married and had not seen Emil for almost ten years. Fuchs once said that his father always did what he wanted, and it seems that he was very domineering and judgemental. Else, Fuchs's mother, committed suicide in 1931, by the ghastly expedient of drinking prussic acid. Emil wrote a long letter to Klaus on one anniversary of this event, spending more time describing the tragedy of his own life, left alone to raise his children, than on the tragic turmoil in his wife's mind that led her to kill herself in such an agonizing way.

Similarly, when his daughter Kristel became mentally ill and was struggling with a failed marriage, Emil complained to Klaus that she had never achieved anything and was a great disappointment to him. Klaus must have been deeply wounded by the suicide of his mother, but barely made any mention of it throughout his life.

Klaus became politically active, as did his brother and sister Elisabeth, as they grew into their teens. He joined the SPD and later recounted how he went to his school on an anniversary celebration of the Weimar Republic. The school building was draped in the flags of the republic, but once inside the classroom he discovered that the other pupils and some of the teachers were wearing the red-and-black badges of the old imperial flag. Fuchs defiantly pinned his SPD badge to his lapel. This enraged his schoolmates and they fell on him, ripping his badge off and throwing him out of the class.

By the time Fuchs was at Leipzig University, he had joined the Reichsbanner, the paramilitary organization set up by the Social Democrats. It was a serious move. The Reichsbanner had an estimated membership of three million in 1930 and it was highly organized, structured along military lines. The Nazis and the far right had grown, and the marauding thugs of Hitler's Sturmabteilung (SA) were eager to attack members of the SPD physically in the streets. The violence of the German political scene was all pervasive and it took courage to be an active member of a political party. Reichsbanner members acted as bodyguards for election meetings, rallies and the defence of socialist neighbourhoods. Clearly, Klaus had by now rejected his father's pacifism.

As a student it was impossible to escape the political turmoil that was engulfing Germany. The KPD, which had now grown to a respectable size and could gain 15 per cent of the votes in a general election, was heavily influenced by the Communist Party in Moscow, which by this time had been purged of the old Bolsheviks and was dominated by Stalin. The Communist International, set up by Lenin to spread the revolution, had been transformed and its activities were manipulated to suit the needs of the Soviet Union's foreign policy. In constant arguments and debates in the bars and student cafés around the university, Fuchs was dismayed by the intellectual confusion of the German Communist Party members, who often held to a line with which they privately disagreed. At that time the Party saw the Social Democrats as their biggest obstacle in Germany and attacked them with more vehemence than they did the Nazis.

In 1932 the situation came to a head with the elections for chancellor (*Reichskanzler*). The SPD took a decision not to put up a candidate, but refused to support the communists. They argued that they had to support the re-election of Paul von Hindenburg, an old war leader and a pillar of the right-wing establishment, in order to keep out Hitler. Fuchs was appalled at the decision. The Social Democrats controlled the government of the Free State of Prussia, an area that encompassed a large part of Germany and included Berlin and Hamburg. Their control of the state's police was the party's main line of defence against the violence of the Nazis and the Brownshirts, as the SA were called. Fuchs knew that a victory for Hindenburg would jeopardize this.

By now, Fuchs had moved from Leipzig University to study maths at Kiel. He had joined the Socialist Student Society, and in public meetings he started openly to support the communist candidate during the elections. It was not an easy decision for him, nor for his brother, Gerhard, or sister Elisabeth, both of whom were active members of the SPD. In fact it was Gerhard who made the first move to join the Communist Party. Klaus Gysi, who had first met Gerhard Fuchs while they were at school, remembered a long conversation that he had at the time with the two brothers. Gysi had been a member of the KPD's youth wing while he was at school and now he was about to become a full member of the Party. Their argument went on for hours, almost through the night, and they talked about the whole gamut of KPD policy, from the united front to the possibility of collaboration with the SPD. Gysi, who went on to become a member of the KPD underground in Nazi Germany and later served as a government minister in East Germany, realized that this conversation was more than just a political debate. The two brothers were on the verge of joining the Party, and for them it was a serious intellectual commitment. Gerhard joined, but Klaus Fuchs was more cautious. He worked for the communists in the election because he believed that the other parties would not be able to stop Hitler, but his collaboration with the KPD became intolerable to the SPD and they expelled him in March 1932.

Hindenburg was re-elected in April, and in June he appointed the right-wing Franz von Papen as chancellor. He immediately came to an arrangement with Hitler to remove the ban on the SA marching in uniform in return for his support in the Reichstag (the German parliament in Berlin). With this deal done, von Papen and his fellow ministers started to plan the removal of the socialist government of Prussia and that province's integration into a greater Germany. For Fuchs, the fact that the SPD remained inactive in the face of this threat was the last straw. He joined the Communist Party.

With the lifting of the ban on the SA Brownshirts that June, the latent civil war that had simmered throughout the history of the Weimar Republic came back to the boil once more. Violence on the streets rose dramatically. That same month there were seventeen political murders. In July eighty-six people died in political clashes. Also in July, the Brownshirts staged a rally and marched through Altona, a working-class suburb of Hamburg. Local workers' committees composed of SPD and KPD members mobilized to stop the fascists marching. In the fighting that followed eighteen were killed and over a hundred wounded.

Fuchs must have been aware on a daily basis of the increasing danger from the Nazi organizations on the streets. Any lefty handing out leaflets, selling the Party newspaper or even leaving a meeting would be on their guard against attack from Nazis armed with blackjacks, knuckledusters and firearms. Communists were active in their communities, and at Kiel University in the autumn term Fuchs's communist cell started to organize. He was the leader of a group known as a Nazi Commission, whose task was to engage with Nazi groups in order to split them and influence some of their members to leave the organization. It required a sense of tactics, and of course courage.

The Nazis had started a campaign against high tuition fees, and Fuchs decided that the communists would engage with them and join their campaign. By calling for direct action, which the Nazis would not support, Fuchs hoped that some of the Nazi student members would become disillusioned. This tactic, known as a united front, was a potent weapon. Fuchs talked to the Nazi leadership in the university and proposed that they should jointly organize a strike against the university authorities. The Nazis hedged, and finally Fuchs decided to expose them. The communists distributed leaflets telling students that the talks had been going on but that the Nazis were not serious about taking action. The tactic was a success, isolating the Nazis in the student body and reducing their support. In the wider world, however, Hitler and his party were going from strength to strength.

Von Papen and his colleagues used the deaths at the march in Altona to argue that the Prussian government had failed to maintain law and order, and with the backing of a decree from Hindenburg he dissolved the assembly, replacing it with his own right-wing nominees. With this job done, the Nazis reneged on the deal to maintain their support for von Papen, and by November it was clear he no longer had the votes in the Reichstag. The next two months saw manoeuvring between Hindenburg and von Papen that resulted in the appointment in January of Hitler as chancellor. Von Papen believed that the conservatives in the Reichstag would be able to control Hitler. As Alan Bullock succinctly wrote, Hitler was jobbed into office by a backstairs intrigue.

The lives of millions would ultimately be destroyed by this shabby deal, but Fuchs and thousands of fellow communists in Germany were faced with an immediate threat. The drumbeat of violence and murder rapidly escalated after Hitler took over the chancellorship in January 1933. The *Munich Post*, a conservative but anti-Hitler newspaper, was filled with stories of political assassinations. That month a socialist Reichstag deputy was murdered. In the week of 26 January the *Post* reported, "19 shot in a terrible political bloodbath". After Hitler took office, socialist newspapers in Berlin were banned and the Nazis mounted a huge parade through the city. In Prussia the ban on fascist militias, which had been lifted some months previously, was now completely reversed and they were recruited as auxiliary police.

Fuchs continued his fight. After Hitler came to power the Nazi students organized a campaign against the rector of Kiel University and the local SA militia were called on to make a show of force in front of the university. Fuchs refused to be intimidated and went to the university every day with his copies of *Die Rote Fahne*, the KPD daily newspaper. He was by now well known to the Nazis and in one of his confrontations with them the SA attacked him, beating and punching him, then carrying him from the university and throwing him in the river. He was lucky to escape with his life. As it was, he lost a few teeth and had to wear a dental plate.

Fuchs never gave up his Party activity, but it must have been obvious to him, and to many other communists, that the Nazis were going to crush any opposition when they felt strong enough.

Elections for the Reichstag were scheduled for 5 March and, as well as increasing the level of violence against their opposition, the Nazis were ramping up the propaganda war. Then, on the night of 27 February, something happened that allowed the Nazis to make their move. The Reichstag caught fire and burned to the ground. A Dutch communist, Marinus van der Lubbe, was arrested at the scene and that same night Reichsminister Hermann Göring ordered the arrest of four thousand Communist Party officials.

Fuchs learned of this the next morning when, on his way from Kiel to Berlin to take part in a KPD conference, he picked up a newspaper on the train. He was sufficiently politically astute to know immediately what the outcome would be. Whoever had started the fire, Fuchs knew that the communists would be the target of a massive crackdown by the Nazis and their right-wing allies. Under the cover of his opened newspaper, he took off his Party badge with its hammer and sickle. It would be a long time before he wore it again.

Fuchs continued his journey to Berlin and attended the now secretly held conference. He received considerable recognition for the campaigning work that he had carried out in Kiel. But those days were over. Fuchs did not return home. The government, with Hitler and his cronies now in power, called on Hindenburg to back their demands for a state of emergency. The Communist Party was banned, its regional offices and committee rooms were stormed, duplicators and typewriters were smashed. Fuchs's house in Kiel was raided by the police on 1 March, and piles of leaflets and pamphlets were taken away. Five days later the election gave Hitler a majority with 43 per cent of the votes. It was a farce. Ernst Thälmann, leader of the KPD, had been arrested on 3 March, and any of the eighty-one communist deputies who could be found were thrown into prison. The communists still managed to get over 12 per cent of the vote, but the Nazis' reign of terror had begun.

The first concentration camp was set up at Dachau, just outside Munich, on 22 March, and in Bavaria alone ten thousand communists were arrested, with the local leaders sent to the camp as the first political prisoners of the Third Reich. The whole of society had collapsed in the face of violence and fear, and a gang of political thugs had taken control of an entire country.

Fuchs was by now living underground. Remarkably, he was able to enrol at Berlin University to gain some legitimacy for his presence in the capital, but he never attended classes. He later said that he spent most of his time with the students of the Berlin Technical School, who were more active in anti-Nazi circles. He may also have worked with his brother Gerhard's wife, Karin, who taught there. While Fuchs remained in Berlin, his father was expelled from the staff of Kiel University and arrested and questioned for five weeks. The streets of Berlin—hung with banners of black and red, giant swastika flags on every official building, and filled with jackbooted Brownshirt and Nazi troops—were now a foreign country for Fuchs. A year before it would have made sense for him to stay in a group for defence against attacks by fascist gangs. Now it was important to remain alone, not to draw attention to oneself, to remain inconspicuous.

His brother, Gerhard, had moved to Berlin earlier, and so too had his sister Elisabeth. Elisabeth had married a member of the Communist Party, Gustav Kittowski, and they were all involved in underground work. Emil, their father, owned some shares in the giant chemical conglomerate IG

Farben, future manufacturers of Zyklon B, the gas used at Auschwitz. Emil sold these shares and gave the proceeds to Gerhard, Gustav and Elisabeth. They bought a few cars and set up a small car-hire company that was used to smuggle Jews and Communist Party members out of the country via fishing ports on the Baltic coast. The company also provided a courier service for the German Rote Hilfe (Red Aid), part of an international organization set up by the Comintern, the Communist International established by the Bolsheviks to coordinate policy for all the different national communist parties. The aim of Rote Hilfe was to provide aid and support to political prisoners and now it tried to establish itself in exile, along with the rest of the KPD. Two centres were set up, in Paris and Prague, where the Party hoped to be able to continue to function and to support any illegal activity in Germany.

Gerhard was active in the Berlin Communist Party, was an organizer for Rote Hilfe and was also Party organizer for a large part of northern Germany. Klaus Kittowski, his nephew, believes that Gerhard was friends with the two daughters of General Kurt von Hammerstein-Equord, an anti-Nazi General in the Wehrmacht. His daughters, Maria-Luise and Helga, were secret members of the KPD and had been informed by their father about Hitler's speech on 3 February 1933, in which he outlined to members of the General Staff his intentions to defy the Treaty of Versailles and expand German territory to the east. The information was passed through the Party apparatus to Moscow. The general's daughters also provided other information about forthcoming arrests—information that allowed many Party members to escape the clutches of the Gestapo.

What Klaus Fuchs's role was in the Party in this period is a mystery, but it is most likely that he was involved with some of the operations that his elder brother organized; we will see later that he was well aware that family connections were a good cover for political activity.

In July of 1933, the Party organization in Berlin decided that Klaus Fuchs should also go into exile. Fuchs says that he was ordered to do so to continue his studies, because they would be of benefit to the Party when Hitler was defeated. It was arranged first that he should go to Paris, where he could work for the Party in another capacity before going on to find a place in a university.

So in July he left Germany. He was a young man, still only twenty-two years old. He was highly intelligent, a very promising mathematician, but he had, over the past year and a half, become an experienced and hardened political organizer, who had witnessed at first hand the violence and brutality of fascism. Over the next few years he was to see his family practically destroyed by the Nazis. He had learned how policies of racial hatred, backed up by ruthless violence, had trapped and destroyed a society. However, his political activity during a time when fear and violence gripped Germany taught him a lesson that was to stay with him for the rest of his life. "The only people who had risen above the fear and demoralization of the victory of Hitler and the Nazis, who had kept their strength and optimism, were those who had fought. Only amongst those", he wrote many years later, "were there happy people."

The people who had fought were the communists. He was one of them.

And so he went to Paris.

FOUR

We'll Always Have Paris

Klaus Fuchs spent only a few months in Paris, but while he was there he met someone who would surface again, much, much later, to become a key part of his life. He always claimed that while he was in Paris he worked with other volunteers of the KPD in exile organizing the Congress Against War and Fascism, which was part of the very well-organized and well-funded Comintern propaganda effort. The congress was ultimately the brainchild of an entrepreneurial member of the KPD named Willi Münzenberg, who, as well as having been the youngest communist member of the Reichstag, had also put together a successful group of newspaper and magazine publishers and film production companies. He had established the congress a year earlier in Amsterdam and, while its driving force was the Comintern, it also attracted a large international following of people who were alarmed about events in Germany and believed that the old conservative governments in the West were once more allowing the world to drift towards war. The congress had therefore proved successful, and local committees Against War and Fascism had been established around the world.

The latest congress promised to be a big event, particularly after the rise to power of the Nazis, and delegates were expected from all the European organizations as well as from the United States, Australia, Canada—anywhere, in fact, where a local Communist Party was able to generate enough concern from sympathetic individuals about the rise of militarism.

We only have Fuchs's word that he was in Paris to attend the conference. It may be that he had had to leave Berlin quickly and the congress provided an opportunity to get him out of Germany so that he could wait in a safe place before going to university. Or there may have been some other, more conspiratorial reason. We will never know.

What we do know is that while he was in Paris, presumably working for the congress, Fuchs met a married German woman who was six years older than he was. Margarete Keilson—or Margot as she was known in Paris, or Grete as she was known elsewhere—was clearly attracted to him. She says that she took pity on him and invited him back for meals at her flat at the end of the day. She enjoyed his company and they had many interesting and enjoyable conversations, although in retrospect she believes that she was doing most of the talking. According to her account, her husband, Max Keilson, asked her why she brought Fuchs back to eat so often because he was poor company and had little to say, although most records suggest that Max was in Prague for much of this period.

At the time that she and Fuchs met, Grete had already spent several years working full time for the Comintern. She may or may not have had a significant influence on his later activities in Britain and Los Alamos, as we will see in due course, but it is illuminating to look at her career. It provides a taste of the type of people with whom Fuchs was associating in the KPD, and an insight into the future culture of the Party in exile.

Margarete Keilson came from a working-class family of eight children, three of whom had not survived into adulthood. She left school at the age of sixteen and trained as a stenographer, a shorthand typist. From around that time she was an active member of the KPD, doing the grassroots work of a Party member: organizing public meetings, selling the Party paper, *Die Rote Fahne*, and distributing leaflets; by 1926 she owned a Party card. After a while she took over the role of organizing a Party newspaper for workers in the gas and coking plants in Berlin, an illegal publication called *Der Rote Kammerhof*, which was edited by her husband, Max Keilson. She rose in the hierarchy and in 1928 went as part of the KPD delegation to Moscow for the sixth Congress of the Communist International. In the preparations for this she started to work closely with Ernst Thälmann, general secretary of the KPD's Central Committee.

The work that she did and the contacts that she made at the Moscow congress meant that on her return to Germany Grete was put into a post where she had to be both highly efficient and highly secretive. She moved out of the German Communist Party and its regular work in the daily life of the districts to take up a job as assistant to Georgi Dimitrov, head of the western European section of the Comintern, which had its headquarters in Berlin. Dimitrov was on the run from his native Bulgaria, where he had been sentenced to death in 1924 for his role in leading an uprising against a military coup. He had several aliases, but in March of 1933 he was travelling under the name of Dr. Rudolf Hediger. Many of the international comrades based in Berlin used to travel on forged papers, some of which were stolen, but many of which were produced by a small counterfeit unit of the KPD in the Kaiserallee in Wilmersdorf, a working-class suburb of Berlin. Grete quickly became familiar with these covert activities; in fact, one of her tasks was to keep track of all the aliases and visa applications made by Comintern members who were working underground. It was a common practice, and special visa applications for travel to Moscow had a section to be filled in if the applicant needed the visa for a false identity. During this time Grete herself worked under the name of Marianne, and she and Dimitrov carried out their undercover activities from a rented apartment in Berlin. Dimitrov was a large, flamboyant figure, with a reputation amongst his comrades for being untidy and disorganized. Grete became his Girl Friday, imposing discipline and organization on his work and insisting that she know where he was, what his arrangements were and when he was going to be late.

On 9 March 1933 Dimitrov and two of his companions were arrested and accused of being part, along with the Dutchman van der Lubbe, of the plot to set fire to the Reichstag. They were held in Spandau Prison while Reichsminister Hermann Göring prepared the case against the alleged conspirators. On the day that he was arrested, Grete became extremely worried that Dimitrov had not arrived at the office, nor telephoned to say that he was going to be late. She knew that he was in Berlin and would not have made any journey without her knowing. It dawned on her that her boss had been arrested. Relying on her own judgement, she immediately took action.

The Berlin Post Office operated a system of sending messages around the city via pneumatic tubes; it was as quick as an ordinary telegram, and more confidential. Grete rushed to the nearest post office and sent a message to Dimitrov's comrades in the Comintern saying that she was concerned that the doctor had not arrived. She then proceeded to get any incriminating papers out of the apartment.

With Dimitrov's arrest, the outlook for Grete in Germany was extremely bleak, so she quickly joined the sixty thousand German communists who fled abroad. She had already made her preparations to go underground. She had a variety of contacts in Europe and false documents with which to travel. Her first port of call was Copenhagen, where the Danish Communist Party was active. Then she was drafted to Paris to work on the Congress Against Fascism and War, and no doubt to help pick up the pieces of the organization that had been based in Berlin.

In March the Nazis also arrested Ernst Thälmann. He was kept in solitary confinement in Bautzen Prison for eleven years; the Gestapo then moved him to Buchenwald concentration camp and executed him. Dimitrov stood trial for the Reichstag fire, but conducted a brilliant defence and was acquitted. He went to Moscow, where he became general secretary of the Comintern, and eventually president of Bulgaria.

With the close of the Congress Against War and Fascism, Grete continued in her role as a courier for the Comintern, travelling between Prague and Paris, and as a member of the KPD Central Committee. She had several work names, notably Agnes and Alma, and acted as secretary for the section of the Party that maintained contacts with the underground organization in Germany. The bulk of this work was intelligence about conditions in the country, but it included, of course, details of the state of the Party cells and their activities. Many of these reports were encrypted and Grete would decode them before forwarding them to the KPD Central Committee. Correspondence in a Moscow archive indicates that she was also forwarding these reports to Moscow; whether to the KPD, the Comintern or another organization is never made clear. She also made personal visits to Moscow, in 1936 for example travelling under the name of Anni Grob with a Swiss passport. Her Russian visa applications came with the personal recommendations of the KPD leadership of Wilhelm Pieck and Walter Ulbricht, the two major figures of the Communist Party in exile who later became leaders in East Germany, the DDR.

With the partition of Czechoslovakia in 1938 and the declaration of war the following year it became impossible to maintain the Party centres in Prague and Paris, and Grete, along with the Party leadership, sought final refuge in Moscow. The non-aggression pact between Hitler and Stalin, signed in 1939, meant that it was a dangerous time for members of the German Communist Party. A thousand KPD members were sent back to Nazi Germany by Stalin, and Grete, whose husband Max had been a member of a dissident faction, had to be particularly careful.

A brief biography written by Grete to accompany her application for asylum in Moscow, places great emphasis on her role as a stenographer and her membership of district Party organizations, implying that she was a mere lowly secretary. But once asylum was granted and she was living in Moscow, and with the invasion of the Soviet Union by Germany in 1941, the importance of her activities become more obvious. She now worked closely with Wilhelm Pieck as a member of the counter-intelligence section of the Party, and she visited German prisoner-of-war camps, collecting information about morale amongst the armed forces and seeking recruits to the anti-Nazi Free German Army. Throughout her career in the KPD, especially in the years in exile in Moscow, there were two different biographies in her Party file. One, as we have seen, stresses her grassroots Party work and her working-class credentials as a stenographer; the other separate document lists her positions in the Party apparatus, her membership of the Secretariat of the Central Committee and so on. Her role in the counter-intelligence section is particularly sinister. By 1945 she had created an index system on the members of the KPD, recording on small filing cards various aspects of a member's political history, with code words for various types of activities and grounds for suspicion. Grete was one of the first wave of German communist exiles to move back to Berlin after the defeat of Hitler, and she then returned to Moscow to retrieve the card index she had so carefully built up.

We have now got far ahead of ourselves. Grete's future was unknown in the summer of 1933 when she and Klaus Fuchs spent so much time together. Apart from the fact that she appears again in Fuchs's life, why mention her at all?

It is because her next known contact with Fuchs was not merely a coincidence, or the casual meeting of old comrades. Klaus Fuchs and Grete Keilson got married twenty-six years later, within a few weeks of Fuchs's arrival in East Germany. Yet, remarkably, there is no evidence that they were ever in touch with each other again after he left Paris at the end of the summer of 1933. There is no letter, no postcard or address in any of Fuchs's papers—and he was a hoarder of letters and documents, meticulously filing correspondence from past friends and colleagues, even keeping for many years some personal documents that he had brought from Berlin. Yet there was nothing in his possessions from the woman he would eventually marry. If Grete Keilson was so insignificant in the early part of his life, it seems improbable that they would marry so quickly when they met again twenty-six years later. It is more likely that she did have an important influence on Klaus Fuchs to which he never admitted and which he was anxious to keep hidden. Given Grete's lifelong commitment to the KPD and her role in its apparatus, her influence was more than merely romantic; it was Fuchs's final initiation into the clandestine life of the Party—an initiation that stood him in good stead, as an activist and then a spy, for many years to come.

There is one other thing that makes Fuchs's relationship with Grete of more significance than it at first appears. At the beginning of his interview with Jim Skardon, Fuchs says that he travelled to Switzerland via France in 1934 to see his brother Gerhard. Skardon knows nothing about this, makes no reference to it and Fuchs never mentions it again, ever.

Was it a mistake by Fuchs, albeit an unlikely one for a man with a brilliant memory to make? As far as is known, Gerhard was arrested in Berlin in 1934 and then on his release travelled to Prague. He might have made a brief journey to Switzerland to meet his brother, but Klaus Fuchs's German passport had expired in May of 1934 and he could not get it renewed. Furthermore, he was granted only a limited time to stay in Britain, as a refugee, and travelling abroad again would have jeopardized his status and his ability to return to Bristol University. There is also no record of him entering or leaving the UK after his interview with an immigration officer in September 1933.

So the statement that he travelled abroad in 1934 was either a mistake, a slip of the tongue, or he really did travel through France to Switzerland to see either his brother or someone else, which raises the questions who was it, why did he go to see them, and what passport or other papers did he use to make the journey?

Might he have travelled to see Grete, or might he have travelled with documents provided by her? Was his journey to do with the KPD, or was it personal, involving Grete or Gerhard? We don't know, but Fuchs did make one reference to a mysterious love affair in his past.

In a letter written many years later, when he was perhaps at one of the worst moments in his life, he wrote to another woman who had become deeply emotionally attached to him:

I thought many years ago that I was really in love, and even that has lost all conviction. There was I intelligent, (I hope that this does not count as arrogance) idealistic and immature, and she shrewd—very shrewd and unscrupulous. Both working for the same thing. An

ideal partnership for the devil and the devil she was.
Just try to imagine that pair in a collection of left wing
intellectuals. I never had any suspicion how shrewdly
she tackled me.

Again, we don't know to whom he is referring in this letter.
It may be Grete, or it may be someone who will remain
completely unknown, but it's clear that Fuchs believes he
was "tackled" in more than just an emotional way.

All speculation aside, after getting to know him in Paris
Grete would have made some report to the KPD leadership
about Fuchs. This was an accepted responsibility of someone
in her position and Fuchs claimed, in a later interview, that
when he arrived in Britain the German communists in exile
in London would have known who he was. To use his own
words, he came well recommended. That claim was perfectly
justifiable, and it was backed up many years later by leading
figures in the KPD. When he landed in Britain Fuchs was
not, as several writers have portrayed him, a poor, lonely
refugee. He was an active and experienced member of the
German Communist Party, doing what the Party told him,
with connections at high levels of the organization and a
sophisticated awareness of clandestine activity.

Looking at the organizational and conspiratorial aspects
of the KPD, it is easy to forget the broad popular support
that the Soviet Union then had, and that there was a widespread antagonism to the growth of fascism. Fuchs, as a
young refugee from Nazi Germany, would have generated
considerable sympathy.

It is also easy nowadays to dismiss the Congresses
Against War and Fascism and various other campaigns as
the insubstantial creations of a flamboyant chancer like
Münzenberg. But in Paris and in other cities around the
world in 1933 politics was conducted in the streets and
anti-fascism was a hugely popular movement.

On 11 September, just a couple of weeks after the congress had ended, a crowd of fifteen thousand people gathered in the streets of Paris. They formed outside a meeting hall to hear a lawyer, Vincent de Moro-Giafferi, who had originally been appointed by Georgi Dimitrov to appear for the defence of the men accused of the Reichstag fire. The trial was to open shortly in Leipzig. At the last moment the German government barred de Moro-Giafferi from entering the country, so he was prevented from attending the trial. The meeting in Paris had been organized for him to denounce the decision. The press of people was far larger than the meeting hall could accommodate, and the crowd of thousands outside who could not get in to hear the lawyer speak became a spontaneous rally. *The Times* in London reported the incident the next day: "After singing the Internationale, water carafes, chairs and other convenient missiles from neighbourhood cafés were hurled at the police." The riot spread into the surrounding streets. Meanwhile the meeting continued inside the hall and the assembly passed a resolution. "The fifteen thousand citizens assembled at this meeting", it said, "denounce the parody of justice which is being prepared at Leipzig . . ."

Fuchs may have been at the rally, or he may not; but given his Party membership and his close friendship with Grete he would certainly have been closely following the events around the trial. The clash with the police would have come as no surprise to him. These scenes occurred almost daily as the struggle between the forces of the left and the authorities was fought out.

Klaus Fuchs left Grete and Paris a few days later. His destination was the University of Bristol in the United Kingdom.

FIVE

Asylum

F uchs walked off the cross-Channel ferry on to the quay at Folkestone Harbour on 24 September 1933. His conversation with the immigration officer was circumspect. He claimed that he was coming to study at the University of Bristol and showed the officer a letter from the admissions office, which said that there were no courses for the particular branch of higher mathematics that Fuchs wished to pursue but that there were some other alternatives, and Fuchs told the officer that he intended to study physics.

His father was going to be responsible for his fees, and Fuchs, according to the immigration report, described him as a suspended professor of law. The immigration officer concluded that Fuchs was a refugee, or "at least prefers to study outside Germany". As "he appeared to be of good class", he was granted a visa for three months on the conditions that he registered with the police, at the address he had given, and did not take up any employment. So it appears that good manners and a confident bearing would go far!

Fuchs had arranged to stay with a married couple, Jessie and Ronald Gunn. Ronald was a socialist sympathetic to the Soviet Union, and had made a visit to Leningrad in 1927, although his MI5 files have no record of him being a member of the Party. Jessie was a Quaker, and both of them had in the past provided accommodation to a cousin of Fuchs, Grete Martigny; it was she who had put Fuchs in contact with them. Ronald Gunn was also a shareholder and director of the W. D. & H. O. Wills tobacco company, whose factory dominated Bristol and was a major employer. When Fuchs arrived in the autumn of 1933, the wealthy Wills family had given the money to build a modern physics laboratory for the university. So some of the large fortune made from the sale of Gold Flake tobacco, Woodbines and Capstan Full Strength cigarettes was used to challenge, at least in the UK, the duopoly in physics research of the Cavendish Laboratory at Cambridge and Manchester University.

Professor Nevill Mott, who had recently taken up the Melville Wills Chair of Theoretical Physics at Bristol, remembered that it was Ronald Gunn who brought Fuchs to his office at the university. He may have done so, but Fuchs's place was also considered by the university admissions board, which took the view that his qualifications from Kiel and Leipzig were good enough for him to become a research student, under Nevill Mott. Fuchs, of course, was a mathematician moving into physics, and this was a change of academic discipline that was familiar to Professor Mott because he had made the same transition.

Mott had decided to move into theoretical physics because of the revolutionary work that was being done in Göttingen University in 1925 by Professor Max Born, who was head of the physics department there, and a young German mathematician called Werner Heisenberg, who produced a paper outlining a theory of quantum mechanics. In 1927, Heisenberg published another paper describing what he termed his uncertainty principle. These papers took the world of physics—admittedly a small and esoteric one—by storm.

At the time, Mott had been in Copenhagen studying under the famous physicist Niels Bohr. Bohr had developed a theory about atoms that described them as a nucleus with electrons spinning around them like the model of the solar system, with the sun as the nucleus and the orbiting planets, such as Earth and Mars, as the electrons. This is probably how most ordinary people still visualize an atom, if they ever need to. The problem was that this description did not explain what scientists knew about the behaviour of different types of atoms and different particles. At the subatomic level, experiments found that it was impossible to measure more than one thing at a time. Measuring the speed of a particle meant that it was impossible to measure its weight, or its trajectory, and vice versa.

Werner Heisenberg realized that because particles could not be accurately measured with any certainty, then predictions about their future behaviour could only be made using mathematical formulae to predict probability. He developed a mathematical system that had first been put forward in the nineteenth century, a system called matrix algebra that would provide a method for dealing with the uncertainty of the behaviour of subatomic particles.

Heisenberg's system of analysis, quantum mechanics, provided explanations in many areas of science. Mott decided to study German so that he could read the papers of Heisenberg and others at Göttingen in their original language. He saw that quantum mechanics offered a way of understanding subjects in which he was particularly interested, like the structure of crystals. Much of his research work at Bristol led later to the development of semiconductors and transistors.

So Mott saw no problem for a good mathematician like Fuchs to move into the realm of physics. In fact, he encouraged it. He later suggested in an interview that he had turned Fuchs into a respectable physicist. Fuchs might have disagreed. The point, however, is that quantum mechanics opened the door to a new field of theoretical physics through which clever and able mathematicians like Fuchs could walk.

Fuchs worked with Professor Mott on several areas of his research, but an important one was developing a theory for why the resistance of a wire changes with alterations in electrical current. This is something that modern A-level physics students have to demonstrate, but the theoretical explanation for the law was then only sufficiently advanced that Fuchs's paper on it was accepted as a doctoral thesis and the university awarded him a PhD without an intermediate higher degree.

Fuchs was now demonstrating the power of his mind and his deep understanding of mathematics. While it impressed those who met him, it did not necessarily endear him to people. Herbert Skinner, another fellow at the Wills Laboratory, thought Fuchs an arrogant, callow youth. The pipe-smoking Herbert was himself a complex character. He came from a solid bourgeois family, his father a director of the shoe retailers Lilley and Skinner and a founder of the SU Carburettors company. Herbert Skinner was educated at Rugby and Trinity College, Cambridge, and he had married an Austrian Jewish divorcee, Erna, in 1931. At Bristol he was working on X-rays and the excitation of various gases by radiation, and he had developed a skill at glass-blowing so that he could make his own special apparatus for his experiments. Skinner may have found Fuchs arrogant, but he was to admit much later, when their lives had become intimately entwined, that Fuchs taught him everything he knew about nuclear physics.

Other researchers at the Wills Laboratory were probably more immediately friendly with Fuchs. Ronald Gurney worked with Mott on research that led to a textbook on semiconductors and crystals, and he was also a member of the local Communist Party. Fuchs did not join the British Communist Party, but neither did he keep his political views secret, at least not from his friends and colleagues. He was extremely active in campaigns in Bristol and also at national level, organizing for campaigns against Nazism and militarism, and after 1936 for campaigns in support of the Spanish republicans in the civil war. He also helped to send propaganda material into Germany and would have been in contact with other members of the KPD in exile. This activity escaped the notice of the local Special Branch, and Fuchs never talked about it—except, as we shall see later, to say that he was concerned about what records might still exist.

The organization of the KPD in Britain was shaken up in 1936 by the arrival of another exile, Jürgen Kuczynski, who had been a member of the Berlin Party Central Committee, had served on the editorial board of the Party daily *Die Rote Fahne*, and had been working underground in Berlin since 1933. In other words, he was a senior Party organizer, and he claims to have shaken up the cosy world of the London émigrés, which he thought was little better than a bohemian talking shop before he arrived. MI5 suspected that he had some connections with Soviet intelligence, although they never managed to substantiate this beyond linking him with others who clearly had. He galvanized the Party organization, then set up the Freier Deutscher Kulturbund (Free German League of Culture), a wider organization to gather anti-Nazi émigré Germans together, creating, in fact, a useful front organization for the Party. According to interviews he gave later in his life, Kuczynski met Klaus Fuchs after his arrival in London in August 1936 and was well aware of his previous activities for the KPD in Germany.

There were no restrictions on Fuchs's movements

around the country before the outbreak of war in 1939, and there is a possibility that he travelled widely to deliver propaganda or to attend meetings. When war did start in September of that year, enemy aliens, as Fuchs had then become, did have their movements restricted and had to hand over any maps in their possession to the nearest police station. When Fuchs did this he gave in thirty-five maps of various places in the UK. Either he believed that they might become collectors' items, or he needed them as part of his political activity, to find his way to meetings or to other activists' addresses. I think the latter is more likely.

Nevill Mott told a story in later years that at meetings of the Soviet Cultural Appreciation Society in Bristol members would get transcripts of the show trials that were taking place in Moscow in 1937. These grotesque travesties of justice were organized by Stalin as a method of finally destroying the old Bolsheviks of the revolution, and of eradicating any criticism of the brutal methods that his regime was imposing. According to Mott, Fuchs always took the part of the chief prosecutor Andrei Vyshinsky, reading out with extra vigour the absurd accusations that the surviving comrades of Lenin were in the pay of imperialism. Mott suggested that doubts about Soviet communism might have arisen in his own mind, but he did little about it; and in fact very few people in Britain and Europe who had supported the original revolution in Russia were prepared to make a sudden break with communism, whatever Stalin and the regime got up to. Indeed, the stories that were coming out of Nazi Germany—Hitler's aggressive foreign policy and rearmament, and the threat of fascism throughout Europe—encouraged many to cling to the belief that the Soviet Union was the only hope in a brutal world. And the start of the Spanish Civil War, which directly crystallized the fight between socialism and fascism, helped smother doubts about what was happening in Moscow.

The rise of Nazi Germany threw the world of physics into turmoil just as much as the new theories of quantum mechanics. Max Born, who led the Physics Institute at Göttingen University, who had nurtured Heisenberg and the birth of quantum mechanics, and had encouraged a stream of visiting physicists who would dominate the Nobel Prizes for almost a generation, had been dismissed from his post in 1933 because he was Jewish. He left the country, taking his family to a country cottage in Austria. But he had been arbitrarily removed from his life's work and he did not know what to do. He took a job at Cambridge, but then the authorities at Göttingen stopped his pay and in 1935 stripped him of his doctorate. As a final humiliation, his protégé, Heisenberg, who had always been sympathetic to German nationalism, took over the running of the institute. Born, desperate to keep working, considered taking up posts in Calcutta and even for a time in Moscow, but finally was offered a chair at Edinburgh University, which he accepted. Countless less well-known scientists and academics were also victimized in this way because of their race or their beliefs.

Horrified by what was happening to academics and teachers in Nazi Germany, in May 1933 Lord Beveridge, the economist and director of the London School of Economics, along with scientists Lord Rutherford, William Bragg and others, set up the Academic Assistance Council. It was to provide grants and help in finding jobs for the thirteen hundred university teachers expelled from Germany in that year alone. The AAC also helped other refugees and Fuchs received a grant from them in 1934; they continued to help him financially, as well as assisting in his negotiations with the Home Office about the conditions under which he was allowed to stay in the country. The association reorganized itself on to a permanent footing in 1936 when it became the Society for the Protection of Science and Learning. It made a considerable impact, and held a public meeting in the Albert Hall that was addressed by Albert Einstein, who spoke to a crowd of ten thousand people. The issue of Nazi anti-semitism and their assault on academia was a live one.

The financial assistance provided by the AAC to Fuchs was essential, and so too was their lobbying on his behalf. He had travelled to the UK in 1933 on a German passport that had been issued to him in 1929 in the town of Eisenach where his family then lived. The problem, as we saw earlier, was that it expired in June of 1934. Fuchs approached the German consul in Bristol, a gentleman called Mr. C. Hartley Hodder, and asked for a new passport to be issued. He was told that he had to obtain a certificate from the police in Germany showing that there was no reason for a new passport not to be issued. Fuchs wrote to the registration office in Kiel, giving his last official address in the city.

The police authorities in Kiel replied, not to Fuchs but directly to the German secretary of the consul, Carl Herweg. On no account, they stated, should Fuchs be issued with a new passport. The reasons were written on the reverse of Fuchs's original letter. It was an accurate analysis of his recent political history. He had been a member of the Social Democratic Party until March 1932; he had then joined the Communist Party; and he was a public speaker for the KPD in the elections. He was also a leader of a group that was designed to split the National Socialist Party. His house (as we have seen) was raided and Communist Party books and leaflets were found. The case against him had been suspended but would be pursued in due course. All that the consul was authorized to do was to give Fuchs a travel permit to allow him to make a one-way trip to Kiel, where he could discuss a new passport with the police. It would clearly be a one-sided conversation.

The consul's secretary wrote directly to the Bristol police informing on Fuchs. The chief constable, in his role as representative of Special Branch, then passed the information on to Sir Vernon Kell, director of MI5. Fuchs, wrote the chief constable, is a notorious communist, but at the end of his letter he added, "During his stay in this City Fuchs is not known to have engaged in any communist activities." The copies of the German correspondence were sent also to the Aliens Department of the Home Office, who had recently received a letter from Fuchs asking to extend his permission to stay in the UK and to be granted an identity certificate in place of the invalid German passport. His request was backed up by some influential figures. Professor Henry Overton Wills, professor of physics at Bristol University, urged the Home Office to grant Fuchs an extension. The combination of local chief constable and local benefactor and academic clearly had influence, as Fuchs was granted an extension to remain until December; but his request for an identity card was refused on the grounds that he did not wish to travel outside the UK. In December, the Academic Assistance Council wrote to the Home Office requesting a further extension to Fuchs's permission to reside, and he was granted a further twelve months. MI5 took no action over the information they had received from Bristol's chief constable.

It was surely a relief for Fuchs to know that he could stay in the UK for a year, but that was the limit of his security. Every August he had to make an application for another year's extension, with support from the Society for the Protection of Science and Learning. This continued until 1937, when he was offered the chance to take up a scholarship at Edinburgh University under Max Born, the exiled and unsung polymath of physics and co-creator of quantum mechanics.

Perhaps now for the first time Fuchs's mathematical talent was fully engaged on the fundamental problems of physics. He said later in an interview that Born and he complemented each other in the way that they thought about problems. Fuchs saw things in equations, while Born was conceptually more visual. Fuchs developed a profound respect for Born, not only for his intellect but as a mentor and friend, and this never altered. It was Fuchs's impression that Born was deeply depressed by the loss of his institute at Göttingen, his exile and the hatred that he had faced at the hands of his erstwhile friends and collaborators. Fuchs believed that the work they did together at Edinburgh rekindled some of Born's intellectual inquisitiveness and pleasure in the mysteries of the physical world.

Fuchs had now started to establish a name for himself amongst mathematicians and was corresponding with some senior researchers at the Cavendish Laboratory in Cambridge and at other universities. Rudolf Peierls, another German refugee and a leading theoretical physicist, who became professor of mathematical physics at Birmingham in 1937, also wrote to Born and Fuchs about a paper that the latter had written. Professor Born thought highly of Fuchs. "Fuchs is the soul of my research group," he wrote. "He is responsible for about half of the dissertations partly finished, partly in progress. He is in the small top group of theoretical physicists in this country."

With the assistance of the Society for the Protection of Science and Learning, and the efforts of both Mott and Born, in 1938 the Home Office finally lifted any restrictions on Fuchs's residence in the UK. Moreover, he was awarded a scholarship by the Carnegie Endowment to continue his work at Edinburgh with Born. It must have eased anxiety about his future. Yet distress about the fate of the rest of his family never left him.

His younger sister, Kristel, travelled from Germany to the United States via Britain in 1936. She was going to study at Swarthmore, a prestigious Quaker college in Pennsylvania. Fuchs was able to meet her in the few days that she stayed in the UK. He was always writing letters asking the Society of Friends or sympathetic politicians to intervene to help his brother Gerhard, who by now had been released from the concentration camp and sought refuge with others of the Party in Prague, but who needed treatment for tuberculosis. Fuchs was trying to meet some of Gerhard's medical expenses out of his small scholarships, and he wanted his brother to seek the safety of Britain. In 1938 Gerhard moved to Switzerland and also tried to get to the United States. He flew to the UK but was refused entry because the immigration officers decided that his tuberculosis would prevent him landing in the US, so he had to return to Switzerland and Fuchs wasn't able to meet him. His sister Elisabeth and her husband, Gustav Kittowski, had also been imprisoned, escaped and fled to Prague, where in 1939 Elisabeth committed suicide by jumping in front of a locomotive.

People who met and lived or worked with Fuchs at the time often remarked that he was quiet and withdrawn. Given the personal and family problems that weighed on his mind, it is hardly surprising. However, he seemed to have an unerring ability to evoke sympathy in female hearts. He was slim and young. He had a round, childlike face with warm eyes and a full mouth, and he was alone. Jessie Gunn, whose house he shared while he was in Bristol, believed that he lacked a mother's touch. As his mother had committed suicide when he was twenty years old, she may have been right. Jessie thought that he had a deep need for love and affection, and that only she really understood him; her later letters about him suggest that she might have felt slightly possessive over him. The wives of his professors also took him under their wings, offering a sheltering house, meals and sympathy. Hedi Born, like her husband Max, was clearly concerned about both his welfare and the precarious and dangerous situation of the rest of his family. She wrote to him, and he kept her letters, as he did those of almost every person who corresponded with him, though oddly nothing has ever been found of any correspondence with his brother Gerhard, his sister Kristel or, as we have seen, with Grete, the woman he had met in Paris.

As Fuchs developed as a theoretical physicist, papers he wrote were published in various scientific journals and his reputation grew. He produced several in collaboration with Max Born, and two major papers on his own that were eventually published by the Royal Society. His work had shifted over the years from pure mathematics to the application of mathematics to electrons and electromagnetic theory to nuclear physics. It was becoming more and more aligned with the work of other nuclear physicists. Everyone engaged in this field was starting to realize that the atom was the repository of enormous forces, and that it had a potential to be harnessed as a weapon.

In the first six months of 1939, the scientific journal *Nature* published twenty articles about uranium. One of them, written by a group of scientists in Paris, declared that one of their experiments had shown that splitting a uranium atom produced extra neutrons, clearly indicating that a chain reaction was possible. Also, in April 1939 the *Sunday Express* carried a story about the possibility of building a super-bomb from uranium. The whole question of the use of atomic physics was now part of public knowledge, however poorly informed it might be. It was a question that Born and Fuchs frequently discussed. Born was opposed to any work that would increase the world's ability to destroy itself. If war came to Europe again, then the civilian populations would be in the forefront. Born would later remember that Fuchs, on the other hand, had no qualms about anything that would help to destroy the Nazis.

With the conditions on his residence in the UK now completely removed, and the Nazi Party firmly in power in Germany, it seemed logical to apply for a British passport.

He had applied again in 1938 for an identity card, ostensibly so that he could travel to Prague to see his brother, but when the political situation meant that Gerhard, as a communist, was forced to move to Switzerland, the application lapsed. Now, in 1939, Fuchs decided to try once more.

SIX

Interned

Fuchs made the decision to apply to become a British citizen in the summer of 1939 and he sent an application to the Home Office dated 17 July of that year. The referees were his colleagues from the University of Edinburgh, Professor Mott from Bristol and his old friend from his first arrival in the UK, Ronald Gunn. It is hard to know what prompted this. Citizenship was not now legally necessary in order for Fuchs to remain in the UK and at Edinburgh. However, it may be that he thought it would help to get his brother into the UK and away from an increasingly dangerous existence on the run in Europe.

The application had every chance of being successful, and in August the Home Office wrote to Fuchs asking for the £1 naturalization fee. Wider events in Europe were conspiring against him, however, and, through the actions of his nemesis, Hitler and the Nazi Party, he was destined to remain a German for the time being.

The invasion of Poland by German armed forces triggered the doleful broadcast on 3 September by Prime Minister Neville Chamberlain that a state of war existed between Britain and Germany. Suddenly Fuchs found himself an enemy alien.

It was a strange situation, which even his mathematical talent might find hard to rationalize.

It was one shock after another. A month earlier, the foreign ministers of Germany and the Soviet Union had signed a non-aggression pact. This agreement, coming so suddenly into existence, had stunned the whole world, but its effect on the minds of committed members of the German Communist Party, like Fuchs, can only be imagined. There had been rivers of blood between the Nazis and the communists, but now Stalin, the supreme leader of the world communist movement, had signed a deal with the government that had murdered thousands of Fuchs's comrades and was responsible for his exile in the UK. Within days of the British declaration of war against Germany, the Russian army had occupied the eastern part of Poland.

Grete, the woman whom Fuchs had met in Paris in 1933, had been a courier for the Party between Prague, Moscow and Paris, but in August 1938, when the German army occupied Czechoslovakia, the Party apparatus in Prague had to be rapidly abandoned. Fuchs's brother was still active in Switzerland, but now, with the latest events, the future of the Party centre in Paris was in doubt, as was the fate of the KPD leadership in Moscow, whose existence in exile was a permanent rebuke to Stalin. But Fuchs's position never wavered. Then in November of 1939, the Red Army attempted to invade Finland and seize territory that Stalin claimed was historically part of imperial Russia. Such a claim, backed up by military force, would have been anathema to Lenin and the old Bolsheviks. Fuchs and Max Born, and no doubt others at Edinburgh University, argued the pros and cons, but Fuchs's support for Stalin and the Soviet Union remained resolute.

Fuchs and Born might have had their differences about the nature of the Soviet Union, but neither of them would let that get in the way of their friendship and their intellectual relationship. With the start of the war, the government had passed legislation to round up enemy aliens and intern them in camps. A system of tribunals was established to interview any German or Austrian national over the age of sixteen to see if they might be exempt. Klaus Fuchs was summoned to appear before one in Edinburgh's Sheriff Court House on 2 November.

There was no legal representation at such tribunals, but the enemy alien could take a supporting statement from someone who knew them well. Born provided one for his friend, saying that Fuchs was the son of a pastor, now a Quaker, still living in Berlin, and that Fuchs was "a man of excellent character deeply devoted not only to his science, but to all human ideals and humanitarian activities. He is passionately opposed to the present German Government and hopes for the victory of the allies." Fuchs also presented a similar supporting letter from the Friends Service Committee's (the Quakers') refugee liaison officer.

The tribunal took its time deliberating and it was not until March of 1940 that Fuchs was told that he was exempt from internment. With this news he still had to make a further application for permission to continue to live in Edinburgh. Because of the naval shipyard at Rosyth, the city had been designated a prohibited area. Permission was granted, but it was to be a brief respite. With the German advance through Belgium and Holland in May 1940, and the subsequent collapse of France, the enemy was on Britain's doorstep, or at least on the coast of France just 25 miles away, and threatening to cross the Channel fairly soon. There could be no exemption from internment any more.

Fuchs was first taken to a camp on the Isle of Man and then, with several hundred other German exiles, was sent across the North Atlantic, where he landed in Canada at Halifax, Nova Scotia, on 17 May. He was registered as an internee at a camp near Quebec on 13 July. Known as Camp

L, it was a series of huts surrounded by a barbed-wire fence. The huts, which were like army barracks, could each accommodate eighty people. Most of the inmates—and there were about seven hundred in all—were Jewish, the exception being a few, like Fuchs, who were communists or left-wing. There were also around thirty Catholic students in the camp and a few others who had been arrested in Gibraltar while they were waiting for a ship to South America.

Fuchs said later that he never felt any resentment towards the British authorities over his internment, that he understood why it happened. But he must have had alternative feelings. He had spent six years in Britain, building up a network of friends and colleagues, and he had just started to achieve some recognition, when all this was suddenly destroyed. He had great intellectual strength, but the loss of home and career, plus a potentially dangerous journey across the Atlantic to an unknown destination, must have been incredibly unsettling.

In their first weeks in the camp the internees organized themselves in various ways. At first those from the same institution would congregate in one hut, so that those from the London School of Economics would socialize together, as would those from Cambridge or Oxford colleges. Fuchs was with a colleague from Edinburgh, Walter Kellermann, who was Jewish and whose father was a rabbi; but Fuchs quickly gravitated to a group of about ten men known amongst the internees to be KPD members. There was not necessarily an enormous divide in the politics of the inmates, most of whom were socialists of one form or another, and the Communist Party members did not openly advertise their affiliation. What marked them out to their politically astute fellow internees was the sensitivity they felt about the Stalin—Hitler pact, and the care they took to describe Germany and the Nazis in ways that did not appear to reflect badly on the Soviet Union.

Apart from this embarrassment, the organizational talents of Communist Party members quickly brought them to the fore. Fuchs joined the Refugee Committee, which became a focus of negotiation with the camp authorities. Their first dispute was about correspondence and the censorship of letters. The committee demanded an end to restrictions on the number of letters internees could send and receive. Associated with this demand was pressure on the camp authorities to allow them to receive books and magazines, because they had not been permitted to bring any reading matter with them. With seven hundred intellectuals cooped up behind wire it was natural, as a way to stave off boredom, that a series of educational lectures started up, and Fuchs gave several on theoretical problems with physics, displaying, according to another inmate, "a brilliant scientific talent".

Boredom and petty restrictions concerning letters were one thing, but what really caused unrest was the camp administration's attempt to categorize the internees as Jews or non-Jews. Most of the inmates were refugees because they had fled the effects of such racist practices, and it also caused many to fear that the Jews would somehow be repatriated to Germany in return for Canadian prisoners of war. The Refugee Committee withdrew all cooperation with the administration and the inmates started a campaign of passive resistance.

The camp commandant looked around for a figure amongst the refugees who could exert some influence and discipline, in order to appoint him as the chair of their committee. He selected a man called Hans Kahle, who had been an officer in the German Imperial Army in the First World War. Kahle, it was true, had been a young cadet at the Military Academy in Berlin-Lichterfelde and had then fought in the war as a lieutenant. He had been a prisoner of war in France for two years, then on his release he studied

at the London School of Economics and went on to work
in Mexico. He had become a socialist during his war service
and on his return to Germany in 1927 he started writing
for some socialist newspapers, then joined the KPD. There
he put his military experience to use by working in the
armed wing of the party, the M-Apparat, which had been
created in preparation for a planned insurrection in 1923.
Like Fuchs, Kahle had fled the country after the Reichstag
fire and the Nazis' rise to power in 1933. Also like Fuchs,
he had passed through Paris on his way to exile in the UK.
Unlike Fuchs, though, he had not remained there. He went
on to Moscow and later turned up as a commander in the
International Brigades in the Spanish Civil War, taking part
in the battles of the Ebro and Madrid.

Hans Kahle was a product of the close, intertwined
relationship between the KPD, the Comintern and Soviet
intelligence. It was generally accepted that the role of foreign
communist parties was to defend the revolution in the Soviet
Union, and in this the Soviet intelligence services found
ready recruits—none more so than in the ranks of the KPD,
where collaboration with the Soviet Union had long been
established.

MI5 firmly believed that by the time Kahle reached
Spain, if not before, he was an agent of the Soviet Joint
State Political Directorate, the OGPU, which was the fore-
runner of the NKGB. The OGPU's focus, particularly in
Spain, was the eradication of Trotskyites and anarchists in
the ranks of the International Brigades and the republican
government. It is possible that Kahle and Fuchs had met
before, in Paris, but they were certainly working together
now as chairman and member respectively of the Refugee
Committee. They both remained in Camp L for three
months. Then in October 1940 the group of German
Catholics, and a few of those who were Nazi sympathizers,
were removed and a similar number of refugees, mainly

Jews, arrived to take their place. With this new intake, the whole population of the camp was moved to Camp N, where they were housed in two large barracks, accommodating around three hundred at a time.

Fuchs and many others in the camps were not left languishing, forgotten by their friends in the UK. There was a continual campaign by members of the Society for the Protection of Science and Learning to allow the refugees to return. This organization made representations about Fuchs, as did Max Born, who also wrote on his behalf to the Home Office. The campaign was successful and, at about the time that he was moving between camps, Fuchs was placed on a list for return. It was not, however, until December 1940 that he was released and sailed back to the UK to land at Liverpool in January 1941. He was given permission to travel back to Edinburgh, though there were some restrictions on his movements. He had to notify the police of any change of address, and also report to a local police station if he was unable to spend the night at his registered address; but these were more or less the same restrictions that had been imposed on him before his internment.

Hans Kahle also returned to the UK, where he worked for a time with Professor J. B. S. Haldane, the left-wing geneticist, at University College London. He moved on, however, and, perhaps because of his military experience and knowledge, was employed by the US magazines *Time* and *Fortune* as a military correspondent. After the attack on Pearl Harbor in December 1941 brought the United States into the war and the US armed forces quickly established a significant military mission in London, this job gave Kahle access to senior military and political figures. He picked up a lot of confidential background information, which he passed on to an agent of the Soviet Military Intelligence, or GRU.

It might seem that we have gone ahead of ourselves

again, but the Soviet agent with whom Kahle was eventually in contact arrived in Britain in the same month that Klaus Fuchs landed in Liverpool from the internment camp in Canada. This agent, whose work name in the UK was "Sonya", was a German and, again, originally a member of the KPD. Why Moscow told her to go to Britain at this time is unclear. It may be that it was the safest place to send her, or there may have been GRU contacts in Britain that required handling by an experienced agent. Whatever the reason, she was soon to play an important part in Fuchs's story.

Sonya, or Ruth Werner, was born Ursula Ruth Kuczynski in Berlin in 1907, the daughter of the well-known economist and statistician Robert Kuczynski. In the 1920s she became an active member of the KPD and in 1930 she moved to China with her first husband, Rolf Hamburger, who had taken a job with the Shanghai Municipal Council. Before she made the long journey by train on the Trans-Siberian Express, she approached the KPD Central Committee in Berlin, telling them about her imminent move and saying that she wanted to continue to work for the Party once she had arrived in Shanghai. It may have been that she was merely naïve, or it may be that she understood that the Party had extensive and varied international connections. Whatever the reason, hers was an extremely risky ambition. The Chinese Communist Party was illegal at the time, and hundreds of thousands of Chinese communists had been executed or jailed. This didn't alarm her. When she arrived in Shanghai and observed the grinding poverty of millions of landless labourers and the brutal conflict between the Communist Party and the Kuomintang, she was impatient to be part of the fight.

At first she was frustrated that nobody made any contact with her; it was some time before she was finally approached by a fellow European communist. This brief meeting, however, led to a second one, this time with Richard Sorge, an agent of the Soviet General Staff, who gave her the name Sonya. Sorge was establishing a large and successful network of agents in China and Japan. He went on to penetrate the German Embassy in Tokyo, hoovering up such vital nuggets of information as the planned German invasion of the Soviet Union and Japanese intentions in the war.

Sonya worked with Sorge for two years before she was directed to go to Moscow, where she spent six months on a training course. Here she learnt to code and decode messages and send them in Morse, and to buy electrical equipment and build her own clandestine radio transmitter. By this time she was an officer in the GRU, with an army rank of captain. After her training programme Sonya became the link between Moscow and a group of agents in Poland and the free city of Danzig. This operation too proved valuable to the GRU, and in 1938 she made another trip to Moscow for further training, promotion to colonel and also to be awarded the Order of the Red Banner, the Soviet Union's highest military honour. After this she left for Switzerland, where she ran a couple of English communists, former International Brigade men, into Germany and acted as the radio link to another network led by a Hungarian, Sándor Radó, a veteran of the 1919 Hungarian Revolution.

When war broke out in Europe, Moscow decided Sonya should move to the UK. The timing was fortuitous, as some of her contacts and also a woman employed to look after her children were threatening to report her to the Swiss authorities. Sonya's papers were not, as they say, in order: she had an out-of-date German passport and a very fishy-looking one from Honduras. By now she had divorced her first husband, Rolf, who was sadly to end up in the Soviet gulag, and in order to get out of Switzerland she married one of the English agents she was running, Len Beurton. On the basis of this she obtained a British passport from the consul in Geneva and left with her children for the UK, via Vichy France, Spain and Lisbon, arriving in England in January 1941. She found a cottage in a village near Chipping Norton and eventually met with her Soviet contact in the UK. Every two weeks she would travel to London, where she would meet with Hans Kahle; she also ran several other agents, sending her information to Moscow by radio, or passing it to her Soviet contact who would then pass it on to Moscow via the diplomatic bag.

Sonya's information was of high quality. Not only did Kahle provide her with the material he picked up as a military correspondent, but she had good access to other political gossip. She was the sister of Jürgen Kuczynski, who, as we have seen, had re-energized the KPD in the UK and was now its leader. She also frequently met her father, Robert, who had arrived in Britain in 1933 and was now an advisor to senior Labour Party MPs.

Important as her role in China and Switzerland had been, Sonya's most important work for the Soviet Union was about to begin. She had never met Klaus Fuchs, and knew nothing of nuclear physics, but they would eventually be put in touch with each other by her brother Jürgen and it was she who would transmit details of the single biggest secret of the twentieth century.

SEVEN

The Biggest Secret

By the time Klaus Fuchs returned to Edinburgh in January of 1941, two émigré German physicists based at Birmingham University had dramatically transformed nuclear research. Fuchs was to spend the next few years in close collaboration with them, and his first encounter with their work was to prove the most fateful moment of his life.

Otto Frisch was an Austrian Jew who had arrived in Birmingham in July 1939. He was the nephew of Lise Meitner, an Austrian Jewish physicist whose work with Otto Hahn in the Kaiser Wilhelm Institute in Berlin had led to the discovery that uranium atoms would split if hit by a neutron. Lise Meitner had fled to Sweden because of the Nazi persecution, but Hahn had kept her informed about the results of his work. Frisch had helped her write a paper that explained this process, describing it as "fission". He was studying at the Niels Bohr Institute in Copenhagen at the time and, believing that sooner or later Hitler would invade Denmark, he accepted a very loose invitation from the head of the physics department at Birmingham, Professor Marcus Oliphant. He worked with Oliphant for a few months but, when war was declared in September 1939, the professor started working on radar, a subject that Frisch, as an enemy alien, was not allowed to know about.

At a bit of a loose end, Frisch volunteered to write an article about nuclear fission for the Chemical Society's annual report. He agreed with Bohr's analysis that the rare isotope uranium 235 was the source of uranium's radioactivity, and so wrote that a weapon based on the fission of uranium atoms was a very remote possibility because uranium 235 amounted to such a small proportion of natural uranium. While he was writing this article, however, he started to question Bohr's assumption. If the percentage of uranium 235 in natural uranium, which was about 0.7 per cent, could be artificially increased, then Bohr would be wrong. The greater the amount of uranium 235 in natural uranium, the greater the possibility of spontaneous fission, which would lead to an explosion.

Frisch was living at the time with Rudolf Peierls and his wife, Genia. Peierls had studied physics with Enrico Fermi in Rome before moving to the Cavendish Laboratory in Cambridge. From there, with funding from the Society for the Protection of Science and Learning, he had spent two years at Manchester University. He was an engaging, some said arrogant, young and respected physicist who had worked with many scientific luminaries, including Hans Bethe and James Chadwick. In 1937 he had been offered the post of professor of mathematical physics at Birmingham University and when Frisch also arrived in Birmingham they quickly became friends, and Frisch lodged in the Peierls' large house. Pcicrls too had been thinking about various aspects of a chain reaction, so when Frisch asked him, "If someone gave you a quantity of pure uranium 235, what would happen?" he took the proposition seriously.

The question wasn't as far-fetched as it seemed, because some work had already been done on the physical separation of isotopes of gases. Frisch and Peierls realized it might prove possible actually to separate the lighter, radioactive isotope of uranium and produce pure uranium 235. From then on, the calculations to be made were straightforward, if somewhat esoteric. They sat down and wrote up the results of their work.

The outcome was a concise document of just three pages entitled "On the Construction of a 'Super-bomb'; based on a Nuclear Chain Reaction in Uranium". The conclusions it came to were alarming. It suggested that separating uranium 235 was possible, and that about one kilogram would be enough to create a bomb. It outlined ways of triggering the explosion, proposing that the gadget, as they called it, would have to be assembled rapidly from two or more parts.

The opening paragraph of the covering letter that Peierls and Frisch sent with their memorandum to Professor Mark Oliphant sums up the enormity of their conclusions:

> The attached detailed report concerns the possibility of constructing a "super-bomb" which utilises the energy stored in atomic nuclei as a source of energy. The energy liberated in the explosion of such a super-bomb is about the same as that produced by the explosion of 1,000 tons of dynamite. This energy is liberated in a small volume, in which it will, for an instant produce a temperature comparable to that in the interior of the sun. The blast from such an explosion would destroy life in a wide area. The size of this area is difficult to estimate, but it will probably cover the centre of a big city.

This paragraph is frighteningly prophetic. There cannot be many examples in history where two people armed with nothing more than their own scientific knowledge and their mathematical skill have been able so accurately to predict the future. Their document was completed in March 1940, just a few weeks before the German invasion of France and the Low Countries, the event that triggered Fuchs's internment.

Professor Oliphant understood immediately the significance of the two scientists' work and sent their memorandum, which became known as the Frisch—Peierls Memorandum, to Sir Henry Tizard, who was rector of Imperial College and, more importantly, chairman of the Air Defence Research Committee, a key body that coordinated scientific research. In typical fashion, this committee set up a subcommittee to investigate further. It was a small one, made up of the leading British scientists in the field, chaired by George Thompson, professor of physics at Imperial, and it included Professor James Chadwick of Liverpool University, Sir John Cockcroft at the Cavendish in Cambridge, and Professor Oliphant himself. They met under the auspices of the Ministry of Aircraft Production, a wartime department that enjoyed special status, as well as priority in the war economy.

Peierls and Frisch, the authors of the memorandum, were told that they could not take part in the work of the committee because of their alien status, even though Peierls's certificate of naturalization had been granted in March. Frisch, of course, had avoided internment, perhaps because he was an Austrian, and Jewish, although he had been asked to attend Birmingham police station for an interview, where he thought a decision had been taken about what sort of security risk he was. Peierls complained to Professor Oliphant about their removal from the work of the committee, which had been given the name of MAUD, and eventually the decision to ban them was rescinded. The committee was called MAUD because of a telegram sent by Niels Bohr from Copenhagen during the German invasion of Denmark. He asked Frisch to inform Cockcroft and Maud Ray Kent. It was thought this was some sort of message about uranium or radium, but it was in fact a reference to a former governess of the Bohrs' children, Maud Ray, who lived in Kent. The confusion helped, however, to provide a name that seemed to camouflage the work of the committee and it was adopted.

When Chadwick read the Frisch—Peierls Memorandum he too realized how groundbreaking it was. He had been working along similar lines at Liverpool University, and later in his life he said that after realizing the potential of nuclear fission he never got a good night's sleep again. He quickly invited Frisch to Liverpool to investigate whether uranium 235 could be separated by a process called thermal diffusion. To separate the 0.7 per cent of atoms of uranium 235 from the 99.3 per cent atoms of uranium 238, the metal had to be turned into a gas using nitric acid, chlorine and hydrogen. This produced uranium hexafluoride, which was highly toxic and corrosive. It was a difficult and expensive process, and, to the disappointment of Frisch and Chadwick, thermal diffusion did not result in any separation of the two isotopes, in the gas.

Peierls, meanwhile, had also continued to work on the problem, and proposed the idea of allowing the gas to diffuse under pressure through membranes with extremely small holes. The experiments with this method proved promising, and a newly created technical sub-group of the MAUD Committee decided to follow this route for the separation of uranium 235. To move forward and take the process of separation out of the laboratory, some of Britain's engineering giants were called in. Metropolitan-Vickers in Manchester, busy building Avro Manchester bombers, was contracted to make a ten-stage separation machine, and ICI was approached to manufacture the required quantities of uranium hexafluoride gas.

With Otto Frisch in Liverpool, Peierls had to bear a lot of the theoretical work for the MAUD Committee on his own, and at some time early in 1941 he wrote to various university physics departments asking if they could recommend any promising theoreticians to be his assistant. This in fact is Peierls's explanation and he claims he received only one reply, from Professor Max Born in Edinburgh, who suggested that Peierls consider making an offer to Klaus Fuchs, who had of course been released from internment that January.

The truth is that Peierls and Born were in correspondence about employment for Fuchs from November 1940, when Fuchs was in Canada. Born wanted to find some paid work for him because his Carnegie grant was running out and he could not renew it. Peierls had met Fuchs before the war, and was no doubt aware of his last scientific paper, about the use of the statistical method to calculate the energy of heavy atoms, which had been published by the Royal Society. Peierls initially wrote that he might be able to offer Fuchs a part-time lecturing post, then later mentioned to Born that he had some war work that might be useful to Fuchs and the correspondence continued when Fuchs was released.

Born would obviously have discussed this with Fuchs, and both of them would have known what the nature of the research work might involve. Both Fuchs and Born later said that they discussed the possibility of a nuclear weapon, and the morality of whether to work on it or not, although neither of them ever mentioned specific dates. The implication is that this was an ongoing discussion, triggered by the prospect of military use starting to tap on the window of nuclear physics. A direct letter from Peierls, though, would clearly have triggered an immediate and focused conversation.

The first documentary evidence of Peierls making direct contact with Fuchs is a letter that he wrote on 10 May 1941. It said:

I have for some time been busy with research for a committee of the Ministry of Aircraft Production and I need someone to help me with this work ... It is theoretical work involving mathematical problems of considerable difficulty and I have enjoyed doing it quite apart from its extreme importance ... it is the sort of work for which a good theoretical physicist is best qualified ...

The plot now thickens, because on 3 April, a month before this letter was sent, Fuchs caught a train from Edinburgh to London. Because of his status as an enemy alien, he had to observe a curfew between 10.30 in the evening and 6.00 in the morning, and he had to inform the local police about any movements that would prevent him from complying with this; he also had to register with the local police station wherever he was. He was due to return to Edinburgh on 15 April. He was delayed, possibly because of an air raid, so he reported to the police station at King's Cross railway station to tell them that he had missed his night train to Edinburgh. The desk sergeant took a note, with a record that the "alien" had been told to sleep on the station and catch the first available train in the morning.

Fuchs himself later said very little about this visit to London. He claimed, in a conversation with Skardon, that Kahle, his KPD fellow internee in Camp N in Canada, had made efforts to contact him in Edinburgh, that he had travelled to London to meet him, and that after that he broke off any contact with his old KPD associates. The only other clue that he gave is that they met somewhere in Hampstead— Fuchs was vague about the exact location, except he remembered that they had gone to a café that had been set up by the Freier Deutscher Kulturbund.

The only place in Hampstead with a café set up by émigré Germans was in Lawn Road, a block of flats built in

1934 and inspired by the German Bauhaus movement. Lawn Road is a street off Haverstock Hill, midway between Camden Town and Hampstead, and lies behind Belsize Park underground station. The flats were designed as a four-storey, minimalist building that would encourage communal living. Jürgen Kuczynski stayed there when he first arrived in Britain, before moving around the corner. His father, Robert, and his family lived opposite the flats in a house, No. 12. The Lawn Road flats became the centre for a large number of Soviet intelligence contacts and KPD members, such as Arnold Deutsch, who recruited the spies Kim Philby, Anthony Blunt and others, as well as the non-political writers Agatha Christie, Nicholas Monsarrat, and the original television chef Philip Harben. Celebrities aside, the café run by the FDK was a central part of their activities. In the month before Fuchs's visit both Jürgen Kuczynski and Hans Kahle had spoken at meetings held there, addressing issues such as Soviet policy towards the war and the future of a post-war Europe. This was a time when the Stalin—Hitler pact was still a reality and both speakers followed the Soviet line, that Britain was waging an imperialist war to dominate Europe.

Fuchs spent twelve days in London—a fairly long time for someone who had very few friends in the city and who claimed to have only a passing acquaintance with the German exile movement. In reality, he most likely started establishing his first contact with Soviet intelligence during this visit. Jürgen Kuczynski, as head of the KPD in Britain, was already familiar with Fuchs and was also in contact with an agent of the Soviet Military Intelligence, the GRU, called Semyon Kremer, who was secretary to the Soviet military attaché in London. An historian of the GRU says that, as the resident Soviet intelligence agent, Kremer was much more important than his ostensible boss. He gave the game away slightly when, shortly after his arrival in London, he was seen walking up and down the Charing Cross Road, the centre of London's book trade, buying the latest edition of *Jane's Fighting Ships* and every book on modern military tactics he could lay his hands on.

While everybody involved—Kremer, Kuczynski and Fuchs—described the first arrangements for meeting, the actual dates are hazy. Each description is coloured by personal motives, of course. Kuczynski, an important member of the KPD, claims a central role and says that Fuchs asked him if the Soviet Union would be interested in a very dangerous and effective weapon? He replied that of course they would, and then he arranged for Fuchs to meet with Kremer. Under questioning, Fuchs told Jim Skardon that he first met Kremer at an address somewhere south of Hyde Park and never provided any more concrete details than that. He didn't know who his contact was, except that he was working for Soviet intelligence, and Fuchs knew him as "Alexander". Kremer says that Kuczynski had a discussion about Fuchs with another diplomat, the Soviet ambassador Ivan Maisky, and claimed to have known Fuchs for many years, since 1936, when Kuczynski first arrived in London. According to Kremer, he was told about Fuchs as a result of this conversation.

By whatever means that first contact was arranged, when Kremer and Fuchs finally met, Fuchs insisted that the information he was going to supply reached Stalin—"was placed on Stalin's desk", as Kremer later said. Kremer replied that he did not have direct contact with Stalin, but that he did have a connection with someone who had and that he accepted Fuchs's conditions. At their meeting, according to Kremer, they started out speaking in German, but then changed to English. Fuchs made it clear that he was helping the Soviet Union for ideological reasons, not for money.

Shortly after their first meeting, it is said that Fuchs made an unannounced, and highly dangerous, visit to the

Soviet Embassy to make sure that Kremer was in fact connected to the Soviet Union. He accidentally bumped into Kremer walking along the corridors and Kremer, after overcoming his amazement, took him into a side room and explained that this was a serious breach of *konspiratsia*, or tradecraft, and was highly dangerous. The story has been mentioned in various publications, but it seems strange that Fuchs, who wasn't even a Soviet citizen, could bypass the strong security at the entrance and so easily walk the corridors of the Soviet Embassy.

The uncertainty about the date of the first meeting between Kremer and Fuchs is important. Before the German invasion of the Soviet Union on 22 June 1941, the Soviet Union was still an ally of Nazi Germany, and therefore an ally of a country at war with Britain. Any offer to pass over wartime secrets would be treason. The only certain date on record is that of the second meeting between Kremer and Fuchs, which was on 8 August. By then Fuchs had been fully integrated into the work of the MAUD Committee.

It took almost no time at all between his receipt of the 10 May letter from Peierls offering him a job for Fuchs to pay a visit to Birmingham to discuss the terms and to have the offer confirmed; he took up residence on 27 May. Peierls wrote that he had to wait for Fuchs to get a security clearance, but this clearly isn't true, because he was quickly collaborating with Peierls and other scientists working on MAUD.

Early in June, just two weeks after arriving in Birmingham, Fuchs accompanied Peierls when he paid a visit to the Cavendish Laboratory in Cambridge. Peierls was going specifically to speak to Professor Ralph Fowler, but he also wanted to meet Dr. Hans von Halban, a French physicist who, with his colleague Lew Kowarski and Frédéric Joliot-Curie in Paris, had investigated nuclear fission using a substance called heavy water. This water has molecules made up of an isotope of hydrogen called deuterium. Deuterium has a neutron, as well as a proton, in its nucleus, so the atom is twice as heavy as an atom of hydrogen, though it will combine with oxygen in the same way to produce water.

Halban and Kowarski had left Paris at the time of the German invasion and were installed in the Cavendish Laboratory doing research for the MAUD Committee into the fission of uranium oxide atoms surrounded by heavy water. Peierls wrote to Halban saying that he was bringing Fuchs with him especially to talk to one of their colleagues, Dr. Nicholas Kemmer, because, Peierls wrote, their problems were the same from a mathematical point of view. It would have been impossible for Fuchs to have any meaningful discussions with Dr. Kemmer or anyone else at the Cavendish without being aware of what they were working on, yet, as we shall see, MI5 had still not provided a security clearance for Fuchs.

When the MAUD Committee concluded its report in July 1941 it was the result of work from several teams from universities around the UK. As well as Peierls and Fuchs and two others at Birmingham, there was Chadwick with Frisch and seven others at Liverpool. The large team at the Cavendish Laboratory of which Halban and Kowarski were part was headed by Norman Feather and Egon Bretscher; they were not directly working on a weapon, but were exploring the possibilities of building a nuclear reactor. Oxford University was represented by Professor Franz Simon and Nicholas Kurti, and Fuchs's former mentor Nevill Mott was working with Herbert Fröhlich and two others in Bristol. Taken all together, they formed a diverse group of world-class scientists representing a broad spectrum of research, and a high proportion of them had fled the Nazis for a variety of reasons. In addition to this academic community, of course, there were the groups of engineers and scientists at companies like ICI and Vickers, all working on the practicality of separating uranium 235 from uranium 238.

The completed MAUD Report was a major advance from the memorandum written by Peierls and Frisch just eighteen months previously. It was really two separate reports, one covering the feasibility of building a bomb, the second about the uses of nuclear energy for power production. The nuclear weapon report said that the feasibility of an atomic bomb was proven, and that production of such a device would be possible within two years. It described the diffusion method of separating and enriching uranium, and put a price on the development of the weapon. Other parts of the report raised the possibility of building reactors to produce energy, of using nuclear energy to power ships, and the production of radioisotopes for use in medicine. It was a remarkable and far-sighted work, produced at a time when even the survival of Britain was still in doubt.

The report was submitted to Lord Hankey, secretary of the War Cabinet, with a request that it go before the Scientific Advisory Committee to decide on how to take the matter forward. This committee took its time examining the assumptions and calculations in the MAUD Report, and questioned other experts who had not been involved in the work. When it finally reported in late September the committee accepted the positive tenor of MAUD, but was sceptical about the time frame for making a bomb, saying that it was more likely to be five years than the two the report had suggested. The committee also wanted more investigation of uranium 235 and more research on the diffusion method of separating the isotope out. In short, the committee sat on the fence. The development of the uranium bomb should be regarded as a project of the very highest importance, it recommended, but it called for no further work to be done on a full-scale diffusion plant until two other things had been done: design work for the plant should be completed in the laboratory;

and then a pilot plant of two units, each of ten separation stages, for gaseous diffusion should be built to prove the process.

The members of the Scientific Advisory Committee believed that ultimately the project should be a collaboration with the United States. If the work were done there, it would be free from interference from air raids, the United States had the resources, and it would help bind the United States to Britain in the post-war world. The problem was that at the time the United States was neutral. For the moment the work should therefore be sited in Canada. So the committee recommended that one of the pilot plants and the full-scale separation plant ought to be assembled in Canada, and another pilot plant should be constructed in Britain, "provided the necessary priority can be assigned to it".

In order to carry on the work that the committee had recommended, a new organization was created—the Tube Alloys Directorate, a name chosen to be as misleading as possible about the true nature of the work. It operated under the control of the Department of Scientific and Industrial Research, and a Technical Committee was created, composed of Professors Chadwick and Simon, Dr. Halban, Rudolf Peierls and a representative of ICI, Dr. Slade, with Wallace Akers, from the board of ICI, recruited as its director and chairman and another ICI man, Michael Perrin, as his deputy. These people met as part of the new Tube Alloys Directorate in November 1941.

While the bureaucracy dithered and called for more research, Klaus Fuchs had acted. Before the Tube Alloys Directorate was established, he met his GRU contact, Semyon Kremer, or Alexander, on 8 August in a side street in London. There is no record of which street, or whether they quickly passed over material in a "brush by" contact or made their way to a rendezvous. It's probable that they caught a taxi and had a conversation while travelling. This, according to Fuchs, was Kremer's favourite way of meeting. It irritated Fuchs because he felt that taking a taxi was conspicuous, as was Kremer's habit of telling the driver to retrace their route to see if they were being followed. Accounts also differ about what Fuchs handed over. Kremer, in a later interview, said:

> . . . he gave me a large note pad, of around 40cm by 20cm in size which was full of formulations and equations. He told me, "Here is all what is necessary for your scientists to know how to organize production of nuclear weapons." All the material was sent to Moscow and an instruction was received back not to lose contact with Fuchs. But as usual, there wasn't anything said about how useful the material was.

Another Soviet account says that Fuchs handed over a short paper, which stated among other things that if only 1 per cent of the energy of a 10-kilogram nuclear bomb is used it will be equal to 1,000 tons of dynamite. This is a comparison that is used in the Frisch—Peierls Memorandum, and is repeated with more accuracy in an appendix of the MAUD Report itself. Whatever the complete set of documents was, a transmission from London was made on 10 August which included not only details of the documents but a briefing about the person who had supplied them. He was, the signal said, "a member of a special group at Birmingham University whose research focuses on building an atom bomb. Another group is active in Oxford on the practical side. The work should be finished within three months and then everything will move to Canada where the bomb will be produced."

Upon receipt of this signal, the director of the GRU in Moscow, Aleksei Panfilov, sent a reply to Kremer: "Do everything possible to obtain information about nuclear bomb." The material that Fuchs supplied was eventually passed on

22 September to Sergei Kaftanov, who was the Soviet State Committee for Defence's "plenipotentiary" for science, appointed shortly after the German invasion of the Soviet Union. In July he had established a Scientific Technical Council that coordinated the work of leading Soviet scientists in the defence of Mother Russia.

So, eight years after deciding that the Communist Party was the only defence against the Nazi threat in Germany, Fuchs had done all he could for the defence of the revolution and for the Soviet Union. That autumn the German army seized territory that supported 45 per cent of the Soviet population and produced 60 per cent of the country's coal, iron, steel and aluminium output. Worse was to come. That same autumn, however, Fuchs had handed over information that would ultimately transform the Soviet Union into the world's second superpower. Not even Fuchs understood the road he had started down.

EIGHT

A Lady from Banbury

While Klaus Fuchs worked on the problems of building an atomic bomb for Britain and started passing his work over to the Soviet Union, he was still an enemy alien and the restrictions this imposed on his movements were a severe hindrance to him and to his colleagues. Professor Rudolf Peierls, as we have seen, happily ignored any of the restrictions, but the Home Office and police were not so easy to avoid. When he arrived in Birmingham on 27 May 1941 Fuchs became a lodger with Peierls and his wife, Genia. Immediately on changing his address, he had to register with the Birmingham police, whose chief constable wrote to the chief constable of Edinburgh for any information that they might have on Fuchs. The reply was prompt and short. On 9 June the Edinburgh chief constable wrote back that nothing detrimental was contained in their records: "He is understood to be a Quaker and to have been persecuted by the Nazis."

That was one bureaucratic hurdle over, but the Ministry of Aircraft Production, then still responsible for the MAUD Committee, had to get a security clearance for Fuchs from MI5 so that they could issue an Aliens War Service permit.

The written application took its time, and receipt of the request was not registered by MI5 until 6 August. By then, of course, Fuchs had already made visits to some of the other university departments working on the questions of the separation of uranium. On 9 August MI5 sent a letter to the chief constable of Birmingham requesting details of Fuchs's background, mentioning in their letter that the German authorities had refused to renew his passport in 1934. In considering this request, the Birmingham police again wrote for further clarification to the chief constable of Edinburgh, who in turn sent back a much more detailed response.

The Edinburgh force's letter, written by Plain Clothes Police Constable Johnston Swan, is a very detailed description of Fuchs's arrival in the UK, his work at Bristol and the changes that had been made in the conditions to his visa over the years. It detailed his internment, and quoted the reference that Professor Max Born had given to the Internment Tribunal hearing in 1939, that Fuchs was a former member of the Socialist Student Clubs and, moreover, that he was an outstanding mathematical physicist. "There is nothing in the Records of this Force detrimental to the character of the alien," Constable Swan concludes. On the same day that this letter was received, the chief constable of Birmingham wrote to MI5 that nothing was recorded against Fuchs and that his only known associate was Professor Peierls. Peierls had vouched for Fuchs, and he would of course, the police pointed out, be working under Peierls's supervision.

MI5 were not satisfied with this and made other inquiries, casting their net amongst the émigré community and their handlers. These investigations took some time and the Ministry of Aircraft Production began to get impatient. The MAUD Report had been submitted formally in July, Fuchs was continuing to work on various aspects of atomic energy and the civil servants at the ministry were no doubt unhappy about this loose end. On 18 September they wrote again to MI5, asking for an explanation of the delay in replying to their original request. MI5 did not respond to this, because their inquiries were still taking place.

On 8 October an MI5 contact, Dr. Kurt Schreiber, codenamed Kaspar, had reported to his MI5 officer, Mr. Robson-Scott, that Fuchs was very well known in communist circles. The problem was that Schreiber had been unable, so far, to find out if he was a Party member, or to come up with any more details of Fuchs's activities. The MI5 officer handling the case wrote in the file that it would be difficult to hold this case up for much longer, so perhaps the best option would be to inform the Ministry of Aircraft Production of Fuchs's communist connections. This was a curious line for the Security Service to take, and on the face of it seems to be an abdication of responsibility.

There were no objections to this proposal, however, so on 10 October an MI5 officer, Wing Commander John Archer phoned the head of security at the Ministry of Aircraft Production, Mr. W. Stephens, and asked him if it would be serious if information about this work left the country? It was an impossible question. It is unlikely that Stephens fully understood the nature of the work going on in Birmingham, or what Peierls, Fuchs, Frisch and the other scientists around the country were really doing. It wasn't just because of the secrecy surrounding it, but also the abstruse nature of the highly theoretical work itself. The MI5 man went on to say that it was impossible to assess the risk, but that if there was any leak the information was likely to go to the Russians rather than to the Germans. Naturally, after listening to this statement Stephens wanted to go away and think. The crux of the matter, they agreed, was whether it was possible to employ someone else instead of Fuchs on this particular work.

Stephens made his inquiries and got back to MI5 a few days later, replying in writing: "We find that Dr. Fuchs assistance is urgently required at present, and since he will only have knowledge of such part of the work as is necessary for the performance of his duties, we think that there will be no objection to employing him, and we should be glad if the necessary formalities could be expedited." Anyone who knew what Fuchs's work was would find the idea that he would be told only what he needed to know absurd. Fuchs knew just about everything there was to know.

Along with Peierls, he had begun to examine the scientific literature brought over from Germany to London via Switzerland and Sweden to see what mentions there were of any work on nuclear physics and whether it revealed any signs of progress on atomic weapons. Peierls wrote a letter to Professor Chadwick in Liverpool on 23 September about such a visit: "I heard from Simon that you had suggested looking at German periodicals and Fuchs and I had just been in London for this purpose . . . I am not having this report circulated to the committee as I think its circulation should be restricted." Clearly either someone at the ministry had no idea of precisely how far Fuchs had become embedded in the atomic project, or they regarded MI5's objections as an irrelevance and Stephens' letter was merely intended to keep MI5 happy. The letter did exactly that: Wing Commander Archer replied in writing that MI5 had no objection to Fuchs getting his Aliens War Service permit.

By this time Fuchs had met the GRU officer Semyon Kremer three times and two bundles of documents had made their way to the Soviet State Committee for Defence. Fuchs was now providing valuable theoretical analysis on various aspects of the work being done at Tube Alloys. By the end of 1941 he had produced, in collaboration with Rudolf Peierls, two scientific papers on the separation of the isotopes of uranium 235. In 1942, as the project advanced and the design of the pilot diffusion plant developed, Fuchs started to look at the practical problems that would be experienced, attempting to work out theoretical solutions. The major problem with a diffusion process was how long it would take before the plant was producing a stream of gas with a higher concentration of the radioactive isotope. This was known as the equilibrium time, because the plant's output needed gas pressures to be equal from the inlet to the outlet and all through the various filter stages. Two papers were produced on this problem. Fuchs also worked with Peierls on a major analysis of the size and effect of the blast from nuclear fission, as well as the amount of uranium required to create a weapon.

In February 1942 Peierls flew to the United States with Professors Cockcroft and Chadwick for meetings with American scientists who were also working on nuclear energy. Peierls and Fuchs wrote a paper that comprehensively described the work that had been carried out in Britain and Peierls took this with him in the hope that it would lead to a mutual sharing of research and information between the US and Britain, who were now of course allies since the Japanese attack on Pearl Harbor two months earlier. The document detailed calculations of the critical mass of enriched uranium assuming the fast neutrons had constant energy, or if the neutrons' energy had variations. It made these calculations for different shapes, bearing in mind that the critical mass needed to be assembled by firing two hemispheres together, and that distortion of the metal might occur. They made other calculations about the reaction if the sphere was surrounded by material that reflected more of the neutrons back into the sphere of uranium.

The paper detailed calculations made to assess the energy released by the reaction, and what would be the mass of the uranium in the microseconds after the start of the chain reaction. Then it went on to consider the effect of the blast wave in air at temperatures that would be enough to separate the electrons from molecules of oxygen and nitrogen. Finally, it looked at what factors—such as impurities in the metal and the presence of hydrogen, for example—might precipitate a premature chain reaction. In fact, the paper described sufficient work to have answered a great many of the questions that were raised by the decision to create a nuclear weapon based on enriched uranium.

While Peierls was in the United States, Fuchs acted as his deputy back in Birmingham, handling correspondence with other research departments working for Tube Alloys and continuing to monitor German literature for information about what German scientists were up to.

The Aliens War Service permit that had been arranged for Fuchs did not remove the restrictions that were imposed by his registration as an enemy alien. He was still subjected to limits on his movements. If he wanted to visit Max Born in Edinburgh, for example, he still had to tell the Birmingham police and the police in Edinburgh before making the journey. He also had to do this if he ever stayed overnight in Liverpool when he was visiting Frisch or Chadwick, going to the ICI factory in Billingham or visiting Professor Simon in Oxford.

Fuchs, of course, had applied for a certificate of naturalization shortly before the outbreak of war, and he decided in April 1942 to try another application. If successful, it would make his work much easier. Once more, officers in the Security Service had the file of Klaus Fuchs on their desks. The application came in a memo from the Home Office to MI5, headed "National Interest Case for the favour of your early report". It was dated 30 April.

Mrs. Wyllie of Department C3 forwarded the request to department F2B, asking if that department had any remarks to make, while at the same time she sent a letter to the Birmingham chief constable with yet another inquiry about

Fuchs, posing the question why would his naturalization be in the national interest? Birmingham police responded that Fuchs was employed by the University of Birmingham on research work for the Department of Scientific and Industrial Research. The letter went on to say that "the Chief Constable is assured that if Fuchs still has any interest in politics it is not an active one and he has not been known to associate with communists in this District."

Following this, Mrs. Wyllie sent a memo to the Home Office stating that the Security Service had examined their records for Klaus Fuchs and they saw no objection to this application being granted. Fuchs became a British subject on 30 July 1942. He was now free of the restrictions and controls that had limited his movements, although they had been more of a hindrance in his work for Tube Alloys than in his activities as a spy.

Subsequently, however, MI5 received two reports from their émigré informants. One source, Kaspar, has already been mentioned, and his latest report triggered a request from MI5 to the chief constable of Birmingham for Fuchs's Aliens registration cards. These were sent in the post, no doubt examined, and returned on 26 July 1942. They would have shown MI5 nothing that they did not already know. Then in February 1943 source Kaspar provided another report on Fuchs. It is detailed, and describes Fuchs's family connections, but Kaspar made the fatal error of confusing Klaus with his brother Gerhard. Gerhard, of course, was a KPD official in Berlin and had sought refuge in Prague, but Kaspar states that so too did Klaus, and makes no mention of the fact that he entered the UK in 1933 and studied at Bristol University. MI5 followed this up, however, with fresh inquiries to Birmingham police, who responded, for the third time, in a letter dated 28 July 1943. The chief constable showed signs of exasperation. He enclosed the report written by them at the time of Fuchs's naturalization in

1942 and said that he was unable to learn anything to Fuchs's detriment. "You will appreciate", he wrote, "that the information regarding his being a communist originated from the German consulate at Bristol, and their report was possibly biased. There is no doubt that Fuchs is a man of high intelligence but he has caused no adverse comment at the University and we are assured that the work he is doing is of importance to this country."

Some departments of MI5 were undaunted by this. Mrs. Daphne Bosanquet of section F2B decided to take action. She obtained a warrant, described as a Return of Correspondence, that allowed MI5 to request the Post Office to record mail coming to an address. She reported that the Return, taken out for a fortnight, showed that Fuchs did not get a single letter. From this, said Mrs. Bosanquet, it appeared unlikely that he was in close touch with anyone of interest. She could not, of course, have been more wrong. Fuchs's contacts with Soviet Military Intelligence were still very much alive.

MI5 not only missed Fuchs's contact with Kremer, but there were other less conspiratorial aspects of his life that do not seem to have been followed up by them. Several MI5 sources reported that Fuchs was a member in Birmingham of the 70 Club, as well as an associate of the "Co-ordinating Committee of European Clubs", both of which were associations of refugee Germans and East European Communist Party members. The 70 Club in particular seems to have attracted the attention of some right-wing émigré Czechs, who were informants of the Security Service. The membership list of the club was stolen when the secretary was treated to large amounts of alcohol, which eventually made her pass out. The list of members prompted a German ex-communist, Hans Ripel, to tell an MI5 informer, "Victoria"—who was herself an associate of source Kaspar—to visit a German family in St. Albans who had been refugees in Prague and were associated with Fuchs's brother Gerhard when he was one of the KPD organizers there. Nothing in the MI5 files suggests that these leads were followed up.

Fuchs met Kremer four times, and in total handed over two hundred pages of information about his work for Tube Alloys. Then came an interruption in the regular contacts. Kremer returned to Moscow, and most Russian historians suggest that he went back to become an active soldier. If he did, it seems odd that the GRU did not make any arrangements to hand over Fuchs to another agent, especially as the GRU centre knew how important his information was. Yet in this period there was a constant turmoil in the leadership, with directors of Military Intelligence changing rapidly. Soviet scientists had not yet been given very much access to the stream of information that was coming from London.

As we have seen, Klaus Fuchs had first made contact with a representative of the GRU through Jürgen Kuczynski, leader of the German Communist Party in London. Now, left in limbo by the sudden departure of Semyon Kremer, he sought out Kuczynski again.

Ever resourceful and confident, Kuczynski had the solution. His sister Ursula, an equally resourceful woman with many identities, had arrived in Britain at the beginning of 1941 and by the time that Kremer left, she had set up her clandestine radio and established contact with GRU headquarters in Moscow.

She made regular visits to London to meet her brother and her parents at their home in Hampstead. On one of these visits, Jürgen told her about a comrade who had access to important information but had lost touch with the Soviet Union for some time, and that he had turned to Jürgen for advice. Sonya, as he was to know her, met Fuchs in a café in Birmingham. What she said to him no one knows, but it was enough for her to gain his trust and he started to give her information. She had arranged this liaison without any instructions from Moscow and the GRU was told about these contacts in a radio message from her on 22 October 1942. They radioed back that she should continue to maintain contact, and continue to take any information that he handed over.

After that first meeting, the venue changed. Sonya chose to meet in the countryside, because anybody attempting to follow them would have been very conspicuous, and because it allowed her and Fuchs to talk naturally, as though they were close friends. So they established a routine of meeting on a country path near Banbury, an old market town between Birmingham and Oxford. Sonya would ride her bike there and leave it nearby, then their clandestine meeting would take place under the guise of a man and woman taking a friendly walk, strolling arm in arm through the countryside. According to Sonya's account, she found these meetings pleasant. Fuchs was attractive, and she described him as calm and cultured, able to talk about books, films and current affairs.

It was an enormous relief to Sonya to be able to spend time talking to a member of the German Communist Party; it made a welcome break from her life of secrecy and isolation. It must, she believed, have been the same for Fuchs and, according to her, they became close to each other. In a passage that reveals much about Fuchs and his effect on women, she described how on a walk through some meadows to the edge of a wood she dug a small hole for a dead letter box, where messages could be left and later collected without the danger of a meeting. As she dug the hole, Fuchs watched. She thought this was quite all right because "I was more of an ordinary person and more practical than he. I looked up at him once and thought 'oh you dear, great professor.'" This, it must be remembered, is from a woman who had been a radio operator for spy networks in China, Poland, Switzerland

and now Britain, and had attended two long courses in secret GRU training schools.

Sonya was a trained radio operator, but the information handed over by Fuchs was too long and too esoteric to be condensed into coded radio signals, which in wartime Britain had to be as short as possible and irregularly scheduled to avoid detection. Sonya must have made significant changes to her modus operandi to pass the documents to someone who would be able to get them to Moscow; the most convenient way would be to get them to the London embassy, where they would then have some diplomatic cover. Sonya never revealed how she achieved this.

Fuchs's knowledge about the work that was being done in Britain on nuclear research was extensive, and he saw it from the point of view of a Soviet agent. In April 1943 Sonya reported to Moscow that Fuchs had identified another scientist as a possible spy. He was Engelbert Broda, an Austrian refugee who was at the time at the Cavendish Laboratory in Cambridge, and had worked for the Halban group on their research into heavy-water reactors. He was an active member of the Austrian Communist Party, as was his wife Hildegard, who eventually divorced her husband and married one of his colleagues, Allan Nunn May. Nunn May also passed information over to the Soviet Union, via the NKGB, but it isn't clear that Fuchs was aware of this until Nunn May was arrested in 1946. The GRU decided not to recruit Broda, however.

Fuchs must have felt demoralized and frustrated in July 1942, when the link he had established with Kremer was allowed to collapse and it seemed that Moscow did not appear to react with any urgency to his information. The new contact with Sonya must have restored his belief in what he was doing, but it was not until early in 1943 that the first serious response was received from Moscow, and at that point it would have been clear to Fuchs that someone understood the material that he had delivered. It had, however, taken some time before it was brought to the attention of Soviet scientists.

Originally, Soviet physicists had shared in the advances made in nuclear science in the 1920s and 1930s. A physics institute had been opened in Petrograd—as St. Petersburg, or Leningrad was called at the time—in 1923 under Abram Ioffe, and one of Russia's leading atomic physicists, Pyotr Kapitsa, had worked with Rutherford at the Cavendish Laboratory for twelve years. Ioffe's institute had set up a nuclear department under the direction of a young scientist called Igor Kurchatov, who had moved into the study of nuclear physics in 1932; later he became head of the physics department at the Radium Institute in Leningrad. The rise of Stalin had gradually isolated Soviet science, however. Kapitsa had been prevented from returning to Cambridge in 1934, and the purges of 1937 and 1938 saw many scientists jailed or shot. But while physical contact with the West diminished, the scientific journals were still available and the Soviet physics community was able to remain current with research in the rest of the world.

Three scientists wrote to the Soviet deputy premier in 1939 suggesting that he create a Uranium Commission, and in May of 1940 Georgi Flerov, in Kurchatov's department, ran an experiment that led to his discovery of spontaneous nuclear fission. On 29 August 1940 Flerov, with Kurchatov and Yulii Khariton, submitted a plan called "On the Utilization of the Energy of Uranium Fission in a Chain Reaction". The paper led to some initial research at the Radium Institute by Khariton and Yakov Zeldovich, but their work was principally concerned, as was the original proposal, with the study of natural uranium. No one had considered the concept of artificially increasing the concentration of the radioactive isotope in natural uranium to increase the efficiency of the chain reaction in the way that

Frisch and Peierls had proposed. The research carried out by the Uranium Commission looked at a variety of ways of enriching uranium, but not from the point of view of creating a weapon.

However, the information that Fuchs supplied in his two meetings with Kremer in 1941 would not have been met with loud cries of "Eureka!" in Moscow. The German invasion of June 1941 brought a halt to everything. Most nuclear scientists abandoned their research and started work on immediate wartime technology such as radar, armour and naval mine defences. Flerov began training as an aeronautical engineer to work on developing dive-bombers, although he kept returning to the question of uranium and chain reactions. The German advance was astonishingly quick and the Red Army, whose officer corps had also been damaged by the purges of 1938, was in poor shape. In October 1941, as catastrophe seemed absolutely certain, Stalin gave an order for Moscow—that is, the ministries and government apparatus—to be evacuated to Kuibyshev in the east. In this chaos it is no surprise that almost no attention was paid to the information coming from Britain until March 1942, when Lavrenty Beria, head of the NKGB, wrote a letter to Stalin and the GKO (the State Defence Committee) recommending that steps were taken to evaluate intelligence about work in Britain on the uranium question.

What had spurred Beria to action was the receipt of a copy of the MAUD Report, along with minutes of the British Cabinet's Scientific Advisory Committee. The NKGB had many spies in Britain and it is assumed that one of them, the civil servant John Cairncross, who worked for War Cabinet Secretary Lord Hankey, was the source of this material. Although he confessed to working for the NKGB, Cairncross denied this particular allegation, saying that by the time the MAUD Report was completed Lord Hankey had very little to do with it any more. A Russian historian,

Vladimir Lotta, with some access to the GRU files, says that the intelligence material that was in the possession of Military Intelligence triggered the first steps in the Soviet work on the atomic bomb. It is not clear whether this material included the MAUD Report or, if it did, who the source was.

What Vladimir Lotta does claim is that Igor Kurchatov started to work with Military Intelligence in October 1942. Kurchatov was at the time employed at a university in Kazan, the capital of Tatarstan, to where Leningrad University had been evacuated. He was invited to Moscow by Sergei Kaftanov, given access to the intelligence documents and asked to make a report based on them.

A few months earlier, in April 1942, Georgi Flerov was stationed in Voronezh, and although the nearby university had been evacuated, the library still had copies of various periodicals. Flerov looked through them and noticed that there were no articles in the US *Physical Review* or in *Nature*, about questions of nuclear physics. He suspected that this might indicate that the topic was now considered too sensitive to publish. He wrote to Kaftanov suggesting that this issue be investigated. Kaftanov did not reply. Flerov, still convinced that he was right, then took the final step of writing directly to Stalin, saying that he felt that he was facing a brick wall, and called for a conference of scientists to be convened. Again he got no reply, but this letter was probably forwarded to Kaftanov as well.

So, despite the terrible losses that the Soviet Union had suffered, there was some pressure on Kaftanov. He and another member of the GKO responded by saying they had talked about the question of a uranium-based weapon to several other scientists, but that only Kurchatov had responded positively to the idea. The story goes that Kurchatov was brought to Moscow and put up at the Moskva Hotel, around the corner from Red Square, where he worked for a month.

The information he was given was contained in three separate bundles, all of which had been received by the GRU over a short period in August and September 1942. Altogether, there were about 280 pages of information for Kurchatov to read and subject to close analysis.

He produced his report for Kaftanov at the end of November. His conclusions were that Soviet science was some way behind Britain and the United States, and that a nuclear bomb would be a dreadful weapon. He recommended that work start on a bomb in earnest.

The report went from Kaftanov to Vyacheslav Molotov, who was Soviet foreign minister and also Stalin's deputy; he then passed it on to Stalin personally. By February 1943, when the battle of Stalingrad was in its final stages, the GKO made a formal decision to start work on a bomb.

After looking at the intelligence material, he produced a list of questions to which he wanted answers and handed it to Molotov to pass on to the GRU. He wanted to know if Metropolitan-Vickers had successfully manufactured the membranes for the diffusion plant and what the results were. He also asked for plans and a technical description. In all there were, according to Lotta, twelve points on which Kurchatov wanted more information. These were passed back to Sonya, who in turn asked Fuchs if he could supply the answers.

Kurchatov was officially appointed as scientific director of the Russian project on 1 March. He had a great deal of information to assess, and one of the first questions was whether the whole package of documents he had been given was an exercise in disinformation? Was this a genuine description of a real and serious project to create a frightening new weapon, or was it designed to make the Soviet Union waste scarce resources on a chimera, and so weaken their fight against Nazism?

Kurchatov decided, crucially, that the documents were

genuine. There were some mistakes, but these seemed minor errors in calculations that were easily spotted. However, he also saw something to which the scientists working on the Tube Alloys project had not paid sufficient attention. This was the results of the research carried out by Halban and Kowarski, whose research was concerned with heavy water in a reactor; it showed that a by-product of burning natural uranium in a reactor would be a metal called plutonium, and that this would be an easier route to creating a bomb than using highly enriched uranium. There were problems with this approach, which Kurchatov did not know about. But it was this that made him decide that the first task of his team was to build a nuclear reactor.

While Fuchs's material was slowly absorbed by Soviet physicists, Sonya continued to meet him regularly every three months, passing on the requests for information made by Kurchatov and receiving new material from him. Fuchs now knew that the importance of his information was understood in Moscow and that it was triggering action, as indeed it was. Kurchatov planned a new research centre in Moscow and called up a team of scientists, including Flerov, to work with him. As the project got under way, Sonya was ordered to stop working with her other contacts and to meet Fuchs with increasing regularity. The GRU gave him a code name, "Otto"; later in his career he was called variously "Charles" and "Rest". There were more questions to ask him, and he produced a contents list of all the documents that he had provided since his first contact with Kremer in 1941.

In September 1943 Fuchs became aware that he would probably be going to the United States. He told Sonya, and obviously wanted to maintain the link with Soviet intelligence. Sonya was asked by the GRU to arrange an initial meeting place with Fuchs in America, and to establish some visual signals and passwords for a new contact. Fuchs suggested to Sonya that he would be going to a remote location, but until he knew more about it she proceeded on the basis that a meeting would take place in New York. She had had a job in a bookshop there some years ago before starting to work for the KPD and the Comintern, so she dredged up a likely location for a covert meeting from her memory of the city.

Fuchs now took a huge gamble. He suggested a possible fallback arrangement through which he could be contacted if the New York rendezvous wasn't possible. He gave Sonya the address in Boston of his sister Kristel and her husband, Robert Heinemann. It was radioed to the GRU and a recognition code was arranged, which Fuchs would have to pass on to Kristel. It was an uncharacteristic mistake for Fuchs to make and it was, as we shall see, one that would come back to haunt him.

Sonya's final message concerning Fuchs was received from Moscow in November. "The meetings location and arrangements in New York are clear. Please give 'Otto', our thanks. Tell him that we hope that his collaboration with us in this new place will be as successful as it was in England." This was an understatement by the GRU centre. Between 1941 and 1943 Fuchs had handed over 570 pages of calculations and description of the construction of an atomic weapon and the process of enriching uranium. It was almost the sum total of the research that had been produced in Britain on the subject.

NINE

Allies in Name

When Klaus Fuchs started working with Rudolf Peierls on the MAUD Report, the scientists working on it were at the cutting edge of nuclear weapons research, more advanced than in any other country. In August 1940, a small group of British officials and scientists, headed by Sir Henry Tizard, chairman of the Air Defence Research Committee, visited Washington, taking with them details of British developments in radar, proximity fuses for shells and so on, in the hope of being able to increase US assistance to Britain. Professor John Cockcroft was part of the team. American research into the nuclear question was also under way and Cockcroft visited Enrico Fermi at the University of Chicago, where Fermi was working on building a nuclear reactor. Fermi was also investigating the possibility of using plutonium as a substitute for uranium 235 in a weapon. Other teams in New York and California were looking at different methods of separating the isotopes of uranium, but Cockcroft's impression was that the work carried out in the United States did not have the same urgency as the work being undertaken in the UK.

In October 1941 copies of the MAUD Report were sent

to two American scientists, Dr. Kenneth Bainbridge and Professor Charles C. Lauritsen, who had in fact attended a drafting meeting of the MAUD Committee in London earlier in July. On their return to the United States they made sure that the report's conclusions reached Dr. Vannevar Bush, head of the National Defense Research Committee and his deputy, Dr. James Conant. The report impressed them, and this was reinforced by Professor Ernest Lawrence at Berkeley in California, who urged them to take notice of the work being carried out on the question.

Bush took the MAUD proposals seriously and sent two US scientists, Dr. Harold Urey and Dr. George Pegram, to the UK. They arrived in October 1941 and went to all the universities where work was being carried out. They met those running the new Tube Alloys organization, and Chadwick, Peierls and others. They told their hosts that they wanted to pool all the information about nuclear research and the various organizational approaches to the problems that currently existed.

There had been similar approaches at a diplomatic level. Charles Darwin, the British scientific liaison officer based in Washington, had written to Lord Hankey in August of 1941 to say that Dr. Bush and Dr. Conant wanted to treat work on the uranium problem as a joint Anglo-American programme. In October, Roosevelt wrote to Winston Churchill, "It appears desirable that we should soon correspond concerning the subject which is under study by your MAUD Committee and by Dr. Bush's organization in this country in order that any extended offers may be coordinated or even jointly conducted." The overtures and the desire for collaboration could not have been more obvious or more explicitly stated.

But they were not taken up by the British government. There were several reasons. One was a basic belief that the work on the bomb should remain in British hands. This view had been expressed by both the Chiefs of Staff Committee in their comments on the MAUD Report, and by Lord Cherwell, Churchill's chief scientific advisor, who had written in his memo to Churchill:

> However much I may trust my neighbour and depend on him I am very much averse to putting myself completely at his mercy and would therefore not press the Americans to undertake this work: I would just continue exchanging information and get into production over here without raising the question of whether they should do it or not.

The failure to respond to the US proposals at the time when the British programme still had something to offer was to have profound consequences, and events quickly changed the relationship between US and British scientists. President Roosevelt had agreed to set up a nuclear weapons programme in October 1941, but the Japanese attack on Pearl Harbor, naturally, galvanized the United States and their nuclear scientists were soon to be given massive resources.

Robert Oppenheimer, a former student of Max Born at Göttingen, was put in charge of the programme and held a series of meetings around the country, culminating in a conference at Berkeley, California, in June 1942. Oppenheimer was tall and slim, with a clean-shaven, ascetic face—the perfect image of an East Coast WASP. Riddled with personal conflicts, his demeanour was normally calm and patrician. He was the perfect foil for many of the more excitable émigré scientists. Assembled together at this meeting were people he had worked and studied with in the past, like Hans Bethe, Edward Teller and many of the leading theoretical physicists in the US. They were attempting to pull together all the work that had been done so far on creating a nuclear weapon. They also had many of the papers written for MAUD and the Tube Alloys project, and the official Los Alamos history states that particularly useful was material from Fuchs, Peierls, Paul Dirac and Boris Davison.

The Berkeley conference led to the conclusion that a completely new organization was necessary if a weapon was to be built in any reasonable time scale, and in a short while the Manhattan Engineering District, as the weapons programme was called, was established. Oppenheimer became the chief scientist and in overall command was General Leslie Groves from the Army Corps of Engineers. By August 1942 the US bomb programme was seriously under way.

The same could not be said for the British Tube Alloys Directorate. The cautious approach adopted after the MAUD Report had proved fatal. Wallace Akers returned from a visit to the United States impressed with the speed of progress and the resources that had been shifted to nuclear research. All the various theoretical possibilities of separating out uranium 235 from natural uranium were being developed into full-scale plants. Fermi, in Chicago, was also pursuing the proposed alternative to uranium 235, plutonium, with the construction of a reactor using graphite blocks and uranium oxide as a fuel; it went critical—in other words, a chain reaction started—on 2 December.

The biggest indication of the change in US attitude, and the main difference from that in the UK, was that the reactor was built and allowed to go on stream, even though the difficult problems of extracting plutonium from the uranium fuel had not yet been completely worked out. Contrast this with the position adopted by the two former ICI men, Wallace Akers and Michael Perrin, who put their conclusions to the Tube Alloys Consultative Council in July 1942. A full-scale British-type separation plant could not be built in Britain, they said, and they hoped arrangements would be made at once for the design and erection in the United

States of a pilot plant for the British process. This hope was doomed.

In December 1942, Conant, Bush and General Groves worked on a new policy on atomic collaboration that took into account the advances that the US had achieved and the sums of money they had spent and were committed to spending. The new policy memorandum was handed by Dr. Conant to Akers in January 1943, and it crushed any British hopes of equal collaboration. It ruled out any exchange of information on plutonium production, the designs of nuclear power plants, the production of uranium hexaflouride, and any further information on the design or construction of a nuclear weapon. The overriding principle was announced bluntly in the memorandum's opening paragraph: interchange on design and construction of new weapons and equipment is to be carried out only to the extent that the recipient of the information is in a position to make use of this information in this war. In effect, the exchange of information was now to be a one-way street that headed in the direction of the United States.

Sir John Anderson, the minister responsible for Tube Alloys, told Churchill that the whole memorandum was shocking. He urged the prime minister to take the matter up with President Roosevelt at the forthcoming Casablanca Conference. Anderson wrote, "The pretext for this policy is the need for secrecy, but one cannot help suspecting that the United States military authorities who are now in complete control wish to gain an advance upon us and feel that they will not suffer unduly by casting us aside." But there was no discussion at Casablanca, and none of the president's advisors was inclined to take up the issue. Churchill sent telegrams and letters, but there was no reply.

The decision for Britain to go it alone could no longer be avoided. Rudolf Peierls wrote to Akers in May 1943 pointing out that he and other scientists felt that they were in limbo, with a complete loss of momentum. He was very critical of the amount of indecision at high level:

> As soon as there was a serious possibility that collaboration would fail it was in my view the duty of the Policy Committee to consider this possibility and make up their minds what to do if it failed. As long as there is a possibility that one will want to go on with the project every week lost in preparing for it is a week of postponement of its completion.

But there was little faith in the programme. The costs in money, manpower and raw materials were considered to be too great. The estimate was that capital expenditure was required of the order of £70 million, and that around twenty thousand workers would be needed, a good quarter of them highly skilled craftsmen. In the context of the vast sums spent on Bomber Command, the amount wasn't great, but the forecast was that the programme would not produce a useable weapon until 1947. If these considerations were not enough to squash the idea of a full-scale project, the news that the United States had secured the whole output of the Canadian uranium mines and the output of heavy water was another bombshell. It meant either that another mine in Canada had to be financed or uranium shipped in from the Belgian Congo.

Under pressure from Churchill, President Roosevelt eventually shifted his position and at the Quebec Conference in August 1943 a new agreement was signed between them about access to atomic secrets by Britain. This new agreement accepted that the United States had borne far more of the expense of developing atomic energy than the United Kingdom. Both governments agreed that they would never use the weapon against each other, that it would not be used against third countries without each other's consent, and that no information about Tube Alloys would be communicated to third parties. In particular, the agreement said that Britain disavowed any rights over the commercial and industrial exploitation of the technology after the war. The working of the agreement and oversight of the collaboration would be by a Combined Policy Committee in Washington. One inconvenient detail was that the exchange of information would be "full and effective between those scientists engaged in the same sections of the field". This still seemed to limit exchange to those areas where British scientists had already carried out research, so a great deal of crucial work on plutonium and reactor design, for example, might still be off-limits. All the work would be carried out in the US, but there was a promise that US assistance would be provided for Britain and Canada to build a heavy-water reactor in Montreal. It was all that would be on offer, and everyone knew it. So keen was Akers to get men from Tube Alloys into the heart of the US programme that, on hearing the news of the agreement, he telegraphed to London urging Chadwick, Oliphant, Simon and Peierls to come at once. They arrived the very day that the Quebec Agreement was signed.

A telegram from Chadwick to Sir John Anderson, the Cabinet secretary, summed up the situation and revealed the strategy that was now the only hope for Britain. "The American effort is on such a scale that we could not compete with it even in peace time." The conclusion was that the closest collaboration with the United States was essential. It was vital for Britain:

> We should acquire the fullest possible knowledge and experience of all phases of the project so that we shall be in a position when the time comes to start work in England on the right lines, profiting by American experience. There is no question in my opinion, or in that

of the Technical Committee that this policy is in our
own interest.

The team of British scientists to go to the United States was
assembled in great haste. It can best be judged by the speed
with which Otto Frisch was transformed into a British
citizen. The driving force in this whole effort was Akers,
with ingenuity and focus provided by his secretary, Miss
Mayne.

Oppenheimer and Hans Bethe had asked that Frisch,
as one of the originators of the Frisch—Peierls Memorandum
and a highly respected theorist, join them at Los Alamos,
the secret camp in New Mexico where work on the bomb
was carried out. Yet as an Austrian citizen, Frisch was still
an enemy alien and under General Groves's instructions was
not allowed to receive any information about the Manhattan
Project. Miss Mayne organized his application for naturalization and his certificate of citizenship was rapidly granted.
He then took the Oath of Allegiance, which made him a
British subject, and as such, under the wartime regulations,
he registered for military service, but was immediately
granted a deferment. He then applied for and was issued
with a passport, which was stamped with an exit permit and
a United States visa, the whole business being completed in
two days. Frisch took absolutely no part in this process,
apart from riding in a taxi from office to office like a parcel,
with paperwork and letters that were all typed up and
witnessed by Miss Mayne.

Seventeen scientists were organized as part of the
British Mission, and their passage on a ship leaving for New
York was provisionally arranged for 24 November. Michael
Perrin, at the Tube Alloys Directorate in Old Queen Street,
wrote to the Privy Council offices urging them to put pressure on the Ministry of War Transport to make sure that
they all got tickets.

At the beginning, most of the people who went, including Fuchs, did so because of their knowledge of the diffusion process for separating uranium 235, and this would clearly limit the information they would be able to bring back to the UK. The British government tried to push Rudolf Peierls into a position where he would not only be employed with the diffusion team in New York, where this work was being done, but would also travel to take part in the work of Los Alamos where the work on the bomb was being carried out. General Groves was adamant that this should not occur, because it would breach his policy of compartmentalization, a policy that would ensure that as few people as possible had a complete picture of the total effort devoted to the creation of an atomic weapon. Groves was one of the few men who had such an overview, and he was prepared to grant this to Chadwick, who was to become head of the British Scientific Mission. No other British scientists were to be given this privilege. Sir John Anderson was tempted to argue about this, in the belief that a dual role for Peierls would be acceptable for most of the groups of scientists in the project, but Groves insisted and Anderson backed down.

There was one other slight issue, and that was General Groves's request that the British give a security clearance for the members of their mission. This they did, and according to the FBI Wallace Akers wrote to General Groves saying that Fuchs had been given special clearance. What did this amount to?

Fuchs's name appears on a list for passage to the United States that was dated 11 November 1943, and it is likely that he was selected much earlier. The question of his security clearance, however, appeared to arise quite late in the Department of Scientific and Industrial Research, because it wasn't until 17 November that they sent a telex to MI5 about Klaus Fuchs, who had been granted a certificate of naturalization on 30 July 1942. The telex said that he was a mathematical physicist and was leaving the country for the United States as part of a government mission. It asked if there were any objections to his journey to the United States and requested a reply by 18 November, the next day.

The response by the MI5 officers was one of outrage. Millicent Bagot of Department F2B, an expert in communist infiltration, wrote "we knew that his naturalization was under consideration but the report did not state that it was a fait accompli". Sadly for MI5's Soviet experts, it was. Another pre-war communist subversion expert, Michael Serpell, realized that not only was Fuchs now a British citizen, but there was probably nothing they could do to hold up his trip. Trying to keep his hand in the game, he asked of Major G. Garrett, MI5's security liaison officer with the Department of Scientific and Industrial Research, whether any period had been set on Fuchs's stay in the US?

The reply came back on 8 December, when Fuchs had already landed in the United States, that they could not yet give a firm statement about how long Fuchs would remain in New York. Serpell pressed on. "I should be grateful if you could discover the address of Fuchs in the USA, and perhaps at the same time it might be possible to inquire whether he does belong to the particular batch of workers referred to in your minute." It was all bluff. Serpell could do nothing with the information about Fuchs's address, and what did it matter if Fuchs was on an original list or not? Serpell was not going to be told the reasons for Fuchs's urgent journey to the United States and he must have been aware of that, and also aware that MI5's views were now irrelevant.

However, Michael Perrin at Tube Alloys must have known of the disquiet. He wrote to Major Garrett on 10 January 1944 to say that Fuchs's visit was intended to be a short one, and that he would probably return with the rest of the scientists. However, Perrin had received a telegram from Peierls saying that he wanted Fuchs to stay out there with him. Perrin wanted from MI5 their most detailed views on the question of Fuchs from a security angle, writing:

> This is a very important matter vis-à-vis the Americans and I want to be quite sure that we do not slip up in any way. I know that you people have had at one time slight doubts about some of Fuchs' connections, and I should be much obliged if you could let me know the present position as quickly as possible.

This letter does not seem to have been passed to either Serpell or Millicent Bagot in MI5 headquarters, and it is impossible to say why. It went to Ms. Daphne Bosanquet, now of D Branch, which was security and travel control. She replied to Major Garrett, pointing out that a full picture of Fuchs's communist activity could be obtained from Michael Serpell. However, she wrote "Clarke's opinion [David Clarke was another officer in F Division] is that he is rather safer in America than in this country, and that for that reason he is rather in favour of his remaining in America where he is away from his English friends." Also, she went on, "it would not be so easy for Fuchs to make contact with communists in America, and that in any case he would probably be more roughly handled were he found out."

The note was dated 16 January 1944. It must rank as one of the more significant blunders of any intelligence agency in history. There is no record of Garrett's response, nor is there one of his reply to Michael Perrin. But we know that Fuchs remained in New York, and how difficult it was for him to make contact with communists in America we shall shortly find out.

TEN

Mission to New York

The scientists, Fuchs among them, who were part of the British Scientific Mission embarked on the former cruise ship RMS *Andes*, now converted to wartime use as a troop transport, for a fast passage across the Atlantic to dock at Newport News in Virginia on 3 December 1943. From there they went by train to Washington, where the large British presence in the US was coordinated through the offices of the British Supply Council in North America. Remarkably, this small group of men were the physical result of months of argument and haggling between supposed allies. Seen by the British government as their foot in the door of the atom bomb project, they were viewed with suspicion by many Americans.

The party was introduced to General Groves, then those who were going to work on the diffusion project continued on their way to New York and put up in the Hotel Taft in Times Square. The hotel was like many in wartime New York: long, narrow, dimly lit corridors, filled with the comings and goings of people who didn't actually seem to be occupying rooms. Times Square also had a brash, sleazy atmosphere, particularly noticeable to Middle European scientists with an intellectual upbringing. It was a far cry from Vienna, and an enormous change from Britain.

The first time that Fuchs had crossed the Atlantic he had been heading for a Canadian internment camp. There he had shared a large bunkhouse with a hundred or so other internees. On his return to the UK he had been confronted with a country at war. Liverpool, the port where he had disembarked, had been severely bombed and the working-class streets around the docks had been hit by German air raids time and time again. Once in Birmingham, Fuchs had not only experienced the effects of nightly air raids, but he had learned to live with the blackout and to carry out his nightly fire-watch duties for the university. Everything was rationed. Here in New York, even he, committed communist that he was, couldn't fail to be affected by what he saw and felt of the vibrant life in the streets. Another émigré scientist who had arrived from the UK was overwhelmed by the simplest sights. A street market with oranges piled high on fruit stalls, their peel glistening in the glow of acetylene lanterns, brought him to the verge of tears.

The New York offices of the British Supply Council were headquartered on Wall Street, on the twenty-fifth floor of a skyscraper, and this is where Fuchs and the other scientists worked.

General Groves had drawn on the assistance of several major US corporations and brought them into the Manhattan Project as lead contractors. The work to build the diffusion plant had been given to the large civil engineering company M. W. Kellogg, and they had set up a subsidiary called Kellex to do the research and construction of the planned diffusion plants. Some theoretical work on various options for separation had been done at Columbia University and by 1942 work on the full-scale plants had started. Three different separation methods were being adopted. One was the British system based on diffusion, one was based on a series of centrifuges, while another, developed by Professor Lawrence at Berkeley, used rings of electromagnets wrapped in silver worth $300 million. This last one was facing recurrent breakdowns because of manufacturing problems.

All these big industrial plants were under construction at a huge site known as Oak Ridge in Tennessee. A whole new industry was being built from scratch. Oak Ridge eventually encompassed over 268 buildings, with sewage-treatment plants, warehouses, shops, a foundry, a generator building, nineteen water-cooling towers, eight electricity substations, canteens, laboratories and so on. Twenty thousand construction workers were housed to develop the site. This was just one of a number of enormous facilities for the Manhattan Project that were mushrooming across America.

But Fuchs, Peierls, Tony Skyrme, Frank Kearton and others who were part of the diffusion team saw nothing of all this. Fuchs stayed in the Taft Hotel for a while, then in February moved into a small furnished flat on West 77th Street. The impression formed by his colleagues was that he was entirely devoted to his work for the mission; that he occasionally visited Columbia University, where he became friendly with Dr. Karl Cohen, who was also doing some research for Kellex; and that he went to the Kellex offices for discussions. He made one visit out of New York, at Christmas 1943, and this was to his sister Kristel and her husband Robert Heinemann, who lived now in Cambridge, Massachusetts. It was the first time he had seen her since 1936 and there was a lot to catch up on. He also had to give her the details that he had arranged with Sonya in case Kristel was contacted by a stranger looking for him. She would probably have understood that she should not ask her brother for too many details. Fuchs claimed that he did not provide her with any.

Rudolf Peierls was the leader of the British delegation in New York and he devoted a lot of his time to corresponding with Chadwick and Akers, as well as pursuing his scientific contacts in the Manhattan Project. This was a role that he had performed since his first visit to the US with Oliphant and Chadwick in 1942, and it is obvious that he was trying to find ways for himself and others in the British Mission to penetrate further into the work of the project. There was far more to building a bomb than separating uranium 235, and the more that he and others could find out about the US programme the better it would be.

Fuchs wrote a detailed report of the work of the New York scientists before they moved back to the UK, in which he made reference to the liaison and general advisory work that Peierls carried out. It is a document that explains a great deal about the work undertaken in the theoretical unit of Kellex and that of Columbia University. They were responsible mainly for analysing various fluctuations in the efficiency of the separation plant. The fluctuations could be caused by changes in temperature, or variations in the volume and pressure of gas flowing through the separators. The effect of withdrawing individual diffusion units for maintenance was also calculated. At the end of the work—which resulted in the production of seventeen papers, more than half of them written solely by Fuchs—an important aspect of the diffusion process had been closely analysed. The papers had titles like "Fluctuations and the Efficiency of a Diffusion Plant" and "On the Effect of a Time Lag in the Control of Plant Stability". The work was not of enormous theoretical significance, but formed a comprehensive analysis of the problems and solutions of running a diffusion plant that had been constructed on an industrial scale.

One other part of the work that Fuchs's report didn't mention was that he was the joint applicant of several patents that were filed by the Department of Scientific and Industrial Research. These patents concerned designs for diffusion equipment and were part of an agreement between the British government and the scientists working on Tube Alloys. Fuchs's co-signatories were Rudolf Peierls and Franz Simon. They related to work carried out in Britain and clearly Fuchs was a key figure. Fuchs's philosophy, which he expressed in the interview that he gave towards the end of his life, was that the more useful he was to Britain and the United States, the more useful he could be to the Soviet Union.

Fuchs's papers were written in longhand, shown to Peierls and then typed up by the secretaries in the Supply Council's office. They were then duplicated and numbered, before being distributed to the members of the team; the printing was done at first in the British offices and later, after the mission had been working for a few months, by Kellex staff. Fuchs received back his original and a carbon copy, as well as his copy of the duplicated report. His original notes or the carbon copy could then be handed over to a contact. Other material needed to be copied either in longhand or on a typewriter, which he could do in his apartment, and Fuchs developed the habit of working at home so that he had a legitimate excuse if anyone questioned why secret material was in his possession. Of course no one ever did.

At Fuchs's last meeting with Sonya in Britain, she had given him the details for the secret liaison with his new contact in New York. The place she had picked was the Settlement at Henry Street, a building in a working-class Jewish area in the East Side, just three blocks from the East River. She told Fuchs what to carry and what his contact would be carrying, and what passwords they should use so that they could identify each other.

Fuchs later claimed that the first rendezvous in New York was within days of his arrival there, just before Christmas in December 1943, but "Raymond", or Harry Gold, his latest handler and most other sources claim that it was in February 1944. What isn't in doubt are the details of the meeting. It was just before four o'clock on Saturday, 5 February. Fuchs carried a tennis ball and a green-bound book, while Gold was wearing a pair of gloves and carrying a spare pair. They were on opposite sides of the street, so Gold crossed and asked Fuchs the way to Chinatown. Fuchs replied, "I think Chinatown closes at five o'clock." Harry Gold, or Raymond, was now Fuchs's connection to the Soviet Union. He was short and tubby, with a liking for wide, colourful ties, and he had been a spy for the Soviet Union since 1935. He was born in Switzerland in 1910, to Russian Jewish émigrés who moved and settled in the United States in 1914. Harry studied chemistry, then worked at the Pennsylvania Sugar Company in Philadelphia. His first work for Soviet intelligence was passing on industrial secrets, and over the years he handed over information about most of the secret processes that his company was developing. In addition, he was the contact for other spies who worked for Eastman Kodak, or who had information about various chemical-engineering processes and equipment. Gold rarely questioned what benefit the relatively mundane information he supplied might be to the Soviet Union. When he did, he was assured that the Soviet Union could not obtain this information any other way. It didn't occur to him that the risks that he and others like him were running might be more geared to promoting his handlers' careers and guaranteeing their continued presence in the United States than to benefiting the workers of the Soviet Union. Gold had joined the Communist Party not through a profound understanding of Marxism, but partly because of a belief that the Party and the Soviet Union were the only real bulwark against anti-semitism. But he had principles, and he stuck with them. During a strike at his factory in March 1937 Gold was the only white-collar worker who refused to cross the picket line and he continued to stay away from the factory even when his boss threatened him with blacklisting and when the company's strike-breaking efforts became violent.

Gold had had a variety of Soviet handlers in his spying career. One, known as "Fred", who arrived on the scene in 1937, was a thug and a bully, probably the product of the turmoil that was occurring in the NKGB in Moscow at a time of show trials and purges under Stalin. Fred tried to intimidate Gold into blackmailing contacts to recruit them as agents. He also pressured him into spying on Trotskyite organizations and their membership. Gold might have severed his links with Soviet intelligence at this point, but a change of handler, and a nasty anti-semitic attack by a drunk at a railway station, changed his mind.

His new handler, an intelligent and urbane man called Semyon Semyonov, but known by Gold as "Sam", reactivated him. Gold was able to obtain a sample of a new high explosive, RDX, for Sam and in appreciation Gold was awarded the Order of the Red Star. He made sacrifices for the NKGB for many years. Reluctant to be seen as mercenary, he subsidized the extensive travel costs incurred in meeting his various contacts. Then, late in October 1943, Gold was called to a meeting with Sam and told to drop all his former NKGB or OGPU contacts, because he now had a special and extremely important task.

In Britain Fuchs had been dealing with agents of the GRU, Soviet Military Intelligence. The NKGB, the Soviet State Security Service, also had its spies and had instructed its agents in the United States to do everything they could to find out more about the Manhattan Project, or *Enormoz*, as they called it. The head of the NKGB, Lavrenty Beria, had been appointed to the GKO (State Defence Committee), where under the auspices of Georgi Malenkov, a senior member of the GKO and a close ally of Stalin, he took on responsibility for arms production. The GKO took a decision that responsibility for all the material gathered about the Manhattan Project was to be coordinated by the First Chief Directorate of the NKGB. This was decided in August 1943,

and in January 1944 the GRU received a formal letter from
Pavel Fitin, the newly promoted head of the NKGB
Directorate of Foreign Intelligence. It asked that the handling
of Klaus Fuchs be transferred to the NKGB. From that time
any intelligence about Problem No. 1, as nuclear research
was called, was given directly to Beria.

Fuchs knew nothing of this bureaucratic reorganization
in Moscow, of course. From his last meetings with Sonya he
was aware that his information was being received in
Moscow by people who understood it and were taking its
implications seriously. He could only hope that would
continue. He had plenty to be concerned about. He was in
a foreign country and on unfamiliar ground. The stranger
he was about to meet might already be compromised and
be a threat to his safety. A new contact was always a leap
into a black pit.

On the day of the rendezvous, Gold, with his extra pair
of gloves, reached New York early. The location he had been
given appeared deserted. The Henry Street Settlement
seemed closed; one of the lots on the street was vacant, with
excavations for a new building; and on the opposite side of
the street was an empty school playground. It was already
growing dark, and Gold thought that it was a very good spot
to have selected. He saw a young man slowly walking towards
him out of the gathering dusk. To Gold, who was short, the
stranger appeared tall and very thin, with large horn-rimmed
spectacles and a pale, intellectual appearance. When they
introduced themselves, with their coded conversation, Gold
thought that Fuchs spoke with a very pronounced and much
clipped British accent. Gold introduced himself as Raymond,
and according to him Fuchs gave his real name. The NKGB
had given Fuchs the code name of "Charles", but Fuchs had
no knowledge of this.

They walked along the waterfront of the East River for
ten minutes, then went by subway and taxi cab to the

Lexington Avenue and 42nd Street junction. Fuchs was wearing tweeds, and Gold reported that he was well, but not fancily, dressed. They continued to walk east to Third Avenue, where Gold suggested that they go for a meal at a steak house.

They didn't talk very much, but Fuchs was clearly paying a great deal of attention to his new contact. Gold remembers that he criticized him for meeting in a public place like a restaurant. Gold was impressed: Fuchs was right about this, and it suggested that he had already been involved in espionage. Gold didn't know how critical Fuchs was. He observed that Gold had kept looking behind him while they were walking to see if they were being followed, which Fuchs found irritating; it was pointless, in his view, and merely brought attention to them. There were more subtle and effective ways of checking if they were being tailed, he thought.

After their meal they took to the streets again and continued their discussion. Fuchs laid down some ground rules. The meetings should be for the shortest possible time, and strictly business. They would never meet in a restaurant and never in the same place twice. The best time was Fridays, after staff meetings, when he was left "pretty much alone". On other days of the week his colleagues sometimes asked him to dinner, and he preferred to accept these invitations so that he did not arouse any suspicion. He was adamant, however, that neither he nor Gold was to wait longer than four or five minutes at the rendezvous. Fuchs believed that there was the possibility he would be followed when he left the offices and so might have to abandon a meeting without any warning.

Fuchs had no documents or papers to hand over to Gold; it would have been foolish of him to carry something so incriminating to a first meeting with an unknown contact. But on their long walk that evening he told Gold about the Manhattan Engineering Project and the British Scientific

Mission; that there was a possibility that he might be transferred out of New York; and that he would probably be in
the United States for the duration of the war. Fuchs was not
very clear about the location of some of the other facilities
but thought that the electromagnetic separation plant, which
had been developed in Berkeley, was being built at Camp Y
in New Mexico. Obviously he hadn't yet discovered the existence of the Oak Ridge compound in Tennessee.

Fuchs also filled Gold in on more of the reasons for his
presence in New York. He told him about the other members
of the British Mission, mentioning Sir James Chadwick and
Rudolf Peierls. According to Gold's report, Peierls was Fuchs's
superior but they had divided the work up between them.
Fuchs also described the diffusion project and its purpose,
to separate the "fissionable isotope of uranium from the more
stable one". As Gold had studied chemistry back in 1937, he
knew something about isotopes and the thermal diffusion of
various gases. His recognition of the subject of Fuchs's work,
even if only partial, gave a clue to Fuchs that this contact
was more scientifically literate than any of his others had
been and he suspected that Gold might have been a chemist.

He told Gold that the process was part of a very complex
project, with a long-term perspective, and that he did not
expect it to be completed before the war was over. He said
that he would deliver a package containing a complete
written account of just who was working on the project and
how far it had progressed. He would put on paper as much
as he could possibly obtain. They arranged to meet again.

Before their second meeting, Gold's Soviet handler, 'Sam'
Semenyov, had been recalled to Moscow and replaced with
another resident, "John"—in reality Anatoly Yakovlev—and
Gold met him in New York near Pennsylvania Station. They
went to a restaurant where John introduced himself and,
like a new broom, announced some changes in the rules for
clandestine meetings. Gold was to arrive at the rendezvous

one hour before the appointed time and carry out a sweep for any form of surveillance. He was never to wait more than five minutes for the contact to arrive, something that Fuchs had already told him. To set up an emergency meeting, rather than make phone calls, John would send two tickets for an event, say a ball game or concert, in the mail. Gold was then to make a meeting three days after the date on the tickets in a seafood restaurant near the Astoria stop of the elevated railway on Broadway.

At their second meeting, on the corner of 59th Street and Lexington, Fuchs and Gold walked along First Avenue, under the Queensboro Bridge and along the East River. It was cold, with a chill wind coming off the water, and again there were few people about. Fuchs wanted to have some sort of alibi if they were ever questioned about their meeting: they would say that they had met, purely by chance, at a concert at Carnegie Hall and had struck up an acquaintance because of their shared interests in classical music and chess.

Fuchs wanted to know how his information had been received. Gold told him that it was fine, but lacked an overall description, and they needed a plan of the whole set-up. Fuchs was not happy hearing this. He had already given Sonya a complete list of the materials he had worked on in the reports he had handed over, and someone in Moscow needed to analyse his latest information in the light of that. It is quite likely that the GRU had not transferred all their material to the NKGB, or that all the papers they claimed to have passed on to the GKO had not been seen by Beria. But Fuchs agreed to produce something, even though it would be dangerous because much of the work he had done in the UK wasn't relevant to his work in New York and it would be suspicious if he was found with it.

Fuchs worked hard on the diffusion project and at his third meeting with Gold, in March 1944, he delivered the fruits of his labours. They met in Park Lane, in the 80s block.

It was a dark night, and Fuchs walked slowly down the pavement, listening to the footsteps of a man approaching from behind him. When Gold caught up with him they turned quickly into a side street and continued towards Fifth Avenue. Fuchs thrust what Gold described as "a very bulky package" into his hands and then they parted. After a few minutes Gold was overcome by curiosity, so he opened the package. Inside was a bundle of twenty or twenty-five closely written pages. He pushed them back into his pocket. Continuing with his walk, he met John, his Soviet handler, and the package of immensely secret information was once more transferred. Its contents would be in Moscow in a few days.

Several weeks later Fuchs and Gold met again. This time Fuchs broke his own rule and they went to a restaurant in the Bronx, where he told Gold about the construction of a big diffusion facility somewhere in the south—near Georgia or Alabama, he thought. Fuchs would spend time with Gold only if he was carrying nothing incriminating; these longer meetings were where he could fill Gold in on less scientific and precise information. This time he told him that there was a lack of cooperation with the Americans and that his work might be wound up in July. This meant he might either go to Camp X, as he called it on this occasion, or return to the UK, where he would be in charge of his own line of work. If this was the case, he would be able to give more complete general information but with less detail. He asked Gold to find out what Soviet intelligence would prefer.

They had dinner again at another meeting in April; Gold reported that it was a little seaside restaurant in Long Island City. The two of them appeared to have lost their initial reservations about long meetings. Fuchs reported that Peierls had just returned from a three-week visit to Camp Y, as Los Alamos was called, where he had been working with a group whose goal was to develop the project into a weapon. At the next two meetings Fuchs had little to report, except that the question of whether he would leave for the UK or go to Camp Y remained uncertain.

Their next rendezvous was a very brief and more dangerous meeting. It took place in July, in the Long Island City area of Queens, across the East River from Manhattan. There was more material in this package than in the last delivery of documents. Again, Gold could not control his curiosity and he opened the envelope and rifled through the pages. This time there were about forty pages of closely written notes and formulae. Fuchs had handed over all the work on the diffusion project that he had done in New York.

After this, the next two meetings were more leisurely. Fuchs was worried about his sister Kristel in Cambridge, Massachusetts. Her marriage was not going well and there was a possibility that she would leave her husband and move with her children to New York; Fuchs wanted to know what Moscow would make of this. Gold had nothing to say officially about the wisdom or otherwise of Kristel moving to New York, but he would soon find out more about her. Meanwhile, Fuchs told him about his brother Gerhard, who was convalescing in Switzerland. He also mentioned that he might be relocated somewhere to the south-west.

At the next scheduled meeting, near the Brooklyn Museum of Art in August, Fuchs did not show up. It was the first time that he had missed a rendezvous. Gold waited for some time, long enough to miss his back-up meeting with his handler, John. He wasn't worried, although it was out of character for Fuchs, normally so meticulous and professional in his behaviour.

Then again, at the next alternative meeting place, there was no sign of Klaus Fuchs. Gold was now worried, but not as worried as John. They had no idea what had happened. They did not know where Fuchs lived and had no way to contact him. John at least was aware that Fuchs was the most important spy that he had ever handled—

perhaps the most important spy that the NKGB currently had. Moscow would demand to know what had happened. John and Gold could also be in imminent danger of arrest by the FBI. An operation that had seemed to be producing the purest, most valuable intelligence had suddenly fallen apart in their hands.

John warned Gold that he should now be extremely cautious. Gold didn't need telling. John would have instructions for him at their next meeting.

In September 1944 they met again and John announced that they had discovered Fuchs's address; he didn't explain how he had done so. Gold was to go there and ask Fuchs directly what had gone wrong. So much for caution. This was more like desperation. Was he, thought Gold, walking into a trap? Why was he knocking on a door and asking for a member of the highly secret British Scientific Mission in New York?

He first went to a bookstore and bought a book by Thomas Mann. Inside the cover he wrote "Klaus Fuchs" and his address, "128 West 77th Street". If he was asked why he was at Fuchs's address, he could say that he had found the book and was returning it.

Gold reached 77th Street and found his way to Fuchs's apartment building. One of the bell-pushes was marked "Dr. Klaus Fuchs", but the wife of the caretaker, who was just opening the door for her husband, allowed him in. Gold was by this time feeling very exposed and nervous, and had a hard time making himself understood by the couple, whom he thought were Scandinavian immigrants. But he grasped that Fuchs had recently left and the two foreigners had no idea where he had gone. The most important contact in Gold's life had vanished.

ELEVEN

Camp Y

Klaus Fuchs had told Harry Gold that he would probably either be moved to another location in the US—which Gold's reports referred to as X or Y—or be recalled to Britain. He had asked Gold to find out what Soviet intelligence preferred, but there was apparently no reply. In the end, the British decided.

The Quebec Agreement between Roosevelt and Churchill, and the resulting presence of some British scientists working in the United States, had not ended the debate about what Britain should do to further its own weapons programme. Chadwick, head of the British Mission in the US, and Wallace Akers, in charge of Tube Alloys in the UK, both wanted Britain to build its own weapon, but could not convince the government to find the resources it needed. In April 1944 Akers wrote to the Chancellor of the Exchequer, saying it was likely that sooner or later the Americans would shut out the British scientists from knowledge of the final stages of the weapon's design and construction, and also from the operation of their large-scale diffusion and electromagnetic separation plants. This would not be serious, he said, if the Tube Alloys people could be certain that plutonium, or an isotope of uranium derived from it, could be used for military purposes as well as for the production of power. With this possibility in mind, there was active consideration of building a low separation diffusion plant, which would enrich uranium to a level sufficient to build a nuclear reactor but would not be sufficient to create a bomb. If this project was to go ahead, Chadwick thought that Fuchs would be invaluable in driving it along. Chadwick, Fuchs and Peierls had a conversation and formed a view that Fuchs, especially after his work in New York, would have a special contribution to make in England to any project to build a diffusion plant there. At Los Alamos, however, he would just be one of a number and would make no really significant difference to the work.

In discussions in the UK, however, Wallace Akers, Michael Perrin and Professor Franz Simon had come to the conclusion that even if the low separation diffusion plant was to go ahead, a theoretician of Fuchs's calibre would be wasted on it. Perrin cabled Peierls, saying that Fuchs would be better used at Los Alamos and should go there rather than return to the UK. Chadwick tried his best to prevent this. He wrote a letter to Peierls saying that he did not agree with Akers. He felt that if Fuchs did not go back to Britain there would be almost no work done in the UK on the diffusion problem. Chadwick suspected that General Groves might soon ask Fuchs to go to Los Alamos and if there was a direct request, then Chadwick could not refuse him, particularly if Fuchs's work was being denied to Groves in favour of an independent British project. This would be a serious breach of the Quebec Agreement. So Chadwick asked Peierls to try to persuade Hans Bethe, head of the Theoretical Division in Los Alamos, to tell Groves that Fuchs would not be specially useful to him: "This means some tactful work on your part, and I hope you will be able to do what is necessary by suggestion rather than direct action."

Whatever Peierls said to Bethe when he was in Los Alamos, Chadwick was frustrated. Peierls wrote later to Akers in London saying that there had been a difference of opinion about whether Fuchs should return to Britain, but he did not elaborate. Whether Peierls secretly wanted Fuchs with him, or Hans Bethe or others in Los Alamos also prevailed, is a mystery. The result of the argument isn't. Fuchs left for Los Alamos on 11 August 1944. It was a fateful decision that was, of course, to have profound consequences for everyone concerned.

Los Alamos, or Camp Y, had been chosen as the location for the secret laboratory and workshops where the final stages of creating a workable weapon would be undertaken. It was originally a boarding school. Robert Oppenheimer, scientific head of the Manhattan Project, picked it out in early 1943, and with a small team of scientists he moved to nearby Santa Fe in March to oversee the construction of what he and General Groves intended would be the site of the most secret project of the war. It was extremely remote, but this was part of its attraction. Rudolf Peierls had already made a brief visit and he described the first views of it as breathtaking, coming out of the New Mexico desert with its dry sagebrush and jagged sandstone formations to a border of wooded hills surrounding a plateau which housed the camp. The dry mountain air, along with its altitude of 7,500 feet and its view of distant mountains, gave the place a beauty marred by the army huts that made up most of the town.

Los Alamos was designed to solve the communications problems caused by having most of the scientific and technical work on the bomb done in universities spread across the continent. Oppenheimer had to cajole and bully those scientists employed on the Manhattan Project to move themselves and their families to this remote desert outpost, but a few short months later, by the time that Peierls arrived there, there were theoretical physicists and mathematicians to work out the behaviour of chain reactions, a cyclotron had been moved from Los Angeles and installed, and there were laboratories and workshops where chemists and metallurgists could carry out experiments.

Fuchs was given a room in the "big house", the main building of the former school, and was a neighbour of Richard Feynman, a young American physicist, whose wife was in hospital in Albuquerque with tuberculosis. Fuchs eventually obtained a driver's licence and bought a car, a second-hand blue Buick. He would often lend it to Feynman, or sometimes even drive him to the sanatorium where his young wife was dying. The slowly unfolding tragedy must have reminded Fuchs of the fate of his brother Gerhard, also suffering from tuberculosis in Switzerland.

Fuchs shared an office at Los Alamos with Peierls, part of the Theoretical Division headed by Hans Bethe. Peierls had been put in charge of the hydrodynamics group, replacing Edward Teller, who was determined to push forward with his own proposals for a hydrogen bomb. This weapon would release its energy not by encouraging heavy atoms of uranium to split, but by forcing light atoms of hydrogen and its isotopes to fuse together, a process that occurs naturally in the sun. To Bethe and Oppenheimer such projects seemed a luxury. There were seemingly insurmountable problems already with the development of a plutonium weapon, and Peierls and Fuchs arrived at a time when they could make a significant contribution to possible solutions.

The Manhattan Project and the scientists at Los Alamos were working on two possible atomic bombs. One of them, the same type that the British MAUD Committee had envisaged, used uranium 235 as the explosive critical mass. This was a relatively simple device to create and the calculations for it were fairly straightforward, at least for physicists like Bethe and Frisch. However, creating highly enriched uranium 235 was time-consuming and very expensive. The other weapon under development at Los Alamos was a bomb using plutonium 239. The advantage of this was that plutonium is produced when uranium is irradiated as a fuel in a reactor. The uranium for a reactor does not need to be so highly enriched as uranium for a bomb, so plutonium is cheaper and quicker to produce. But irradiated uranium is turned into both plutonium 239 and plutonium 238, and this makes the plutonium highly fissionable; it is therefore far more unstable than concentrated uranium 235 and there was a risk that the critical mass in a plutonium bomb would detonate prematurely. Either a method had to be found to separate the plutonium 238 from the plutonium 239—something that would be as enormously expensive as and more complicated than, enriching uranium—or an ingenious new way of creating a critical mass of plutonium had to be thought up.

Eventually an answer to the problem was found. A hollow ball of plutonium might be squeezed into a critical mass by surrounding it with explosives. The two people working on this, John von Neumann, a brilliant Hungarian mathematician, and George Kistiakowsky, a chemist and explosives expert, started to experiment with ways to do this, but the possible solution brought other problems in its wake. In particular, there was the question of whether the core could hold its shape long enough, and just how the explosives could be detonated to create a uniform inwardly moving shock wave. The dynamics of explosions had never been studied in such detail before, and there was a lot of work for Fuchs and Peierls to do in association with the rest of the theoretical division and with experts like Kistiakowsky. The plutonium bomb was a daunting task and success was not guaranteed, so work on the uranium bomb continued as a fallback measure.

Groves had introduced a principle of compartmentalization into the Manhattan Project at the very beginning.
Similar to the principle of "need to know", it ensured that
the thousands of engineers and contractors working on the
project were allowed to know only what they needed to
know for their own particular job. This principle had been
relaxed at Los Alamos, however. Oppenheimer knew that,
to most of the leading scientists he needed to recruit, any
limits on their ability to share ideas or discuss problems
with each other would be anathema and would severely
limit their ability to do their work. In addition, Los Alamos
was so remote and cut off from the rest of the Manhattan
Project's factories that it could be considered sufficiently
secure anyway. The town and the laboratory were surrounded
by a large barbed-wire fence and movement in and out was
controlled. None of the living quarters had private telephones. Contact with the outside world was severely
restricted. The nearest towns, Santa Fe and Albuquerque,
were also under surveillance. Many of the taxi drivers
worked for Army Intelligence, as did the waitresses in the
Hilton and Alvarado Hotels. Inside Los Alamos there was
freedom of movement and debate. Every week a colloquium
for all the scientific members of the laboratory was held in
the cinema. There were more discussions at the meetings
of the coordinating council, which was made up of all the
group leaders plus other senior scientists like Fuchs.

There was, in fact, a free flow of information, and anyone
working in Los Alamos would quickly be able to grasp the
extent of the problems that had been solved or still needed
solving to produce any useable nuclear weapon.

Arriving at Los Alamos, Fuchs understood for the first
time the enormous complexity and effort behind the
Manhattan Project. Up until this point he had been mainly
concerned with the production of enriched uranium and
with theoretical work on the creation of a uranium bomb.

Now he could see that another option, the plutonium bomb, was also being actively worked on and that there was an altogether different layer of complexity to the Manhattan Project. He started to make a significant contribution. Hans Bethe thought of him as a quiet, industrious man who worked eighteen hours a day and enjoyed what he did. He attended many of the weekly lectures and seminars. One of the first was in October 1944, where the problems of using shaped charges for the implosion were talked about. Later, in January, he went to one of Bethe's seminars on explosive lenses, where he presented his calculations on the formation of turbulence in explosive gases. He went to others on the yield and blast effects of the weapons. He must surely have realized that coming to Los Alamos was more interesting, and of more use, than returning to Britain.

Fuchs appeared to thrive in the atmosphere of Los Alamos, intellectually, but also physically. There were plenty of opportunities for hiking and skiing in the mountains, and as a single man he was invited to dinners and drinks, at parties that the tightly enclosed society of a few thousand scientists and their wives organized for their own entertainment. Genia Peierls and some of the other women arranged walks and hikes and Fuchs went with them. He also had time to form liaisons with some of the single women who worked in the camp—a young schoolteacher named Evelyn Kline, and another woman, Jean Parker.

Fuchs was working alongside the most brilliant nuclear and mathematical physicists in the world and he was accepted as a leading mathematician in his own right. He was also making friends outside the narrow émigré field that he had known in the UK. Feynman and Fuchs got on well. Feynman was anti-authoritarian, constantly trying to outwit the security officers, claiming that he could break the code of the combination locks on the secure filing cabinets. They were overheard once discussing who it was who would most likely be a spy, and they both decided that Feynman would be the most obvious candidate. The conclusion helped Feynman's ego, no doubt. For Fuchs the conversation must have seemed bizarre, and highly amusing.

Fuchs's comrades in the Soviet intelligence services were feeling less amused. They had lost contact with an exceptionally valuable source, who was of the utmost strategic importance to the Soviet Union and of vital importance to the intelligence services themselves. More than careers and jobs were on the line. Under Stalin, negligence of this order could literally cost people their lives. Fuchs had spoken to Gold about his sister in Cambridge, Massachusetts, but neither he nor his controller, John, knew her name or her address. But before he left the UK, when Fuchs was arranging the details of his handover to the Soviet agents in New York, he had supplied Kristel's name and address to Sonya and told her that if ever contact with him was lost, Kristel would be a back-up. For security there was to be an exchange of dialogue. The visitor was to say "I'm a friend of Max." Kristel would reply, "I heard that Max has had twins", and the visitor would say "Yes, two weeks ago."

In September, after his abortive visit to Fuchs's old apartment in New York and under instructions from John, Gold made the journey from Philadelphia to Boston. He crossed the Charles River into Cambridge and made his way to Kristel's house on Lakeview Drive. A housekeeper opened the door. Kristel and her family, it turned out, were on holiday and not expected back until some time in the next month. Gold returned to New York for a meeting with John. Nothing seemed to be going right for them.

Gold agreed that he should make another trip to Cambridge the next month, when he hoped that Kristel would be at home, and at a time that her husband would be out. Once more, he rang the doorbell and a woman he had not seen before opened the door. He introduced himself, using the agreed formula. Gold gained the impression that Kristel was not surprised to see him. He had brought some candy for her children and a book for her, which she took. He said that he was a friend of Fuchs from New York and was travelling in the area, and wondered if she knew where her brother was. She didn't, but she suggested that he may have gone to England.

If this was true, it was disappointing news, but Gold made another trip a month later, on 2 November, a Thursday. He took more candy and another book, and this time he had some very good news. Fuchs had called from Chicago, where he was on business from New Mexico, and he expected to be able to visit Cambridge for two weeks at Christmas. Gold was so happy that he stayed for lunch. He told Kristel that he would pay another visit in a month's time, which he did, this time on 7 December.

Kristel had heard nothing more from her brother, but expected him to be in Cambridge for at least two weeks. She also told Gold that Fuchs might have to spend a day or so in New York. Gold was pleased to hear this, because it suggested that Fuchs expected him to get in touch. Then he left a small piece of paper with a message, which contained the name and telephone number of someone at Amtorg, the Soviet Trade Mission in New York. Gold then made his way back to New York and Philadelphia, after spending just three quarters of an hour with Kristel. All he could do now was wait.

In Los Alamos Fuchs was seeking answers to many of the difficult questions posed by the plutonium bomb. The shock wave that imploded the plutonium core had to be consistent, otherwise the globe of metal would be distorted and might fragment before becoming critical. Achieving this uniformity in a blast that moved inwards to a centre proved extremely difficult. The original conception of explosive charges formed into sections of a sphere proved to be impractical, because the shock waves from each explosive interfered with the others and the turbulence disrupted the front of the shock wave. Working out what was taking place inside the complex set of explosions, which took just a millisecond to ignite and disperse, required the construction of high-speed cameras and X-ray machines, as well enormous theoretical calculations. After examining this problem, it was decided to use two different types of explosive lenses, with different rates of combustion that might even out the blast.

Solutions were also needed to urgent questions about how much plutonium was required, and whether other ways could be found to trigger the nuclear fission without any danger of a premature chain reaction. One solution actively worked on was the idea of placing a small ball of radioactive polonium and beryllium in the centre of the plutonium sphere. Polonium is highly radioactive, but the radiation could be shielded by a thin layer of boron, which would be stripped away at ignition, allowing a stream of alpha particles to displace neutrons in the beryllium and initiate a chain reaction in the plutonium. But a method had to be found to keep the beryllium and polonium separate, and then to make sure that they combined effectively in the heart of an explosion. Finally, a layer of dense uranium placed around the core would help to reflect neutrons back into the plutonium, increasing the rate of fission and the explosive power of the bomb.

Fuchs worked hard. Oppenheimer had come to the conclusion in March 1944 that the plutonium bomb had to be tested before it was used in anger. Los Alamos had been reorganized into separate divisions working primarily on explosives and on the critical mass. Progress was slow. It was not until December 1944 that the test of an explosive lens system looked as though it would work. Meanwhile there had still not been any delivery of useable plutonium.

Fuchs was lending his mathematical skills to many of these problems, and with Bethe, Peierls and von Neumann was producing papers on blast waves, shock hydrodynamics, methods of calculating the effect of the uranium tamper around the plutonium core, and other questions.

Christmas 1944 and then New Year passed, and Harry Gold heard nothing from his handler John. Then, on a weekday in January, Fuchs telephoned the contact number left with Kristel. He was in Cambridge. Gold had an emergency meeting with John, who told him to get to Cambridge as soon as possible. Gold didn't telephone before his arrival, because he was worried that the phone might be tapped. When he got to the Heinemann's address, he could see Fuchs in the living room, but Kristel answered the door. She had more bad news. Her husband was at home and Fuchs was expecting a visit from the British Consulate in New York. Gold would have to come back in two days' time.

Gold left. He walked around Cambridge pondering what to do. Fuchs didn't know that Gold lived in Philadelphia. These journeys weren't easy, so he decided to phone Fuchs and speak to him. It was a strange thing to do—a product of indecision or stress, or fear that Fuchs no longer wanted to talk to him. He telephoned, a strange male voice answered, and Gold hung up. He decided there was no option but to make another return trip two days later.

On the 21st, at 10.15 in the morning, he knocked again at the door of the Heinemanns' house. This time he was let in and met Fuchs. After saying hello, Gold and Fuchs left the house to make a trip into Boston to do some shopping. Fuchs explained the situation at Los Alamos: he had to make a report for Los Alamos security on everyone he had met on his trip, and he didn't want his brother-in-law to meet Gold. Fuchs had made a careful check and was sure that he was not being watched. They returned to the house in Cambridge, had lunch and then went upstairs to where

Fuchs was staying. He described the state of affairs at Los Alamos. It was growing: when Fuchs had arrived in August there had been about three thousand people there; now it had grown to forty-five thousand, and production of a bomb would begin in about three months' time.

Fuchs had reported nothing to Soviet intelligence for seven months. He had a lot of information to deliver and had prepared for this meeting thoroughly. He did not want to meet in Cambridge again. Gold's repeated visits had possibly drawn attention to his sister and it was no longer secure, he said. Anyway, Fuchs could not guarantee when he would get another period of leave. He was able to get to Santa Fe once a month; Gold or another contact would have to meet him there. He had a time and a place for a rendezvous worked out. He had brought a map of Santa Fe and a bus timetable, and told Gold the recognition signs and exchange of passwords if someone other than Gold was to be his contact. Fuchs would say, "How is your brother Raymond?" The reply would be, "Not well, he has been in the hospital for two weeks." Fuchs said that the next meeting would be in June. Gold was in no position to argue. Fuchs was calling the shots.

Gold had been given an envelope by John with $1,500 to hand over to Fuchs, but Fuchs refused it. He didn't need the money, he said, and that wasn't why he was working for Soviet intelligence. Gold had been concerned that offering the cash would be offensive, but apparently Fuchs wasn't disturbed by it. As well as all the details of the next meeting, he handed over a large sealed envelope.

Before Gold finally left, Fuchs had another request. Clearly he was feeling vulnerable, very much aware of the risks he was running, and he was anxious about his past. He wanted Gold to pass a message back to Moscow. When Soviet troops entered Kiel and Berlin, they must search the Gestapo headquarters for his dossier and destroy it before it fell into other hands. Perhaps, given the status of the war, it was not such a bizarre request. Fuchs would have thought about his home town and the places where he had lived as he followed the news of Germany's collapse, but his first concern was not with his father, or other relatives, or past comrades, but with his secret past, which he knew might trap him. It was an indication of the fear that he lived with every day.

Gold left. He did not know what John would say about the next meeting being in four months' time. It meant another long break in contact with Fuchs, and the trip to Santa Fe would be difficult for him and a big security risk. But there was little Gold could do. It was better to have a meeting arranged, however unsatisfactory the circumstances, than to say goodbye to Fuchs and have no idea when they would meet again.

In any case, Fuchs was obviously still delivering. Gold had a bulky sealed envelope thick with papers. He didn't know it, but they were descriptions of the problems with the spontaneous fission of plutonium, and the need to use the implosion method with high explosives rather than the gun-type assembly that was proposed for uranium. Fuchs had also provided the latest calculations for the critical mass of plutonium. It was an up-to-date description of the current research at Los Alamos on the plutonium bomb—everything that Fuchs had discovered since August 1944. The secrets of the Manhattan Project, the deadliest scientific invention of all time, were wrapped tightly in an envelope and on their way to Moscow. Fuchs was taking them from the very heart of the project, the Theorctical Division where he worked. It is no wonder that he wanted the Soviet Union to destroy any trace of his communist past.

TWELVE

The End Result

Work at the Los Alamos laboratory was gathering pace. When Fuchs returned from his trip to Boston, the massive investment in plants around the country was beginning to show results. The first useable quantities of uranium 235 were delivered from the Oak Ridge enrichment plant in Tennessee, and work on the uranium bomb was progressing well. Castings of plutonium also began to arrive from the separation plant at Hanford on the banks of the Columbia River in Washington state.

The pressure was on. Because the plutonium bomb was so complicated compared to the uranium 235 weapon, Oppenheimer wanted the plutonium bomb tested, in a trial explosion, but the small amount of plutonium that they possessed represented millions of dollars of investment. To ensure that that test was not a waste, and didn't set the project back by months, everything about it had to be meticulously calculated in advance. Fuchs looked at all aspects of the hydrodynamics of the explosion, developing his own methods of calculation for some of the expected characteristics. He examined again the propagation of instabilities in the implosion of the explosive lenses. He analysed whether the proposed initiation of the reaction by a polonium neutron source was theoretically feasible, and what would happen as the unbelievable pressures of shock waves from thirty-two pieces of high explosive converged on the walnut-sized initiator at the heart of the bomb. Once the nuclear reaction had started, how big would the resulting explosion be? Fuchs worked on that question too, calculating the spread and form of the explosive wave in air, at variable air pressures. He worked on the critical dimensions of the tamper system and the layer of uranium that surrounded the plutonium, which reflected neutrons back to add fuel to the reaction and also transmitted the shock waves to the core of the bomb. It had been decided that a gap between the plutonium and the uranium tamper would increase the energy transmitted to the core, and the correct size of that gap had to be calculated. In order for his figures to be accurate, Fuchs needed information about everything that was going to make the plutonium and uranium bombs work. Hans Bethe, the man who had wanted Fuchs to come to Los Alamos to take up some of the pressure of work, valued his presence.

The problems with the explosive lenses were a serious concern to everyone. They had to be free from any imperfections and built to very precise dimensions, but the way they were manufactured—cast in a mould from a liquid of the various chemicals, which then hardened—meant it was almost a certainty that some air bubbles or cavities would develop, making the charge unusable. But the production improved and in April 1945 the experiments with the explosive lenses, which had continued to disappoint through the winter of 1944 and early spring of 1945, finally started to work.

There were other advances. Otto Frisch, with whom Fuchs had worked in the early days of Tube Alloys, assembled small ingots of metallic uranium hydride and finally physically determined the size of a critical mass of uranium 235.

A site for a test shot of the bomb had been picked out in May of 1944. It was an area of 18 by 24 miles at a place called Alamogordo, 200 miles south of Los Alamos. In February 1945, with the project showing some significant advances, Oppenheimer decided that the test shot, which he codenamed Trinity, could take place on 4 July that year. Before that, however, another test was needed—one to rehearse the variety of scientific measurements, the communications and security for the test explosion itself. This rehearsal was going to use 100 tons of explosives, seeded with radioactive material from Oak Ridge, and it quickly became known as the 100 Ton Shot. This was planned to take place on 1 May.

The explosives were set up on a test platform about 800 yards from the planned site of ground zero for Trinity, and the command bunkers, cameras, telephone wires, instruments to measure the shock wave, blast and radiation were positioned where they would be for the real plutonium test. Members of the British team were actively involved in the 100 Ton Shot, as they were going to be for Trinity. William Penney, a mathematical physicist who had carried out detailed research on the effect of bomb blasts on people and buildings during the Blitz, had come to Los Alamos to work on the blast calculations and to participate in the Targeting Committee. Penney had developed his own methods of measuring blast damage, and these were going to be adopted for the Trinity test. Another British scientist, Philip Moon, was responsible for measuring deadly gamma radiation emitted by the nuclear explosion.

The 100 Ton Shot was finally set for 7 May after a meteorological report predicted good weather. A bomber flew over the test site and dropped a series of blast gauges on parachutes. Their release was the signal to switch on all the test gauges and oscilloscopes, then start a twenty-six-second countdown before the explosives were fired.

Moon wrote a report on the test and he said that the theorists and other non-combatants who were not at work inside the shelters saw the explosion, which was a magnificent sight. But he was otherwise critical, saying in his report to Chadwick that it exposed serious problems in the organization, particularly in the military, who seemed to be unprepared and disorganized, and that this would have to be improved for the real test of the atomic weapon.

The next day, 8 May, was celebrated as Victory in Europe Day. Nazi Germany had been defeated and Soviet troops stood in the ruins of Berlin, the Red Flag fluttering from the top of the Reichstag. Hitler had committed suicide on 30 April, and Berlin had surrendered to the 1st White Russian and 1st Ukrainian Armies on 2 May. Over the next two days across the whole of Europe, from Denmark to Italy, German armies marched into captivity.

On Saturday, 2 June, Fuchs drove through the security gates of Los Alamos in his Buick, using his monthly pass-out to Santa Fe. He drove to a spot on Alameda Street, along the river, near to the Castillo Street Bridge where there were trees and benches close by. He spotted Raymond, as Harry Gold was known to him, and pulled up while his contact approached and got into the passenger seat. Then Fuchs continued to drive, over a bridge to a remote spot out of town, up in the hills, where he parked at the limit of a dead end. They sat in the car, talked, then went for a walk. Fuchs told Gold that the project was entering its final stages and that people were working very long shifts. It would not be long before the weapon was tested. He also said that if the test was successful, then an explosion would take place in the Pacific, although Fuchs would have had no knowledge about specific targets.

Before they parted, Fuchs suggested another meeting in a month or so, but Gold said he could not make the journey from Philadelphia so soon. It would have to be some time in September. Before they split up Fuchs passed over an envelope. It contained everything that he knew about the bomb up to that point, and that was a considerable amount.

In the manila envelope that Klaus Fuchs had whisked out from Los Alamos under the nose of the security guards was a longhand description of the plutonium bomb that was the subject of the 100 Ton Shot on 7 May and would be tested in the Trinity shot in July. There was a sketch of the bomb and its components, with the addition of key dimensions. There were details of how the bomb was going to be ignited and a description of the initiator—the walnut-sized piece of polonium that nestled in the middle of the plutonium core.

Gold took the documents back to his handler in New York, where the contents were coded and transmitted in a cable to Moscow on 13 June. There they were sent to Beria, and on 2 July Igor Kurchatov, the scientific head of the Soviet nuclear weapons programme—Russia's own Oppenheimer—received the pared-down information that the bomb was made out of plutonium, or element 94 as the Soviets knew it, with a polonium and beryllium initiator surrounded by uranium to act as a tamper. All of this lodged in a shell of uranium 11 centimetres thick, then an aluminium shell that in turn was surrounded by explosives. There was a reference to two types of explosive as though they were alternatives, not used together. There was also a brief account of the force of the explosion, which was said to be equivalent to about 5,000 tons of TNT, and a calculation of the fission ratio.

The NKGB had several other agents in the United States and Britain. Engelbert Broda, working in the Cavendish Laboratory in the UK, who had been recommended to Sonya by Fuchs, had been recruited by the NKGB in 1944. Allan

Nunn May was working at the Anglo-Canadian reactor project site at Chalk River, and there were at least two others in Los Alamos itself. David Greenglass was a machinist in the explosives laboratory run by Kistiakowsky, and there was another agent, Theodore Hall, the youngest physicist in Los Alamos, a precocious Harvard graduate working on experiments testing the effect of implosion. All these agents' reports were collected, along with those of Fuchs, in a set of documents that was then passed to Kurchatov to read. It is likely that he was aware of the use of implosion, and some of the basic designs of the plutonium bomb, by the time that Fuchs met Gold in Los Alamos.

Kurchatov was very impressed with the materials that he was receiving from Fuchs, however. The information about spontaneous fission in plutonium, he wrote, was "exceptionally important"; so too were the calculations about the critical mass for plutonium and uranium 235, and the intelligence provided very valuable data about the propagation of the detonating wave in the explosive, which was also of major importance.

While Kurchatov was impressed by the results of the NKGB's efforts, the leadership of the Soviet Union was less so. Or it may be that, with the success of their conventional troops on the Eastern Front against Germany and with victory within their grasp, Stalin and the rest of the Politburo did not appreciate the power of the new weapon. Whatever the reason, Kurchatov and his research team had not seen any sign of the necessary resources to build a reactor and get the weapons project under way. They knew they were lagging behind the United States. A test of a nuclear device by the Americans would not be far away. The gap was widening! The latest information from Fuchs must have been intensely frustrating for Kurchatov, because in May he had already written a joint memorandum with Mikhail Pervukhin, Molotov's deputy on the Nuclear Commission of the Defence Council, to the Central Committee and the Politburo. It expressed alarm at the slow pace of work and asked for more favourable conditions to speed up research and development. They didn't get a reply.

The early threat that German scientists like Werner Heisenberg would produce a bomb for the Nazis had not materialized, and the British Scientific Advisory Committee's prediction that the Tube Alloys Directorate would not deliver a weapon before the war had finished was borne out, at least as regards the war in Europe. But other reasons to press ahead with the work at Los Alamos seemed equally urgent. War against the Japanese was still grinding on, the bodies piling high in a dreadful slaughter as US soldiers invaded island after island, and hundreds of long-range B-29 bombers launched air raids on Japanese cities. The Quebec Agreement between Roosevelt and Churchill had created a Combined Coordinating Committee, with delegations from both countries, which had already considered a range of possible targets in Japan for the atom bomb and on 8 May it finally gave formal approval to using the bomb on one of a small group of cities on the Japanese mainland.

There were other motives for pressing on too. The wartime alliance of Stalin, Churchill and Roosevelt had been a superficial matter of convenience, and now the great combined fear of Russia and communism took centre stage. The Soviet Union had driven back the German Wehrmacht and had taken over Hungary, Poland and the Baltic states, expanding Moscow's influence deep into Europe. The governments of Britain and the United States were alarmed about the future of a Europe where the Soviet Union would have a dominant position. Stalin was ignoring the agreements they had entered into about the future of the former occupied countries of Eastern Europe. Churchill and Harry S. Truman, Roosevelt's successor, wanted to confront Stalin at a summit conference at Potsdam, just outside Berlin, and the new US administration wanted to go into the meeting with the new weapon in their pocket.

The pressure to make the test before the meeting of the big three was intense. President Truman had managed to hold off the start of the conference until 15 July to give himself more time, and General Groves had fixed the date of the test for the 16th, subject to the weather and the prevailing winds at the test site. An enormous amount of work still needed to be completed, from laying 25 miles of tarmac roads at the test site, to final inspection and eradicating of imperfections in each explosive lens as it came out of its mould. The two halves of the plutonium core, carefully machined from the ingots delivered from Hanford, were coated in nickel, but as the date for the test drew closer the nickel started to blister. These small patches of corrosion were repaired with gold leaf, but no one knew what, if any, effect this might have on the outcome of the test.

The Manhattan Project had harnessed the best and most acute brains in the Western world to create a nuclear explosion. The possibility of such a phenomenon had been pure speculation in the minds of men like Peierls and Frisch just five years earlier. Now this remote theory was to be turned into reality. Billions of dollars had been spent and hundreds of thousands of workers had laboured to create the fact of a nuclear weapon. No one in the world had ever seen a nuclear explosion before. No one had any idea what to expect. This created an extra tension amongst the scientists as the test date approached. There was not only doubt that the plutonium device on the test tower would work; there was also uncertainty about what would happen if it did work.

In the days before Trinity a sweepstake was organized in which people could bet on their estimate of the explosive power of the bomb. The choices ranged from around 1,000 to 20,000 tons of TNT—an enormous variation.

On the evening before the test Fermi was heard to offer bets on whether the bomb would ignite the atmosphere, and if so whether it would destroy New Mexico. He also said that if the bomb failed, then it would still have been worthwhile, because the best scientists would have proved that an atomic bomb was not possible. These remarks were probably a sign of Fermi's own nervousness and stress, but General Groves was highly irritated by them. He did not want to have to explain to his superiors why a $2 billion project, so secret that it had never been approved by Congress and had been hidden even from the vice-president, had been a failure.

Groves, aware that President Truman, Secretary of State Byrnes and Secretary of War Henry Stimson were in Berlin for the start of the Potsdam Conference, watched the weather reports anxiously and waited that night of the 15th as thunder and lightning rolled across the test site and a storm brought winds of 30 miles an hour. Finally, the meteorologists told him that the weather would ease at 5.30 in the morning.

The final countdown, when it came, was both a relief and a form of purgatory, as each second seemed to stretch to infinity but simultaneously moved forward to the inevitable end. When the explosion came, to the observers it was something beyond any known experience. The most striking first impression was the flash of light. People likened it to an intense sunlight breaking into a darkened room, but Isidor Rabi—a theoretical physicist from Columbia, a Nobel prizewinner and consultant to Los Alamos—described the light as something that physically bored its way through you, so that you wished it would stop. As they looked towards the place where the bomb had been, an enormous ball of fire grew and grew as it rose into the air, covered in yellow flashes that merged into scarlet and green. It looked menacing. It seemed to advance towards them.

The enormously powerful explosion was so dramatic and so shocking that the unearthly fireball and the giant cloud of radioactive material that rose into the sky stunned observers 20 miles away. The bomb had unquestionably worked. The predictions of Peierls and Frisch had come true.

Stanislaw Ulam, already working on ideas for a bigger weapon, the hydrogen bomb, had not gone to watch the test shot. He saw instead the faces of those who returned to Los Alamos from the Trinity site: "You could tell at once that they had had a strange experience. I saw that something very grave and strong had happened to their whole outlook on the future."

Groves and Oppenheimer composed a message to Stimson at Potsdam. He personally passed on the news to Truman and Byrnes. They did not immediately tell Stalin. They waited, partly, as Byrnes claimed later, because Truman had come to the conclusion that it would be regrettable if the Soviet Union entered the Pacific war and tried to exercise some influence over any peace settlement with Japan. Truman was afraid that if Stalin were made fully aware of the power of the new weapon he might order the Soviet army to plunge forward at once, intervening in Manchuria to start fighting the occupying Japanese army.

Truman did not in fact tell Stalin until 24 July, once he had received the news that the first weapon, the uranium 235-fuelled "Little Boy", would be ready to use against Japan by 1 August, and that a bomb of the type that had been tested, "Fat Man", would be ready six days later. Truman knew that the demonstration of the weapons' power would capture Stalin's attention far more than claims at a conference. He also wanted to be sure that the weapons would continue to be available before announcing that the US possessed them. He was told that this was the case. The now relatively smooth manufacturing process throughout the Manhattan Project's plants should be able to produce three bombs in September.

That evening in Potsdam, after the day's session, Truman approached Stalin on his side of the conference table: "I casually mentioned to Stalin that we had a new weapon of unusual destructive force. The Russian premier showed no special interest. All he said was that he was glad to hear it and hoped we would make good use of it against the Japanese." Soviet officials are convinced that Stalin knew that the US possessed the bomb. There was no reason why he shouldn't. After all, he had authorized Kurchatov to start work on a Soviet programme, and it is inconceivable that Beria would not have informed him of the latest intelligence about the Manhattan Project. According to Marshal Georgi Zhukov, back in the Soviet delegation's quarters Stalin spoke to Molotov, who said, "They're raising the price." Stalin replied, "Let them. We'll have to have a talk with Kurchatov today about speeding up our work." So the atomic card had been played in diplomacy against the Soviet Union with no noticeable results.

Next it was a matter of using the new weapon in action, against Japan. There was an energetic debate in Los Alamos amongst the scientists about whether the bomb should be dropped on a Japanese target or should perhaps be exploded in a demonstration so that the world, and members of the Japanese government, could see the power that might be used against them. But as Fuchs recognized after the Trinity test, it was too late to worry about how the bomb would be used. The weapon was in the hands of politicians and the military. Fuchs had also worried about the power of the bomb, and he had done something concrete about it.

Two weapons had been constructed by the time the Potsdam meeting was over. There was a plutonium-fuelled implosion weapon, called Fat Man because of its globe shape, and the uranium projectile-triggered weapon, called Little Boy because it looked taller and thinner than the other. Fifteen long-range B-29 bombers had been specially modified to carry them to their targets in Japan, taking off from Tinian, a small coral island in the middle of the Pacific that had been turned into a huge stationary aircraft carrier. Here, 6,000 miles from San Francisco and 1,500 miles from mainland Japan, six runways, each 2 miles long, were used by hundreds of B-29s on their nightly raids on the cities of Japan.

The components of the two bombs were delivered to Tinian by navy cruiser and air force transport. Little Boy, the uranium weapon, was ready to be hoisted into the bomb bay of a four-engined B-29 by 31 July. At 2.47 in the morning of 6 August, a B-29 named *Enola Gay* took off from the northernmost runway on Tinian, heavily laden with 7,000 gallons of fuel and a uranium bomb that weighed 4 tons. Its destination was the Japanese mainland. Even at this final stage, three cities were the possible target. The ultimate decision would be made when they were closer and weather reconnaissance aircraft could send back a final report on cloud cover and visibility for each possible target.

At 8.15 in the morning, the radio operator on board the bomber received a message that the city of Hiroshima was reported as having the least cloud cover, so that city, which was actually the primary choice, was selected. The *Enola Gay* proceeded to its target, flying high, a single silver speck at the end of a white condensation trail.

At 9.16 in the morning, the inhabitants of Hiroshima saw the cruel, brilliant, intense light of an exploding nuclear weapon.

As we saw earlier, a few days after the successful test of the plutonium bomb at Alamogordo in New Mexico, William Penney, the British expert on blast damage, had revealed his preliminary calculations on the size of the explosion to the seminar at Los Alamos. Fuchs was working on his own figures and later disagreed with some of Penney's calculations, but for the moment they were adequate for the task. One of the scientists at the seminar said that Penney predicted that if used on a city of 300,000 or 400,000 people, the bomb would reduce it to nothing more than a sink for disaster relief, bandages and hospitals.

Hiroshima, a port town, had a population of 350,000 people and the explosion of Little Boy killed 80,000 immediately. Many were vaporized, some leaving nothing but their shadow on walls and pavements. Many thousands more were injured, by blast and heat and by radiation; 10,000 of these wounded were to die in the next months. Almost three quarters of the houses in the city were destroyed, including hospitals, clinics and schools. There had been no air raid warning, the danger from a single high-flying B-29 thought to be inconsequential.

The news about the destruction of Hiroshima initially stunned everyone at Los Alamos. Then reactions were mixed. Fuchs recalled that many were aghast at the final concrete results of their work. Otto Frisch remembered that others were jubilant and decided to make reservations for a night out in Santa Fe. However, the detonation of the Little Boy atomic weapon did not have the expected effect.

The Soviet Union, which had been a neutral negotiator for possible peace talks at the request of the Japanese government, abandoned its neutral status and announced that it would be at war with Japan on 9 August. Red Army units advanced across the border into Manchuria shortly after midnight on the 8th. There was, however, no rush by the Japanese government to capitulate.

The plutonium core, the initiator and the explosive lenses for the Fat Man bomb were already in place on Tinian. The original plan was that it should be ready for use on a target in Japan on 11 August, but now there was pressure to have the weapon ready earlier, to impress on the Japanese military that the destruction of their cities would not stop until they surrendered.

Nightly raids by the B-29 fleet were still taking place, and other cities were experiencing death and destruction, but Hiroshima had been on a different scale altogether. The death rate from a nuclear bomb was far higher than from a conventional mass raid. On Tinian men worked round the clock to get the plutonium bomb ready earlier than planned. It was finally assembled in time for it to be winched into the bomb bay of a B-29, and the huge, four-engined bomber, called *Bock's Car*, hauled into the air at 3.47 in the morning of the 9 August.

The primary target for Fat Man, Kokura Arsenal, lay under thick haze. The pilot of *Bock's Car*, Major Charles Sweeney, decided to head for his alternative, the city of Nagasaki. This too was obscured by clouds. Sweeney decided to make a target run using his radar. He was low on fuel because the pump on a reserve fuel tank had failed. If he didn't drop the bomb on Nagasaki, he would have to jettison his nuclear weapon in the Pacific, or make an emergency landing in Okinawa.

As he made a pass over the city, there was a break in the cloud cover large enough for the bomb aimer to select an aiming point. The first implosion bomb to be used against an enemy exploded at 11.02 in the morning. Nagasaki was surrounded by hills that helped to contain the blast of the fissioning plutonium, but even so the death toll was estimated to be 70,000 people by the end of 1945.

General Groves reported that he could expect to ship another plutonium core and initiator to Tinian on 12 or 13 August, and that it could be ready for use by the 17th or 18th. The components were not, in fact, sent, but instead conventional bombing raids wreaked destruction on two more Japanese cities, Kumagaya and Isezaki.

But the emperor of Japan had already decided to face

down his military leadership, who would have taken their whole country and its people to death with honour, and negotiations with the US government started. On 15 August, Emperor Hirohito broadcast to his people the news of the Japanese surrender. The war was over.

THIRTEEN

After the Bomb

The Japanese government surrendered unconditionally on 2 September 1945 at a ceremony on the deck
of the US navy's battleship *Missouri*, moored in
Tokyo Bay. Whatever the misgivings of many of the scientists
at Los Alamos about the destruction of two Japanese cities,
there was of course an irrepressible wave of celebration
about the end of a horrific war that had lasted for six years.
The world had suddenly become a far safer place, where
young men and women could make plans for the future
and parents need no longer fear they would outlive their
children.

Klaus Fuchs felt no lessening of anxiety or purpose,
however, when the peace treaty was signed. His next meeting
with Raymond, or Harry Gold, was scheduled for 19
September, barely two weeks away. They hadn't met since
June, before the Trinity test and the successful attacks on
Hiroshima and Nagasaki.

When Fuchs set out on his trip to Santa Fe, he wasn't
alone. He had promised to drive there to pick up some drinks
to bring back to Los Alamos for a party later that night,
which would give him a good excuse to make the trip, but

some co-workers had begged a lift and he had taken them along as well. Fuchs made it a habit to be helpful. Arriving in Santa Fe, his companions suggested he tag along and go out on the town, and he had a struggle to part company with them politely. He had pointed out to Gold that it was a mistake to wait longer than five minutes at a rendezvous, so he was probably anxious as he drove to the Bishops Lodge Road, near Hillside and Kearney Avenues. He was almost twenty minutes late.

Harry Gold had had a much longer and more difficult journey. It had taken several days for him to travel from Philadelphia to Santa Fe, so he probably did not feel like abandoning the meeting after ten minutes; but the delay was unnerving. Fuchs had always been very punctual. When Gold got into the car he noticed that Fuchs seemed unusually nervous, perhaps because he was late, but also there were more security police patrolling than there had been the last time they had met in Santa Fe. Fuchs drove slowly because of the bottles of liquor in the boot. He said that it was a mistake to meet in the evening, and probably a mistake to meet in the town at all.

Both men were taking unbelievable risks. It had been barely two weeks since the most destructive war that had ever engulfed the globe had ended. In the second-hand Buick driving around the streets of the small town in New Mexico, one man, Klaus Fuchs, had a bundle of papers that contained the most closely guarded secrets of the weapon that had brought victory and transformed the United States into the world's first superpower. Their nervousness was not surprising. What was surprising was that they both had the courage to go ahead with the meeting.

They travelled up into the hills overlooking Santa Fe until they could barely see the lights of the town below them. Fuchs talked about the bomb, asking Gold if he was impressed. Gold said he was more than impressed, and also a little horrified. Fuchs was pleased, but said that he was shocked at the extent of the destruction the bombs had caused. He was also critical of the local people in Santa Fe, who had warmed to the people in Los Alamos only after they had seen what they had brought about in Hiroshima and Nagasaki.

Fuchs told Gold that there had been a change of atmosphere between the American and British scientists since the end of the war. There was less collaboration than there had been. He didn't expect to stay for long and had received hints from the British Mission that he might soon be returning to the UK. The British were setting up a research institute somewhere in the south of England and by December, or maybe January 1946, he might be in Cambridge, Massachusetts, visiting his sister and then on his way back to England.

It was important that they arrange a rendezvous with a new contact in case he was suddenly recalled. It was to be the first Saturday of the month, either January or February, at eight o'clock in the evening in London, in Mornington Crescent near the underground station. Fuchs's new contact would be carrying five books tied together with string and held under his arm. The dialogue would be, "Can you tell me the way to Harvard Square?" The contact's reply would be "Yes, but excuse me a minute—I have an awful cold", and then the contact was to blow his nose into a handkerchief. The arrangements made, Fuchs drove back into Santa Fe to drop Gold off in a Mexican quarter, presumably to avoid being spotted by any of Fuchs's fellow workers from the laboratory.

As they drove, Fuchs mentioned that many of the scientists at Los Alamos had met at the end of August and drafted a letter to the US government warning against an arms race, and calling for nuclear weapons to be placed under some form of international control. He was doubtful if it would make any difference.

Just before Gold got out of the car, Fuchs gave him another large envelope of papers. Then he drove off, back to Los Alamos. Gold must have looked at the papers, because he said in his report to Moscow that the material was excellent and covered everything. It would certainly have contained any changes to the design of the bomb since the Trinity test, and some of the initial calculations made about the performance of the bombs at Hiroshima and Nagasaki. It also contained the production figures for uranium 235 and for plutonium, so that the NKGB, or the Soviet scientists, could work out the rate of production of further nuclear weapons. It was, as usual, priceless information, from the very heart of the Manhattan Project, and was of absolutely vital importance to the Soviet Union, whose own project had an enormous amount of catching up to do.

Gold first waited at Santa Fe for a bus to Albuquerque; the next day he caught a flight to Kansas City, then took a train to Chicago. Arriving at midnight, he rushed to board another train to New York, where he was to meet his contact, John. Gold arrived the next day, but he was too late for his meeting. There was no alternative but to catch the train back to Philadelphia and make the trip to New York again the following day. To his surprise and anxiety, John again failed to show up. So Gold returned home, still carrying the pages of highly secret information about the deadliest and most powerful weapon in the world. It stayed close with him for the next two weeks until he made the journey once more to New York, where John finally met him and relieved him of his dangerous burden.

According to the documents in the NKGB archives, Fuchs's material on the Hiroshima bomb was transmitted to Moscow on 17 October. It is unlikely that this was a comprehensive copy of his technical material. Gold's personal written report was not received in Moscow until the 26th and another report based on the meeting was dated the

29th. The delay in transmitting Fuchs's latest report was not fundamental to the Soviet scientists, however much of a danger it represented to Fuchs and Raymond.

After the Potsdam summit Stalin had taken some steps to speed up the Soviet project. On 20 August the State Defence Committee, the GKO, set up a special committee to direct the work, appointing several industrial managers essentially to transform what had up until now been a research programme into a full-scale production process, repeating in effect what the US had done with the Manhattan Project. Igor Kurchatov remained the chief scientific representative on this Special Committee on the Atomic Bomb.

The complete dossier of Fuchs's information, collated by the NKGB, was a vital tool for Kurchatov at this stage of his work. It contained all the equations, the dimensions and supporting calculations needed to produce a plutonium bomb. Based on this, and the work of the Soviet scientists since 1942, Kurchatov could take a highly informed view of the material in front of him. One of its great strengths was that it was a design for a weapon that had clearly worked. His team could quickly examine the sketches and the written material that supported them for flaws and inconsistencies. He would have been mad not to accept the documents in front of him as a truly remarkable gift—a clearly defined path through a maze that, as a physicist, he knew might contain a thousand dead ends. Kurchatov decided to take it as the blueprint for the most reliable way to achieve his goal of a workable bomb. On that warm night in New Mexico, as Fuchs handed over what turned out to be the last of the material he would give to Harry Gold, the United States had already started to lose its nuclear monopoly.

However, the evening of 19 September 1945 was also the start of another arms race that was to come to fruition almost ten years later. The envelope that Fuchs handed over to Gold contained even more explosive information, about work that was familiar to only a handful of the nuclear elite. The bombs that destroyed Hiroshima and Nagasaki worked on the principle of nuclear fission. The nucleus of atoms of isotopes of heavy metals like uranium, if hit with a neutron, would split, releasing energy. If enough of them could be made to split in a chain reaction, the resulting release of energy would destroy a city. But another energy-releasing process was also possible. Known as fusion, this was a process where the nucleus of atoms of isotopes of light elements like hydrogen and helium would join together. Scientists calculated that there was no limit to the size of bomb that could be created using this principle.

Work on a bomb based on nuclear fusion, rather than fission, had been continuing at Los Alamos for some years. Edward Teller's refusal to abandon this subject was the reason why Hans Bethe had asked him to step aside from the Theoretical Division and had brought Peierls and Fuchs to work there. There were some seemingly insurmountable problems to building a fusion bomb. One of the most fundamental was that it required enormous energy to make the atoms of an isotope of hydrogen, or deuterium as it was called, combine with each other. These problems were openly discussed amongst the scientists in the Theoretical Division, and knowledge of the current state of work was widely disseminated. Professor Philip Moon, one of the members of the British Mission, wrote in his weekly report to Professor Chadwick in June 1945 about a recent meeting with Oppenheimer on the question of the "super gadget", as the fusion or hydrogen bomb was then called. The letter describes the problems and says that Stanislaw Ulam, the Polish mathematician at Los Alamos, had come up with a suggestion for using the explosion of the gadget, or fission bomb, to ignite deuterium. Ulam worked with Edward Teller on some of the problems of the H-bomb and eventually produced a workable design.

Documents apparently based on lecture notes about the hydrogen bomb from Los Alamos were found in the archives of the Soviet Ministry of Atomic Energy in the 1990s. These led a Russian physicist, German Goncharov, to assert that Soviet intelligence "obtained concrete information that embodied elements of the classical super theory in September 1945". Others have suggested that Fermi prepared these notes for a lecture series he started in July, but the notes themselves don't mention an author. Whoever wrote them, it seems certain that only Fuchs would have been in a position to hand them over to Soviet intelligence in September 1945. Fuchs was certainly aware of current research on the hydrogen bomb and later, as we shall see, he worked on the problem with some of the other mathematicians at Los Alamos, with results that remain classified and which became another strand in the complex layers of Fuchs's espionage.

Los Alamos, whose organization and personnel had been constantly changing with the technical demands of the project, was going through a radical transformation. With the war won, what was its purpose? Rudolf Peierls described the change of mood in one of his regular bulletins to Chadwick that October. "Most people", he wrote, "feel that the development of weapons is not a satisfactory field to work on in peace time." Robert Oppenheimer, who had so successfully led the motley collection of scientific eccentrics and geniuses, resigned on 16 October, and others followed. Hans Bethe, head of the Theoretical Division, Enrico Fermi, mastermind of the first working reactor, and weapons expert George Kistiakowsky all made their way back to academic research.

General Groves addressed a staff meeting at the beginning of October and outlined what the future might hold. Work must go on, he said; it was necessary, because of the demands of international negotiations, to continue to maintain a high level of secrecy and security. Norris Bradbury, who had overseen the final assembly of the gadget, would take over in place of Oppenheimer as director and sooner or later Los Alamos would come under civilian control, but there would be no real policy for the next eight months. The main purpose of the laboratory was to continue weapons production and maintain essential staff.

Bradbury, the new director, was concerned that, with the expected decline in the numbers of staff to about eleven hundred, it would be hard to keep those he needed. He was most concerned about the Theoretical Division, all of whose members were determined to leave. Pcicrls wrote to Chadwick, "the spirit of the placc is very low indeed and is still deteriorating".

The members of the British Mission in Los Alamos now thought about what the future might hold for them and when they would be returning to the UK. A decision of what type of research would continue in Britain after the war had been continually postponed, and the only real independent work that had been done was in Canada in a joint programme that had seen collaboration between French, Canadian, British and American scientists. No decision had been made about what type of enrichment process would be built in the UK, nor if there would be a drive to create an independent British bomb. As these questions loomed, the fact that a large proportion of the knowledge that Britain possessed was in the minds of those who had worked on the Manhattan Project became all too apparent, as did the fact that there remained large gaps in British expertise.

In August 1945 Peierls wrote to Chadwick telling him how to get security clearance for information about Manhattan Project reports on metallurgy so that they could be sent to England. Chadwick was advised to ask for the reports from the Battelle Memorial Institute in Columbus, Ohio, and also to look at the index of the various reports from the Chicago Laboratory. The alternative was to send someone, a qualified metallurgist, over to Los Alamos to spend some time going through the material and talk to scientists who had worked with plutonium and polonium and the other esoteric materials in the bomb. As Peierls pointed out, since the war was now over there was no longer any valid reason to try to get another British expert on the staff. It was best, he felt, to be honest about the reason for making the request: that Britain wanted to know how to build a bomb.

Chadwick knew it wasn't as simple as that. He had received a very confidential memorandum a few months earlier, in October 1944. It was notes of a meeting between General Groves, Ernest Lawrence and Mark Oliphant taken during a visit of Groves to Lawrence's Laboratory in Berkeley, California. It is clear that the document was written for Chadwick by Oliphant, and intended for his eyes only. Lawrence complained to Groves about what he said was excessive secrecy, particularly in relation to some British scientists. Groves responded that he was only following his orders. He then went on to say that it was the opinion of the US General Staff that like it or not the US was bound to make a military alliance with Britain after the war. American policy would be that no manufacture of the materials or storage of the weapon, and here he clearly meant the atom bomb, would be permitted outside the central portions of the North American continent. He pointed out the dangers if a manufacturing or storage centre for these weapons was captured by a paratrooper attack. Pressed about the source of this attack he suggested that it would be Russia. He believed that the US and Britain would maintain its ascendency in the field of nuclear weapons for ten years, and in that time the Allies would have time to prepare for the inevitable war with Russia. But any effort that the UK might make to construct its own weapons, in the view of the US, must be confined to Central Canada.

This was completely incompatible with Chadwick's ambition of an independent British weapon. He couldn't influence the British government to start spending on its own programme, but he could enhance his effort to get as much information as he could from the Manhattan project. Fortunately there was still a lot of work for one or two of the scientists in the British Mission.

William Penney had written to Chadwick shortly after the Trinity test suggesting that he should visit the Japanese cities that had been attacked as soon as Japan had surrendered. He had flown to Tinian for the first attack, but was prevented from boarding one of the escort B-29s to observe the Hiroshima bomb. He did manage to see the Nagasaki explosion and was, as he had requested, one of the first observers on the ground at the sites of the two destroyed cities, calculating the blast effects and assessing the size of the explosion. He suggested that the Nagasaki bomb was extremely large, the equivalent of 90,000 tons of TNT.

In Los Alamos Fuchs was working on the results of the Trinity test, trying to arrive at a satisfactory figure for the size of that explosion. When he received the information from the two Japanese cities, there were clearly some wide differences in the figures of the yield, which suggested that either Penney's calculations were wrong or Trinity had been very inefficient. It was important to find out the truth.

Other work on weapons development was also being done. The safety of the bombs while they were being carried was a concern. Some of the nuclear weapon assembly team on Tinian had seen four B-29s taking part in a major raid crash and burn in rapid succession and this had turned their attention to the safety of the nuclear weapons, particularly the Fat Man implosion bomb. Other improvements were being thought of. In the Theoretical Division Fuchs was looking at the size of the gap between the tamper and the plutonium core to improve the force of the shock wave, and other divisions were working on increasing the number of explosive lenses from thirty-two to sixty. This would make production of the lenses much simpler, but increase the difficulties of detonating them simultaneously.

Fuchs was happy to stay at Los Alamos for the time being and the new director was very keen to see him remain. Hans Bethe had handed him the task of completing the work on the implosion and blast analysis for the Los Alamos Technical Series. He found it interesting, because he could worry away at the apparent large difference in the reported blast for the Trinity gadget and the Nagasaki bomb. He delivered four lectures on hydrodynamics to the so-called Los Alamos University, the series of lecture courses set up by General Groves to maintain the intellectual life of the laboratory and to encourage people to stay there.

One new project that emerged at the end of 1945 to engage the minds of the bomb-makers and the Theoretical Division was a series of tests to be held in July 1946. Organized by the US navy to test the effect of a nuclear explosion on a fleet, a collection of redundant and captured warships was to be moored in the lagoon off a coral atoll— Bikini Atoll—in the Pacific. The plan was that they would be subjected to an air-burst nuclear weapon and then an underwater nuclear explosion.

Bradbury, the new head of Los Alamos, wrote to Chadwick in February 1946 saying that there was a severe shortage of theoretical physicists and he hoped that Fuchs could remain at Los Alamos "during the critical period of our work. In addition to the navy test Fuchs would work on the levitated core, as the new design was known, and the problem of determining the efficiency of the bomb from the ball of fire, a problem which no one here can solve." Chadwick, of course, was happy to agree. The overwhelming opinion at Los Alamos was that the results of the tests would be unpalatable for the navy. Battleships and aircraft carriers had proved to be vulnerable to attacks from the air. Now a single bomb, carried by a single aircraft, that could wipe out a city would surely be able to destroy a whole port, or an assembled battle fleet, so there was some suspicion about how the navy was going to set up the ships and the instrumentation and how they would present the results. Fuchs himself felt that he was being asked to work on the navy test partly out of the belief that he would play an objective role. He wrote to Peierls in February 1946 saying "the feeling around here is that the Navy's motives are not altogether above board, and it would be useful to have somebody around who can see to it that anything that comes from this place is sound."

Whatever Fuchs's views of his usefulness to the Americans, the remaining British scientists at Los Alamos were now the sole source of information available to Chadwick, and some of them knew that what they were being asked to do were at the limits of what the US would find acceptable. George Plazcek, a Czech émigré working for the British at Montreal, had recently come to take up a post in the theoretical division, and he also sent information to Chadwick.

Egon Bretscher, who had been working on the super with Ulam and others, also sent material to Chadwick, but was not altogether happy about it. "I feel rather uncomfortable about this particular type of activity, and to avoid difficulties we did all the typing during Saturday and Sunday night, and the drawing Sunday afternoon. I personally would prefer to memorise information and put it on paper in Washington. My conscience would be considerably easier under such circumstances."

As well as all this work, Fuchs was continuing his investigation of the hydrogen bomb, or "super" as it was known.

In April 1946 Teller chaired a conference to review the current status of the super. Fuchs played an active role and was part of a small informal meeting that included Edward Teller and Von Neumann that examined the effects of a hydrogen bomb. The conference started with the presentation of a paper by a physicist, S. Frankel, called "Prima Facie proof of the feasibility of the Super."

Initially Fuchs was dubious that in fact there was proof. He thought that most work had been done on the problem of ignition of the deuterium, the isotope of hydrogen, and not enough on how to keep the reaction going.

But as the conference continued, he started thinking about some of the problems, and arrived at some promising conclusions. There were still many practical problems. Teller outlined their principle idea, which became known as the "classical super". Deuterium, an isotope of hydrogen with a neutron in its nucleus, would be placed next to a fission bomb of uranium. The explosion of the fission bomb would then ignite the deuterium, whose fusion would release energy. It was still only an idea and many of the practical problems remained unsolved. The thermonuclear fuel had to be placed under intense pressures to create the heat necessary for a fusion reaction to start. There would be just nanoseconds for this to happen before the assembly was blasted open by the initial fission bomb, and so on. The question of a specific design that would work went unanswered.

Fuchs was intrigued by the problem, and so also was John von Neumann, a mathematical genius who had made several brilliant and unique contributions to quantum mechanics. He had been on the target selection committee for the Manhattan Project and worked on the implosion problem. He and Fuchs now worked together on the problem of the "super". They made strange partners. Fuchs was a communist, albeit a secret one, while von Neumann, like

Teller, was profoundly anti-Soviet. Despite this, they both had great mathematical fluency and insight into physical problems.

On 28 May 1946, Fuchs and von Neumann filed a joint patent application which is still classified. The application number is S-5292X, and it was a patent for "Improvements in method and means for utilizing nuclear energy". It is a patent for triggering a hydrogen bomb. Their solution was to place the hydrogen isotope deuterium, or a mixture of deuterium and tritium—a hydrogen isotope with two neutrons in its nucleus—inside a tamper of beryllium. This would be heated and compressed by the radiation from a gun-type uranium 235 bomb. The radiation from the initial explosion would be focused on the beryllium by surrounding both components with a radiation-reflecting case.

This design was the first to demonstrate the principle of radiation implosion, relying on the fact that the initial fast gamma radiation from a uranium bomb has the intensity of a physical shock wave. Before filing the patent, the sketch and presumably the overall concept was shown to Edward Teller and Egon Bretscher, another member of the British Mission who had been working on the fusion of deuterium for some time. So Teller was aware of it, and both Fuchs and von Neumann must have been convinced that it would work; otherwise they would not have taken the trouble to complete the patent.

A document in Sir James Chadwick's personal papers, that are now in the Churchill Archives Centre of Churchill College, Cambridge, reveals more of Fuchs's thinking behind the patent application.

In the last few months of Fuchs's stay at Los Alamos he sent a series of reports to Chadwick, and they reveal a great deal of the work that was currently being carried out at Los Alamos, as well as the wide ranging nature of Fuchs's interests. Some of the information contained in what are often Fuchs's handwritten notes is extremely secret.

Fuchs described, for example, the work that was carried out at the Argonne Laboratories in Chicago, where Fermi started the first critical reaction in 1942. He reproduced detailed figures for the monthly production of plutonium and enriched uranium, and reported on the number of weapon cores that were currently in the stockpile, and what US plans were for future production. As we saw he was asked by Bradbury to continue his work on the levitated core, and his research on this was sent to Sir James.

The lengthiest document in Chadwick's papers from this period, however, was the one produced by Fuchs that details the results of the April conference on the super. It's written in Fuchs's own hand, and while it describes the conclusions that the conference came to it also shows that Fuchs was bringing his own analysis to the problems, and arriving at possible solutions while he was writing.

Fuchs suggests that the problem of igniting deuterium, the isotope of hydrogen with two neutrons in the nucleus, can be overcome by mixing it with tritium, another isotope of hydrogen with three neutrons in the nucleus. This mixture can be compressed, and ignited by a strong radiation field produced by a detonator, which in this scheme would be a fission device of uranium. Fuchs says that a uranium detonator is preferable to a plutonium one because the reaction is slightly slower.

He gives plenty of other details, including the dimensions of the deuterium and tritium container, the distance this needs to be from the core of the detonator and the thickness of the radiation shield, which he suggests should be made of beryllium oxide.

He sums up by saying that he still has some doubts about whether the device that he has outlined will work. "Since the conclusion of the conference I have considered the detonation wave in D (deuterium)." There is a danger, he thought, that the shock wave set up by photons in the deuterium will occur too far in advance of the main detonation shock wave and so would peter out. Fuchs also recommends that more work is done on the affect of the shock wave on the radiation shield and the container.

Whether this is a workable plan for a hydrogen bomb or not isn't clear from the description, and of course Fuchs has his own doubts. The report is, however, an extremely detailed description of the results of the conference, and sums up the current thinking of Teller, Ulam, Von Neumann and Fuchs, as well as the others at the conference.

Chadwick received this information some time in June 1946, just a few weeks after the conference. The ideas in the report, and those in the Fuchs-Von Neumann patent which are surely connected, are significantly more advanced than the information about the "Super" that Fuchs had passed to Harry Gold, his NKGB contact, at their last meeting the previous September. Fuchs had not attempted to get in contact with Gold again. In the absence of any messages via his sister Kristel, agents would be attempting to meet him in London and walking away from the rendez-vous empty-handed. He had effectively severed his contact with Soviet intelligence. As far as Moscow was concerned, he had vanished again, and so too had more information about the explosions in the Bikini Atoll, which took place on 1 and 25 July, and any new research on the hydrogen bomb. Why Fuchs disappeared again in this way remains a mystery. Certainly his situation was changing, and perhaps he felt that it was safer to avoid any contact for a while. When he did make contact again, he had a lot more infor-mation to pass on. That, however, was some time in the future.

FOURTEEN

Dangerous Days

At his last meeting on 19 September 1945, Klaus Fuchs had mentioned to Harry Gold that he might be recalled to the UK fairly quickly because the British government had plans to set up its own nuclear research centre.

The Coordinating Committee of the British Tube Alloys Directorate had met in Washington in 1944 and proposed to the British government that it should set up a nuclear research laboratory along the lines of Los Alamos. This recommendation was repeated several times, but Sir John Anderson, the Chancellor of the Exchequer, who was also Cabinet minister in overall charge of Tube Alloys, had done little about it. The new Labour government, however, had taken up the idea and had got so far as to come up with some possible sites. Four redundant airfields close to Oxford were potential candidates and one of them, Harwell, at Didcot, was thought to be the most suitable.

Fuchs was invited to be head of the Theoretical Division, and there was considerable concern on the part of Peierls and Chadwick to make sure that he was happy with the conditions that were offered. He was told that he would have to work under Herbert Skinner, who had been appointed deputy director of the establishment. Skinner had been a colleague of his at Bristol when Fuchs was a student of Professor Mott, and he had worked on the Manhattan Project in Berkeley during the war. Peierls was anxious that Fuchs did not see this as a downgrading of his authority. He wrote to Fuchs in March 1946, saying it would be a good idea to set a definite date for a return to the UK and assuring him that he would be in charge of all theory, including theoretical engineering. "Whatever the administrative position of your section you will surely be expected to take an interest in any questions within the place on which you have something to say or to do."

Fuchs was not particularly concerned about his status, and he knew that Bradbury, as head of Los Alamos, was keen for him to stay there, so he was able to bide his time. When he was interviewed for the post at Harwell he stressed that it was, for him, a temporary position.

He had another, more personal, concern at the time. His father had made contact with him, through the Quakers, via Birmingham University. Fuchs wrote to Wallace Akers, now ensconced in the Ministry of Supply. After telling him that he was going to stay in the US for a few more months to help with the US navy test, he said he intended to find out if he could bring his father and his nephew Klaus Kittowski to Britain, either for a long stay or permanently. Akers replied on 18 February saying that he had heard of the excellent work that Fuchs had done at Los Alamos; he also told him that he had asked someone in the Cabinet Office to take up the case of his father and nephew and that every possible attempt would be made to help him.

Fuchs continued at Los Alamos, while others dealt with the problems of setting up the new Atomic Research Establishment at Harwell, enmeshed as it was in the red tape of the Ministry of Supply. By May 1946 very little machinery had been delivered and work on building staff quarters and laboratories had barely begun. More important, as Peierls complained to Chadwick, staff returning from Los Alamos were still owed three months' back pay, and it was getting hard to persuade people to come to work there.

In May 1946, while Fuchs was finishing off his work in Los Alamos on the navy tests and the work he had taken over from Bethe on the Los Alamos official history, two stories hit the headlines that must surely have caused him, beneath his calm outward appearance, some moments of fear. They concerned the revelation that there had been a Soviet spy ring in Canada and that a British scientist working at the Chalk River reactor site had been arrested in London.

On 5 September 1945, two weeks before Fuchs met Gold in Santa Fe, a member of the GRU left the Soviet Embassy in Ottawa. Igor Gouzenko was a cipher clerk, who worked not for the Soviet ambassador but for the military attaché, Colonel Nikolai Zabotin. Gouzenko had been in Ottawa since the summer of 1943 and had been allowed to bring his wife, Svetlana, with him; she was pregnant and gave birth to a son shortly after they arrived.

Life in Canada was congenial, and they grew to enjoy its easygoing pace and high living standard. It was a shock for Gouzenko, then, to be told by Zabotin in September 1944 that he was to be recalled to Moscow. He reasoned with the military attaché that it would leave the cipher room under-manned and that there was a lot of work to do. Zabotin agreed and the recall was cancelled, but Gouzenko knew that sooner or later he would have to return to Moscow. He didn't want to go back and neither did his wife. They decided that when the time came for them to go, they would defect. A year later, Gouzenko made a mistake with a secret document and this was reported by the NKGB officer in the embassy. Another recall instruction was received from Moscow, and this time Gouzenko knew that he would have to risk his life if he wanted to remain in Canada.

He worked late at the embassy in the cipher room, then left with a large quantity of signals and documents which he hoped would assist in his request for political asylum. It was harder than he imagined to get anyone in Ottawa to take any notice of his story, and it was not until a group of Soviet agents from the embassy tried to break into his flat that the police took him into protective custody and listened to what he had to say about a Soviet spy ring in Canada. One of the contacts identified from the signals Gouzenko had removed from the embassy was a British physicist, Allan Nunn May, who had worked at the Cavendish Laboratory in Cambridge along with Lew Kowarski and Engelbert Broda, the man whom Fuchs had recommended to the GRU as a possible recruit in 1943, but who had instead been recruited by the NKGB. Nunn May had had an affair with Broda's wife, Hildegard, and they eventually married. Who out of this love triangle had recruited whom as a spy was never discovered.

Nunn May had come to work on the Canadian heavy-water project at Chalk River in January 1945 and had been passing information to the Soviet intelligence services. He had also managed to obtain a sample of uranium 235, which had been quickly flown under diplomatic cover to Moscow in August 1945. The existence of the Canadian group of Soviet agents was announced in March 1946 and Nunn May, who had returned to London to take up an academic post at King's College, was arrested two days later. Fuchs knew Nunn May, having met him when he was at the Cavendish. He probably also met him when Fuchs visited the Chalk River site, and both had made occasional trips to the Argonne Laboratories in Chicago.

The news of the Gouzenko defection, and in particular Nunn May's arrest, startled the British scientists still at Los

Alamos, and Fuchs was with a group of them when it was discussed. Els Placzek had once been married to Hans Halban, Broda's colleague at the Cavendish, and she described Nunn May as a quiet bachelor, helpful at parties, "just like Klaus here". Some accounts of this discussion say that Fuchs was uncomfortable at this remark, others that he laughed it off. He said to his friends that he didn't think Nunn May knew enough about the bomb to be of enormous assistance.

Fuchs had made no attempt to contact Gold since his last meeting in September. He may have felt that he didn't have anything important enough to hand over to justify the risk, but the arrest of Nunn May must have made him exceptionally alert for any signs of extra security service activity.

He left Los Alamos in June 1946. Cockcroft had written to him saying that he wanted him to be in Harwell for a Steering Committee meeting on 1 July, and he should abandon a planned trip to Chalk River. He could find out all he needed to know at Harwell. A seat on an RAF flight was arranged for 28 June. Fuchs took his time. He flew to Washington, where he met Chadwick and handed over some papers from Los Alamos that Bretscher had given him about the deuterium fusion problem. Fuchs had arranged for a case of documents to be forwarded to Chadwick as well. He then went on to Cambridge, Massachusetts, to see his sister, who told him that Gold had paid another visit in February, but Fuchs was not going to do anything about that now. He took the RAF bomber flight from Gander on the 28th and by 9 July he was writing letters from the Atomic Energy Research Establishment at Harwell, Didcot, in Berkshire, trying to find out what had happened to the rest of his luggage, which was being sent by sea; whether the papers that Chadwick wanted to look at before sending them on had in fact been sent; and inquiring if there were any papers in the Washington office about radiation cross-sections, which were urgently needed at Harwell. He had, in other words, quickly got his feet under the desk.

Harwell was 55 miles from London and 18 miles from Oxford. The accommodation was much the same as it was when it had been an RAF base. The officers' mess, called Ridgeway House, had been turned into housing for senior personnel and visiting scientists, and the commanding officers' quarters were taken over by Sir John Cockcroft. Laboratories and workshops were set up in the former hangars. Fuchs had a room in the officers' mess at first, then went to live in a small guest house in Abingdon run by the former manager of Ridgeway House. He stayed here until some prefabricated bungalows became available at Harwell and then he moved in to one of these.

Fuchs was head of the Theoretical Division, and several other scientists from Los Alamos took over some of the other divisions. In fact, Fuchs knew many of these men from the days that he had spent either in Bristol University or working in Birmingham on the Tube Alloys programme. Otto Frisch was the head of the Nuclear Physics Division, working on establishing the first small-scale nuclear reactor at Harwell, the first in the UK. Egon Bretscher, also from Los Alamos, was now head of the Chemistry Division. Herbert Skinner, who had been at Bristol with Fuchs under Professor Mott, had been part of the Manhattan Project in Berkeley, California, working on electromagnetic separation with Lawrence, and was now head of General Physics and deputy director of the establishment. Other divisions were Reactor Physics, Isotopes and Engineering.

It wasn't long after his return to Britain that Fuchs once more came under the scrutiny of MI5. The Gouzenko defection and the arrest of Allan Nunn May had energized the Security Service, of course. MI5 had raked through the personal files in their registry, looking again at the cases of suspected communists working on the wartime Tube Alloys project, with constant memos flying between the officers in B Branch, counter-espionage, and C Branch, responsible for protective security. Sadly, their survey did not throw up the Fuchs files; he came to their attention only because the security officer at Harwell, Wing Commander Henry Arnold, sent MI5 a copy of a note from Fuchs saying that he would attend a meeting of the Physics Club at the Royal Society on 9 October 1946. However, the realization that Fuchs was back in the UK and working on Britain's nuclear programme caused a stir amongst the officers in B Branch, now housed with the director general and his staff in a cramped building in St. James Street, W1.

An MI5 officer contacted Arnold and was told that Fuchs was doing "Atomic Energy work of extreme importance". Arnold had sent the note to MI5 on his own initiative because, he told the MI5 officer, "he had gained the confidence of Dr. Fuchs among other key scientists, and had evolved a scheme whereby they were to report their movements to him so that Arnold would know where they go and what company they keep when they are outside Harwell." Henry Arnold was a strange figure. A member of the Moral Rearmament Movement, he was anti-communist and had a suspicion of foreigners. He saw conspiracies where none existed, and claimed that Fuchs was the centre of a communist network at Harwell. The MI5 officer was persuaded to go to Harwell to visit him and realized that this suspicion was based on no more evidence than that Arnold had seen Fuchs in discussion with another British scientist who had been sacked for being a member of the British Communist Party. The officer's report was scathing.

The MI5 officer did discover, however, that there was a file on Fuchs and he sent it along with a minute to Michael Serpell, the Security Service's leading expert on pre-war communist subversion. The officer who had spoken to Arnold took the presence of Fuchs at Harwell lightly: "It is of course possible that Arnold is having his leg pulled, and that Fuchs may be passing vitally important information which he has in his possession by virtue of his work, through various channels to the Russians." He had absorbed the tenor of the debate from the previous efforts to warn of Fuchs's possible communist connections. "It would undoubtedly be said if Fuchs proves to be a dangerous customer that his technical ability is such that atomic energy research would suffer very considerably if he were removed from his present employment."

Serpell ignored the hint. In a lengthy minute, he launched an attack on Fuchs and on the officers who had cleared him back in 1943. The idea, spelled out in 1943, that Fuchs would be less of a danger on the other side of the Atlantic was a grave error, he wrote. The Nunn May case had proved that. There had been some difficulty back in 1943 in persuading the Department of Scientific and Industrial Research, the DSIR, who managed the Tube Alloys project, that Fuchs was a threat. Now the situation had changed, and Serpell hoped "whatever the value of a refugee scientist's work may be to atomic research, his possible danger to security will be considered as a prime issue." That "refugee scientists" had been the backbone of both British and American work on the atom bomb had clearly passed Serpell by. No matter, he had the bit between his teeth. Fuchs had been a communist penetration agent of the Nazi Party in his youth. There was a suggestion that he had been interned in Canada with Hans Kahle, a man who was a known agent of the OGPU in this country.

Serpell went further. Fuchs was closely associated with R. E. Peierls, also highly placed in atomic research work, and who had a Russian wife. He recommended that an investigation should be launched against Fuchs and that more information should be discovered about Peierls.

At this point Serpell's division head, Roger Hollis, intervened. Hollis had been responsible for monitoring Communist Party members just before and during the war, and had taken a more pragmatic view about the dangers of subversion that they presented. The only action that should be taken, he said, was that the tenor of Serpell's case should be presented to Arnold and more reports from him should be awaited. A few days later, Arnold reported that the arrangement with Fuchs where he reported his comings and goings was clearly breaking down; meanwhile another officer confirmed that Fuchs had indeed been interned at the same time as Kahle.

Then Jane Archer—a senior figure in MI5, the first woman ever to be recruited and an old Russian hand who had helped interrogate the Soviet defector Walter Krivitsky back in 1937—weighed in. They should inform the Atomic Energy Directorate that Fuchs was a probable Russian agent and obtain their consent to his remaining where he was. Her recommendation was that Fuchs should be divorced from all contact with atomic energy and that Peierls should no longer be used as a consultant. She went on to say, "unless my knowledge of Lord Portal [the controller of atomic energy] is at fault he will not allow these men to continue working on atomic energy. To do so may compromise the future of atomic energy secrecy, which is a great deal more important than the fact that such secrecy must be considered compromised up to date."

Hollis had little choice at this point but to submit the case to the deputy director general of MI5, Guy Liddell. He put forward convincing reasons why any evidence against Fuchs was purely circumstantial. There were only two points to be dealt with as he saw it. Fuchs had worked with the German communists in 1933 and he had been associated with Kahle in an internment camp. The latter was easily explained: Fuchs and Kahle had been wrongly interned with

German Nazis, and naturally they would seek out each other's company given the uncongenial nature of their neighbours. Hollis must have known that this was simply untrue. Very few Nazis were interned, and this was the reason that the policy was fairly quickly reversed. But he went on to say, "I can see nothing in this file which persuades me that Fuchs is in any way likely to be engaged in espionage or that he is any more than anti-Nazi." As for Peierls, the only thing against him was his Russian wife.

Hollis, Archer and Serpell had no knowledge of the plans then being worked on, in November 1946, for constructing an independent British weapon. If they had, then Archer and Serpell might have been less confident of the way that Lord Portal would have greeted their recommendations. Hollis perhaps had a slightly clearer idea. "If Lord Portal wishes to exclude people with records such as Fuchs and Peierls, we must I suppose lend our assistance, but I think he should be advised that it will lead to a very considerable purge, which will presumably have to include a number of very highly placed British scientists."

Liddell looked at the case and called a meeting of Archer, Hollis and head of B Branch Dick White. Liddell agreed with Hollis. There was, he said, little real evidence, and anyway, Fuchs had himself claimed to belong to a left-wing socialist youth movement, and the Germans in 1934 made no distinction between Jews, communists and Social Democrats. On the other hand, there was a case for investigation and MI5 could not possibly afford to leave matters as they were. However, it would be unwise to make any approach to the Ministry of Supply until they knew more about both of these people.

So, following a further discussion between White and Hollis, a warrant was applied for, allowing the Post Office to intercept the mail going to Fuchs at Harwell and to the Peierls' home address in Birmingham. There was indeed correspondence between them, but it was personal, concerning a proposed trip to Switzerland which was being organized by Genia Peierls. It revealed little beyond Genia's belief that Fuchs needed a rest and was incapable of organizing things like holidays without pressure from her. Other letters were about technical conferences, from potential employees at Harwell, and so on, but nothing that suggested any connection with Soviet espionage. On 2 April 1947 the MI5 officer responsible for the surveillance recommended to Hollis that the mail intercepts should be ended, and in May Liddell signed off the cancellation.

For six months suspicion had fallen on Fuchs. MI5 had considered the possibility that he might be a spy. They had found nothing, but the investigation had been cursory. An internal argument between officers, who had no more evidence than the fragmentary gossip they had assembled in 1941, was followed by a mail intercept that did not include Fuchs's personal address or Rudolph Peierls's office at Birmingham University. Despite the efforts of two hardened anti-communist officers in MI5, Fuchs had emerged from their attention unscathed.

The well-organized and argued case against Fuchs did Michael Serpell little good. He remains an unknown figure in the annals of MI5, mentioned in a biography of Dick White but with his name spelt incorrectly. A few years later he was shunted out to a colonial posting, and there he remained.

The question of Fuchs's reliability arose again a few months later. Back in 1946 he had been offered a permanent position at Harwell but had turned it down, saying he felt that he would not want to stay there for very long, so would prefer a temporary position. It was a very honest way of dealing with the offer that baffled Cockcroft, who blamed the officials at the Ministry of Supply for failing to make the job appear attractive enough. Now, in November 1947,

Cockcroft wanted Fuchs to be on the permanent establishment. Once more there was a request for a security
clearance, with Cockcroft saying there was "only one other
person in this country who possesses the qualifications and
experience of Dr. Fuchs".

After the recent bruising internal argument inside MI5,
the outcome was not in doubt. A letter from a Colonel
Badham of MI5 went to the Ministry of Supply in January
1948. It outlined the evidence against Fuchs, which was the
accusation by the Gestapo that he was a communist, but
pointed out that this was not objective information and that
Fuchs himself had said that he had been a member of a
socialist student society. The letter also mentioned that he
had had an association with Hans Kahle when he was
interned in Canada, but didn't suggest that this was suspicious. It ended by saying that any security risk presented by
Fuchs was very slight. There was no reply to this letter for
some months. Then in August 1948 Mr. J. McFadden at the
Ministry of Supply finally wrote back to MI5. They had
determined that "the advantages gained to Harwell through
the ability of Dr. Fuchs outweigh the slight security risk".

FIFTEEN

Pillar of the Establishment

Despite Michael Serpell's dismissal of him as a "refugee scientist", Fuchs was now a senior figure in the British nuclear establishment. As an unmarried German émigré it was unlikely that he would be offered one of the top executive posts, which would always be reserved for the more clubbable products of the old school tie, but his job in charge of the Theoretical Division at Harwell was prestigious and a mark of the regard that senior scientists like Chadwick and Cockcroft had for him.

Fuchs could talk as an equal to the most eminent physicists in the Western world. He remained a good friend of Max Born; Edward Teller invited him to dinner when he was in the United States; Hans Bethe at Cornell University entertained him on his way from Los Alamos to Britain; and Robert Oppenheimer suggested that Fuchs take a rest from his busy schedule and spend some time at the Institute of Advanced Study in Princeton.

While Fuchs was riding high, the British nuclear programme, both civil and military, was off to a very shaky start. In the planning stages since the completion of the MAUD Report in 1942 the British government had always baulked at the cost of setting up and running its own factories and research establishments. Now, six years later, the costs of Britain going it alone had not diminished and the economy was, if anything, in a worse state. Victory in the war had brought the expense of feeding and housing millions of homeless and unemployed Germans in their own country, while the situation at home was little better. Rationing was still in force, hundreds of thousands of homes had been reduced to rubble by the Blitz and the V1 and V2 rocket attacks on London, and the government had run up massive overseas debts. Bread rationing had been introduced in 1946—something that had never seemed necessary even in wartime—and it was to last for two years.

In 1945 the new Labour government under Prime Minister Clement Attlee had taken the decision to set up Harwell, but when the McMahon Act was passed in the United States in 1946, Britain really had to go it alone. This piece of US legislation—passed rapidly in the wake of the Gouzenko defection and revelation about Allan Nunn May—stated that all research about nuclear energy, no matter how it was obtained, was secret unless it was specifically declassified. This automatically prohibited the transfer of information to Britain, even if, for example, British scientists working on the Manhattan Project had developed that information. If Britain was to have an independent atomic weapon, then the complete building programme originally called for in the MAUD Report could no longer be postponed.

An important development that had taken place in the last six years was the discovery of plutonium by Glenn Seaborg at the University of California in Berkeley. Plutonium, as we have seen, was produced from the uranium in a nuclear reactor, and this new element could be used as the critical core of an atomic bomb. Three separate industrial facilities were now required in the UK. The first process in the chain that leads to a workable bomb is the extraction and refining of uranium metal from its ore. A factory for this purpose was planned at Springfields, near Preston in Lancashire. The uranium would then be enriched to increase the percentage of uranium 235, so making it more radioactive, and the diffusion plant to do this was built at Capenhurst in Cheshire. The product of this enrichment plant would in its turn be made into fuel rods for a reactor, and the site for this was Sellafield, later to be renamed Windscale. Here also the used fuel rods from the reactor were to be treated in long acid baths to extract their plutonium.

Each of these large industrial projects needed the support of the research scientists at Harwell, and despite Lord Cockcroft's desire to keep the establishment clean of involvement in nuclear weapons, the large nuclear industrial complexes had only one justification, and that was the construction of a British atomic bomb.

William Penney had been asked to lead the work on this as far back as November 1945 and he had accepted, but it wasn't until May 1947 that Air Marshal Viscount Portal, wartime chief of the air staff and now controller of production for atomic energy, gave Penney the orders to build a weapon.

The decision to proceed had been a drawn-out affair. There had been an ad hoc Cabinet meeting in October 1946, where a decision to build a plant for the production of uranium 235 was on the agenda. Hugh Dalton and Stafford Cripps, chancellor of the exchequer and president of the Board of Trade respectively, opposed it on the grounds of cost. But the foreign secretary, Ernest Bevin, intervened in the debate, saying that "I don't want any other foreign secretary of this country to be talked at by a Secretary of State in the United States the way I have in my discussions with Mr. Byrnes." A series of policy differences were exacerbating relations between Britain and the US. The wartime Lend

Lease Agreement had been cancelled without warning, causing a financial crisis for Britain. There had been an abrupt change of policy by the Truman administration over Palestine, which was still a British protectorate, and of course there was the McMahon Act itself.

So the decision to go ahead with the diffusion plant had been taken. Funding for the bomb was not officially part of this decision, but this was considered in a small subcommittee meeting in No. 10 Downing Street in January 1947. Lord Portal was present, but the chancellor and the trade minister were not.

Portal said that as far as he was aware no decision had been taken to proceed with the development of atomic weapons. He had discussed the issue with the chiefs of staff, who were "anxious that we should not be without this weapon if others possess it. About three years' work would be needed to solve the problems of nuclear physics and engineering involved in the bomb mechanism." Bevin supported Portal: "We could not afford to acquiesce in an American monopoly of this new development." Sentiments that were no different from those of Sir John Anderson in 1943, or of Stalin and Kurchatov in Moscow in 1945, or of Klaus Fuchs as a staunch member of the Communist Party in 1941.

The Cabinet subcommittee gave Portal the go-ahead he sought. Portal never explained why he waited several months before telling Penney to start work. Penney was due to go to the United States to have a series of meetings with his former colleagues at Los Alamos, so Portal may have felt that any exchange of information might be easier if Penney could honestly say that he was not working on a nuclear weapon. It may also have been because in January, shortly after the Cabinet committee meeting, Britain was overwhelmed by a snowstorm that was the start of the worst winter ever experienced. It lasted for months, causing food and fuel shortages, power cuts and factory closures. Whatever the reason, it was another delay for the British project.

Stalin, as we have seen, had started directing resources into the Soviet Union's bomb in August 1945. Kurchatov was under pressure to deliver and, with detailed information about the Trinity gadget to hand, had a blueprint that he could follow. Penney, with an equally daunting task in front of him, made exactly the same choice. The British bomb was to follow as closely as possible the design that had been developed at Los Alamos.

Penney assembled his team at the Royal Ordnance factory in Woolwich in June 1947. This was the traditional home of weapons design and manufacture in Britain, and he assumed that much of the work would be carried out there. Portal had suggested that Penney might like to create a completely new establishment to build the bomb, founding something like Harwell for nuclear weapons, but Penney didn't want to take on the effort involved in this. He surmised, probably correctly, that it would divert resources from the primary objective.

There were just thirty-seven scientists, engineers and technicians in the library at Woolwich as Penney addressed them for the first time. He spoke for almost two hours, describing as simply as he could the principles behind a nuclear weapon and explaining what the effort to build one would demand. It was a long meeting, in a warm, stuffy library with the windows kept firmly closed. But no one nodded off.

The task that Penney and his small group faced was extremely difficult. Despite the far-sighted work of Frisch and Peierls in 1940, very few people in Britain had any knowledge or experience of building a nuclear weapon. British collaboration with the United States had resulted in just nineteen or so scientists working at Los Alamos where the bomb was made, and not all of these people had a comprehensive overall picture of the way that the various components of the bomb were constructed or put together. Chadwick had struggled to collect all the reports and documents from Los Alamos and these, along with what was in the minds of Penney and others, was all that the collaboration with the United States had produced.

Penney had produced eighteen pages of notes for this meeting, including a diagram of the plutonium bomb as he understood it, which was similar to the sketch that Fuchs had given to Gold in 1945 and was probably drawn with Fuchs's assistance. Even at this late stage, Penney had wrongly assumed that there were sixteen explosive lenses in the US design, but had then crossed this out and added the correct number of thirty-two. Was this also guidance from Fuchs?

Penney had broken the bomb down into seven different components for his audience. He listed them as the imploder system, the plutonium core, the initiator, the casing of the explosive assembly, the detonator firing mechanism, the proximity fuse device and the ballistic outer casing. He explained that the outer assembly could be broken down further, because the high-explosive shell was made up of an inner and outer shell, and that there were three concentric liners around the core, starting with an aluminium inner liner, a boron 10 shield and a uranium 238 tamper.

The final page of his document was a grid where he asked the rhetorical question, "Could we go straight ahead and make the component?" There were only two items to which Penney could answer yes, and these were the aluminium liner and the uranium 238 tamper. To everything else—the initiator, the core, the boron shield, the high-explosive lenses and the detonators—he had to answer no. The reasons for this depressing conclusion were a combination of lack of special knowledge and experience; and, with the plutonium and polonium in particular, the fact that there were currently no working reactors or separation plants to produce the metals.

Penney was under the impression that the manufacture of the core and the initiator would be somebody else's problem. The Ministry of Supply treated the industrial side of the nuclear programme—the uranium enrichment plant, the nuclear reactors and the plutonium separation units, all of which were built in the north of England—as a separate entity. They were under the control of Sir Christopher Hinton, a man with a strong engineering background whom the ministry had appointed as the deputy controller of production for atomic energy in 1946. Penney quite legitimately focused, therefore, on the manufacture of the explosives and the electrical detonators. There was in the UK after the war a wealth of experience in the production of high explosives, but even here there was ignorance about the necessary shape and composition of the outer explosive lenses. It wasn't only a question of the precise shape; the lenses had to be made with much greater precision and quality control than conventional bombs or shells.

Penney set up his team to develop the explosive lenses at Fort Halstead in Kent, the site of the government's High Explosive Research department. Here they had to work out for themselves everything learned several years earlier at Los Alamos by George Kistiakowsky and his assistants. The explosive shapes had to be almost perfectly homogenous, without any air bubbles or hairline cracks, and this was achieved by controlling the rate of cooling of the explosive mixture. The finished explosives were then detonated at the gunnery testing range at Foulness in the Thames estuary, where the blast and shock wave that was produced were analysed by high-speed film cameras and other instruments.

Penney did not find it easy to build up his organization. He quickly realized that in order to do all the work he would have to increase his staff far beyond his original estimate. This had been based on figures for the number of people employed on the same task at Los Alamos, but he had underestimated the amount of work that was done by some university departments and the extent to which the Theoretical Physics Division staff would move from project to project to solve particular problems. Instead of a planned staff of 220, he would probably need around 500, and this was still a conservative estimate. In the United Kingdom any sort of technical staff, even secretaries, were in short supply, and even if Penney could recruit the people he needed there was nowhere for them to live at Fort Halstead and he could not get the resources to build new housing for them. There were severe shortages in the economy in any case, but the bomb project was so secret that it was impossible to claim any priority over other government programmes. It took Penney more than five months to recruit just six draughtsmen to Fort Halstead. How long would it take to find an extra 250 engineers and technicians? If Penney had known about the effort that the Soviet Union was putting into its own programme he would have been both extremely envious and extremely alarmed.

Realizing that the project was running into the sand, Penney pointed out all his difficulties to Lord Portal, who paid a visit to the head of the Cabinet Office, Lord Bridges. Bridges was at least aware of the urgency attached to building a bomb and he set up a committee to coordinate all the staffing needs across Whitehall. It met with a lot of opposition from some of the other departments, particularly the Air Ministry, eager to hang on to their scientists. They too had some important technical projects, vital to the defence of the country. "What would be the point of having a bomb if there were no jet bombers to deliver it?" was a convincing argument from the air procurement staff. Penney's lobbying did produce more staff, however, and he had taken on another 150 by February 1948.

Klaus Fuchs had also been providing some help. Penney had paid him a visit at Harwell as early as October 1946, before Penney had officially started work. It was a meeting called by Fuchs and included Geoffrey Taylor, an eminent mathematician who had also worked at Los Alamos. As Penney had, of course, been part of the Los Alamos brains trust, the discussion between them in that meeting could only have been about their shared knowledge, which was nuclear weapon technology. Two months later Fuchs sent Penney a key paper from Los Alamos, "The Equation of the State of Air", jointly written by Fuchs, Peierls and Tony Skyrme. It was a paper the three had continually refined, and in it they gave a vital description of a method used to assess the effects of blast and to determine what was happening in the bomb in the milliseconds after the detonators had exploded.

Fuchs also sent Penney another paper from Los Alamos written by Skyrme, this one on the "Hydrodynamic Theory of the Reaction Zone in High Explosive". This was particularly relevant to Penney's work on the high-speed and low-speed explosives that were designed to compress the plutonium core and turn it into a critical mass.

The dual structure imposed on the nuclear project by the Ministry of Supply sometimes appeared unnecessarily complicated. Rudolf Peierls, now back in his academic career at Birmingham University, received a request from ICI, the commercial chemicals giant working with Christopher Hinton. For some reason they asked for information on plane waves in explosives. A plane wave is the shock wave produced when an explosive lens converts the spherical, expanding blast generated in an explosive by a detonator into a single directional impulse with a constant wavelength. Peierls had a copy of the paper on this phenomenon that he had written at Los Alamos, but it was of course in the eyes of the US government still secret and he did not want to pass it on to ICI, so instead he wrote to Fuchs asking him to pass it on to Penney, which Fuchs did. This exchange took place in January 1947, before Penney had even officially started work on the project, but clearly Fuchs, Peierls and no doubt other former members of the Los Alamos team were aware of what Penney was up to.

When Penney started work he believed that he was going to be responsible only for the design and production of the outer part of the bomb, and that the core—that is the uranium 238 tamper, the sphere of plutonium and its small polonium initiator, the "urchin"—would be made and supplied to him by the facilities at Windscale. Really there had been no proper discussion about this but, when the question of who would deliver this part of the work arose, Christopher Hinton, the man in charge of the developments at Windscale and Capenhurst, did not want the extra responsibility. It was proving hard enough to get the resources for his existing commitments. Both plutonium and polonium were unknown quantities and it would most likely prove extremely expensive to his organization to provide the components to Fort Halstead. Hinton believed that they should be made by Penney's organization, from materials supplied by Harwell, and if necessary a brand-new laboratory and factory should be established for the purpose.

It took some time for Penney to accept this. He drew up the plans for a new site, which was eventually to become Aldermaston, the Atomic Weapons Research Establishment in Hampshire, while at the same time he tried to get Portal to reverse the policy. While this argument was going on and the outcome was undecided, Fuchs was receiving requests for information from Air Vice Marshal E. D. Davis, a senior officer in the Ministry of Supply. He sent another copy of "The Equation of the State of Air" and also a vital paper on the problem of spontaneous fission in plutonium. It isn't clear from the correspondence why Davis wanted this particular piece of work by Fuchs from Los Alamos, but it eventually found its way to Penney's scientists.

It wasn't only information in the form of scientific papers

and reports that made their way to Penney and his staff; in addition Fuchs was a regular visitor to Fort Halstead, where he gave talks on a variety of questions about the design of the bomb. He arranged a visit, for example, on 12 March 1948, suggesting that he could talk about implosion and the methods used to determine the critical size of the plutonium core. Fuchs's performance when he addressed the high-explosives team was always impressive. The scientists went to his talks because they knew they would be worth the effort. Two mathematicians on Penney's staff, John Corner and Herbert Pike, were particularly impressed with the way that Fuchs could get across such a vast amount of information and they realized that he had a brilliant, photographic memory. He always had answers for any questions asked of him, and Corner thought that Fuchs was head and shoulders above the other consultants who occasionally came to talk to them. He not only relied on his memory but arrived for the lectures with notebooks that were filled with mathematical equations. Pike thought that Fuchs must have written up everything he did at Los Alamos at the end of each day, because he appeared to have the correct numbers for every problem.

When Penney finally accepted that he was going to be making the whole bomb assembly, Fuchs began to supply detailed information about various aspects of the core and the initiator. Some of his letters suggest that he took part in many of the discussions, and that he felt personally involved in the progress towards a British weapon. He writes in one letter to Penney that he could talk at one of his lectures "about the considerations which have led to the particular designs we believe to be most favourable". In another letter he says that he wants to talk about the "problem of designing the gadget particularly if we are going to consider more complicated types. I will send you the papers, and I hope that we can discuss this." This was in response to a letter from Penney, written in July 1948, in which he specifically requests a paper by Fuchs on a topic described as an "Infinite Tamper System with a gap between Tamper and Core", a paper written in Los Alamos in 1946. This was a theoretical analysis of a type of core more sophisticated than that used at Nagasaki. As we have seen, ever since the assessment of the size of the Nagasaki blast—produced in part from Penney's own observations—had reached Los Alamos, Fuchs had been perturbed by the large discrepancy between the assessed yield of the Trinity test and that of the Nagasaki bomb. Either the estimate of the Nagasaki explosion had been wildly exaggerated, or the Trinity gadget had been flawed in some way. Trying to resolve the problem had led him and others at Los Alamos to consider what might have gone wrong with Trinity and how to avoid these failures in the future. Fuchs thought that Trinity had been at best 20 per cent efficient—in other words only 20 per cent of the atoms of the plutonium had actually released their energy in a chain reaction. Later assessments were that even this figure was far too high.

Fuchs was an inexhaustible fund of information for Penney and his scientists at Fort Halstead. The papers that he forwarded, many still secret as we have seen, covered a variety of topics, such as descriptions of polonium, the substance used in the initiator that was so radioactive it glowed blue in the dark; experiments on implosion with strong convergence waves; a paper on the effect of the boron shield on the behaviour of neutrons; and a survey of the various hydrodynamic calculation methods used in Los Alamos. All of this material had its origin in the work that Fuchs and others had done in the Theoretical Division at Los Alamos. He even supplied the US specifications for the purity of plutonium, to ensure that the product coming out of Windscale would work in a bomb and to save Penney and his staff the labour of having to go through the calculations themselves.

Concerning some of the papers that were still secret,

and had not yet been declassified with the agreement of the United States, Penney assured Fuchs that the information would be used only in internal reports at Fort Halstead, so he need have no worries about secrecy.

Penney had probably also seen some of the other material that Fuchs had brought back from Los Alamos and given to Sir James Chadwick in 1946, including his papers about the hydrogen bomb, the nuclear reactors running at Chicago and at Los Alamos, the figures for plutonium production, and his work on the new design of the levitated core for the plutonium bomb. There is no question that Lord Portal, Penney's superior, had seen these papers, because on 2 July the senior administrator at the Washington office, G.A. Macmillan, wrote to Portal saying, "I enclose four sets of notes written at Sir James Chadwick's request by Dr. K. Fuchs at the time of his departure from Los Alamos. Sir James attaches much importance to them."

Fuchs, continued Macmillan, would by now have taken up his post at Harwell and would be able to answer any queries that Portal might have. There is no record of what Portal did with these notes, which were still extremely secret. They would have been of enormous interest to Penney, and his fellow scientists, but not of immediate use. Penney had his work cut out making Britain's first atomic bomb. The "super" would be ten years down the road.

As well as this collaboration with Penney, Fuchs had other responsibilities at Harwell. There was work to be done on the experimental reactor being constructed there, as well as for the large-scale production piles being built at Aldermaston. All the work that Fuchs had done on diffusion for Tube Alloys and for the Manhattan Project in New York had to be dusted off and applied to the enrichment plant being built at Capenhurst. If the primary aim of the British Scientific Mission to the Manhattan Project had been to acquire as much knowledge as possible for British use after the war, then it had succeeded and Fuchs was a major element in that success.

Fuchs was also, of course, engaged on other projects in the Harwell pipeline that owed nothing to his work in the United States. There were calculations for newer, more exotic reactors, like the so-called fast breeder, which ran on plutonium and uranium 238 and produced more plutonium than it consumed. Fuchs also introduced new computing methods at Harwell. Early forms of computer had been brought in at the beginning just for the Theoretical Division, but the staff and the machines developed to supply a service for the whole establishment. In addition, Fuchs ran the coffee and tea club for the computing section. He took it seriously, as he did everything. One former worker remembers that Fuchs had to put up a notice asking members of the club not to steal the teacups. He had become an established part of the life at Harwell.

For much of the time that Fuchs was working at Harwell and assisting in the preliminary work for the first British bomb he had remained out of contact with the NKGB. It was to be almost two years before they heard from him again.

SIXTEEN

The Third Contact

There were many very nervous Soviet intelligence officers in Moscow at the beginning of 1946. The defection of their cipher clerk in Canada and the arrest of one of their agents, Allan Nunn May, left very large holes in their security and plunged a highly successful network into danger. At the same time, to compound the crisis, a long-term agent in the United States, Elizabeth Bentley, became disillusioned and decided to tell the FBI everything she knew about Soviet intelligence operations. It was a considerable amount and the NKGB, in a massive and unprecedented retreat, took the decision to put all its operations in the United States on ice.

Harry Gold wasn't told of this decision. Still following instructions to maintain contact with Fuchs, and on his own initiative, despite Fuchs insisting that Kristel had already been compromised, Gold went in February 1946 to Boston, then caught the streetcar to Cambridge to inquire if Fuchs had left anything for him. To his dismay, Kristel's husband was at home, but he was invited in and told that Fuchs had not been able to visit at Christmas and was in fact still at Los Alamos. This was very important information in itself, but when Gold returned to New York his handler, John, did not show up for the meeting and he wasn't at the fallback rendezvous either. Unknown to Gold, he had been recalled to Moscow with the suspension of the Soviet spying operation in New York.

There is a report in a NKGB file that seven months later, on 6 August 1946, an agent from the Soviet Embassy in London went to the meeting place in Mornington Crescent where Gold had arranged that Fuchs should meet his new contact. No one was there. In a message to Moscow, the agent claimed that the location wasn't consistent with the description that he had received. It is true that it is a confusing location. Mornington Crescent is an underground station south of Camden Town on the Northern line, but the entrance to the station is located in Hampstead Road. There is also a street called Mornington Crescent, which runs behind what was a tobacco factory in the Hampstead Road. It isn't clear where the agent went, but the result was that the Lubyanka had lost contact with Fuchs. A scientist at the core of the United States bomb programme, and the most important source of intelligence on a weapon vital for Soviet security, had vanished—and this at a time when Stalin had ordered Kurchatov to move forward decisively on the development of nuclear weapons, and the head of the NKGB, Beria, was in overall charge.

Fuchs, however, had not abandoned the Soviet Union. He travelled to Mornington Crescent underground station on the first Saturday in September 1946 but no one was there to make contact with him. No one approached him and asked the way to Harvard Square. It is quite possible that Fuchs was also at Mornington Crescent in August and that two failed meetings were enough to convince him that the arrangements had to be aborted. Fuchs later said that he abandoned contact with the NKGB because of the information about clandestine meetings that were revealed in the trial of Allan Nunn May, but the NKGB files reveal that if this was true he changed his plans only after the failed meeting in September 1946.

At any rate, Fuchs didn't wait very long before trying again to make contact with the NKGB. This effort coincided with MI5's renewed interest in him, and it is all the more remarkable that what Fuchs did next was both extraordinarily risky and, of course, a serious breach of the rules laid down by the NKGB. He made contact with a member of the British Communist Party, Angela Pilley. She was someone he knew from his past political activities before he had gone to the United States and he asked her for a way to get in touch with "Dicke Hannah", the work name of a German communist who had been active in the KPD in exile in Prague and had arrived in the UK in 1938. She would have known Gerhard Fuchs when he was active in Prague, and would have been a comrade of Klaus in the KPD in the UK in the German cultural organization Freier Deutscher Kulturbund.

Angela Pilley eventually responded to Fuchs's request, but only to say that she could not help him. The British Communist Party was no longer prepared to get involved in any arrangements with foreign organizations—"they didn't do things that way"—and Fuchs was on his own.

He then took another tack, one that again relied on his past associations with the KPD in exile. He went to Jürgen Kuczynski, the German communist who had directed him to his first Soviet intelligence agent in 1941. This also didn't prove to be very productive. Kuczynski had fallen out with the Party in 1944 over deals between the Allies at the Tehran Conference, which would have led after the war to the destruction of German industry. The German Communist Party Central Committee, unquestioningly following the Soviet line, accused him of being reactionary and he was removed from his position as chairman of the KPD in exile.

When the war ended, Jürgen returned to Berlin as soon as he was able. His wife, Margaret, still lived at their old address in Hampstead but she was planning to leave the UK in a few days' time. She gave Fuchs the address of another old KPD comrade, Hannah Klopstech, and he finally got in touch with her. She was not an agent, but the NKGB knew her as a "reliable person" with the work name "Martha". After Fuchs approached her, Hannah didn't go straight to her Soviet contacts; instead she passed the message on to Hans Siebert, who was then head of the KPD in England. He informed the NKGB resident, who passed the information back to Moscow centre. Relief that Fuchs was once more in contact was tempered with fear. It was an extremely unorthodox approach and, given the circumstances, was highly suspicious. Fuchs may well have been followed, or be acting as a provocateur.

The NKGB were extremely cautious. They wanted to wait before making contact. Meanwhile Hannah Klopstech had arranged another meeting with Fuchs, but she was unable to get there because her child was ill. Apparently frustrated at the delay, Fuchs then contacted another member of the British Communist Party, an old friend from his pre-war days in Bristol called Angela Tuckett. She also passed a message to Siebert and the centre. The NKGB then decided to make contact with Fuchs via Klopstech, and their instructions were simply to wait. They knew where he was, and he was not to make any effort to contact Soviet intelligence either directly or through another intermediary. The connection would be resumed whenever it became possible.

Throughout the time that these intermittent remote contacts were taking place, Fuchs was working away at Harwell, as well as renewing his links with William Penney and others in the British atomic energy programme. He had also been organized by Genia Peierls into taking a holiday to Switzerland with her and her husband. There, in Davos, he met up with his brother Gerhard—the first time that they had met since 1934. Gerhard was now extremely ill with tuberculosis, and the drugs that he was taking had made him put on weight. He was still active in the KPD, organizing a relief programme for German refugees. What did Gerhard know about his younger brother? It seems odd to think that, after such a long time since they were both politically active in Berlin, Fuchs would not have talked about what he was doing, or that he would have allowed his brother to think that he had abandoned the Party. So far, however, nothing has surfaced to show what Gerhard did or didn't know about Klaus.

On his return, Fuchs set about building up Harwell, putting in motion the construction of the experimental reactor there, and planning the plutonium-producing reactors at Windscale and the enrichment plant at Capenhurst. Finally the NKGB moved. Still cautious, they directed Hannah Klopstech to make contact with Fuchs and arrange a meeting where she could provide him with the details of a rendezvous with a new Soviet handler. Finally, on 19 July 1947, they met in Richmond. Fuchs drove there, picked up Hannah and then continued to Hampton Court, where they went for a stroll. Walking casually through the park, Hannah gave him details of his next meeting. It was to be on Saturday, 27 September, at eight o'clock in the evening in a public house opposite Wood Green underground station in north London, and the meetings would be repeated every three months, so that the next one after that would be on 27 December. There was a series of recognition signals: Fuchs was to go into the bar and order a drink, then sit down at a table. His contact would have a glass of beer, approach the table and say, "Stout is not so good. I generally take lager." Fuchs would answer, "I think Guinness is the best." Then Fuchs would leave and his contact would follow him outside. He would say, "Your face looks very familiar to me", to which Fuchs would reply, "I think we met in Edinburgh a year ago." The contact would then ask the question, "Do you know big Hannah?" The other recognition signals were for Fuchs to have with him a copy of *Tribune*, the left-wing Labour Party magazine, while his contact would carry a red book.

Fuchs did not like the suggested recognition script and Hannah agreed with him. After some discussion, they decided on a new one.

The delay in contacting Fuchs might have suggested that the NKGB did not place that much importance on his information. This was not the case. An experienced and well-regarded officer of the NKGB had been picked to go to London especially to handle Fuchs. Alexander Feklisov had worked under the name of Yuri Modin in New York. Feklisov was a tall, well-built young man, thirty-three years old, with a broad, open face and swept-back hair, the son of a textile worker in pre-revolutionary Moscow. He had been the NKGB contact for Julius Rosenberg, who was later to be caught and interrogated by the FBI, and, with his wife Ethel, was sentenced to death in the electric chair. This spy network had passed back to Moscow information about various weapons projects, such as the proximity fuse and the first jet-powered fighter. Feklisov had also cultivated other contacts associated with the Manhattan Project and had a source in the Kellex Corporation who provided him with some information about the uranium diffusion plant built at Oak Ridge. Feklisov was recalled to Moscow in 1946. This may have been to limit the damage caused by the Gouzenko and Bentley defections, or it may have been because the NKGB had already decided that he would be the best candidate to act as Fuchs's controller. He spoke fluent English, had conducted himself well in New York, and his agents had been highly productive. He was an extremely able and experienced field officer.

Before he went to London, he met Lieutenant General Sergei Savchenko, a protégé of Beria. Savchenko had been in charge of the NKGB in Ukraine during the war and had recently been appointed head of the Combined Intelligence Directorate of the GRU and the NKGB. He stressed to Feklisov the vital importance of his mission. In order to be as effective as possible in his conversations with Fuchs, Feklisov was given several tutorials by a professor of physics from Moscow University, Yakov Terletsky, who explained to him the science behind the bomb and the scientific terminology used by the Soviet Union and Great Britain.

Terletsky was the scientific advisor to Department S, a special office set up by the NKGB to handle all the scientific intelligence about the bomb, under the direction of Pavel Sudoplatov, a senior NKGB officer. Sudoplatov had daily contact with Igor Kurchatov and Generals Boris Vannikov and Avraami Zavenyagin, who had been put in charge of building the industrial facilities for the Soviet nuclear programme. Terletsky's main task was to be the scientific channel between Kurchatov, Feklisov and Fuchs. The NKGB trusted him. In 1945 Beria had sent him to Copenhagen to meet Niels Bohr. Bohr—who had told the Danish government about the visit—listened politely as Terletsky, who was accompanied by a NKGB officer, asked him if he could assist in providing answers to a series of problems that the Soviet scientists had come up against; but he declined to help and Terletsky returned empty-handed—although Bohr did give him a copy of the Smyth Report, the official US publication about the Manhattan Project, which was in itself confirmation of some of the industrial processes used to make the bomb.

Feklisov's cover in the UK was that he was a deputy cultural attaché, but in truth he would be second only to the NKGB resident in London, Mikhail Shishkin. His briefing made it clear how important his task was. Terletsky had given him a list of ten questions that he was to ask Fuchs. They were technical, but Feklisov felt that he had learned enough to understand any answers. A massive amount of resources was being poured into the effort to make a Soviet nuclear weapon. Fuchs was a key element in this programme and Feklisov was to be responsible for his security. He was to make contact with Fuchs only if he was sure that neither of them was being watched. Any disruption in the flow of his information would be a serious setback.

In the early evening of 27 September Klaus Fuchs drove from his guesthouse in Abingdon. He took the A40 to London, but stopped halfway and caught a train for Paddington main-line station. At the station he loitered, on the lookout for anyone who might have followed him on to the train, then he began his journey to Wood Green, which is on the Piccadilly Line of the London Underground. He didn't go directly there, but took a long and roundabout route, changing trains, occasionally leaving the underground system at a main-line station to go into one of London's cartoon and newsreel cinemas that ran continuous shows. Finally, certain that he was not being tailed, he came out of the underground station at Wood Green and walked along the High Road before doubling back and going into the saloon bar of the Nags Head, a large Victorian pub on the corner of the junction opposite the station. It was dark and growing foggy.

Feklisov had also started his journey early. When he first arrived at the residency he had memorized the new code words that Fuchs had suggested; Shishkin had written them down for him on a piece of paper, to avoid saying it out loud in case it was overheard. First he went with a colleague in a car to South London before doubling back using buses and the underground. He had gone to Wood Green a few days before so that he could become familiar with the exits from the station and the side streets leading off the High Road. These were checked on the Saturday evening by another member of the Soviet residency for any signs of surveillance, such as drivers sitting in parked cars, people loitering in shop doorways, anyone who looked as though they did not have somewhere to go. Feklisov arrived thirty minutes early and went to stand by the bus stop outside the station, where he started reading a newspaper. After ten minutes he saw a man whom he immediately suspected was Fuchs walk round the corner and go into the pub. Feklisov waited until he was sure that Fuchs was alone, then he too crossed the road, went into the saloon bar and ordered a beer.

Now was the time for Fuchs to check if his contact had a tail, because anyone following him would soon enter. Two elderly, boisterous men came in and ordered some Guinness. Feklisov relaxed when they greeted the barman and then went into the lounge; they were obviously regulars.

Fuchs had noticed the red book that Feklisov was carrying and he moved over to another part of the bar where there were some photos of British boxers. He said, "I think the best British heavyweight of all time is Bruce Woodcock." This was the cue for Feklisov to say, "Oh no, Tommy Farr is certainly the best."

The recognition signals given, Fuchs finished his drink, then left. Feklisov watched from the window as he walked along the road, then he followed him.

They said hello and kept on walking. Feklisov—who was using the cover name "Eugene"—talked to Fuchs about what he was doing and about his life at Harwell. He wanted details about security, the telephones, the people that Fuchs had to deal with on a daily basis, any information about routine matters that might, if they were changed, suggest that Fuchs was under suspicion. Feklisov had his technical questions, which he had memorized and which Fuchs was able to answer immediately, and he also gave Fuchs a list of topics about which Kurchatov wanted more information. These questions were written on cigarette paper which could be easily swallowed. Fuchs read them, then handed the paper back. He promised to get the information for the next time they met. Then they discussed details of the next meeting, and an alternative follow-up if the first one was not possible. Feklisov was concerned that Fuchs did not write anything down. He pressed him about not making a mistake, and Fuchs recited all of the details he had just been given without any errors. Fuchs's personal file in the Lubyanka had mentioned that he had a good memory, but Feklisov now realized that his agent had a phenomenal ability to recall any information that he had read or been told.

Feklisov knew that the NKGB would hold him responsible for anything that happened to Fuchs. He stressed the security measures that must be taken at every meeting. Fuchs was never to come to a rendezvous if he had any suspicion that he was being followed. Feklisov preferred to meet in pubs, but rather then speak straight after leaving the bar, each of them would take a different direction and walk around the block. In this way they could spot if either one was being tailed and abandon the meeting before talking to each other.

From the questions Feklisov had asked him, Fuchs said he could tell that the Soviet Union had started on its programme and that they might succeed in two or three years. He explained that a British project was under way but it had made little progress. A major reactor was being planned for Windscale and a smaller one was in operation at Harwell, with another larger experimental pile also under construction. According to the notes from the NKGB files, he described some of the work being done by Edward Teller and Fermi on the hydrogen bomb. Feklisov remembers that Fuchs handed over some papers on plutonium extraction from uranium reactor fuel, and a notebook describing the nuclear reactor planned for Windscale. The files suggest that this material was delivered at another meeting, but there is no doubt that at some point Fuchs did give this material to Feklisov. Fuchs also gave some figures for the production of plutonium in the USA and the number of nuclear weapons in the stockpile, which he estimated at around 125 warheads.

Fuchs told his handler that he was going to the United States in November to take part in a conference to discuss declassifying some of the papers produced at Los Alamos for the Manhattan Project. Fuchs thought this showed that the British trusted him. Feklisov asked if it was possible to get in touch with a Soviet contact in Washington, but Fuchs thought this was too risky, and he did not want to leave anything with his sister either. At the end of the conversation, Feklisov raised the question of payment. He said that he knew Fuchs had rejected payment in the past, but that circumstances had changed. He was paying his brother's medical bills in Switzerland and he was going to have to support his father. The Soviet Union wanted to offer to help as a sign of their gratitude. He then gave Fuchs two envelopes. Fuchs weighed them in his hands and asked how much was in them. There was £100 in each. Fuchs said to Feklisov that he had read a file about the case of Nunn May and how Soviet intelligence offered money to bind the spy to keep working for them. He said he was not afraid of that, and would take the money in order to prove that he was loyal. Then he kept one envelope, but handed the other back to Feklisov, saying that it would be too tricky to account for such a large sum. Then they parted.

At subsequent meetings where Fuchs handed over material, Feklisov would immediately leave and pass it to another agent who was waiting nearby. Fuchs never saw this second agent and Feklisov would quickly return to continue the conversation with Fuchs. Back at the embassy, Feklisov microfilmed any papers and documents that Fuchs provided and this film was sent straight to Moscow in a diplomatic bag. When he was sure that the film had arrived safely, he sent the original documents in the same way. Once in Moscow the information was sent to the 10th Department responsible for technical and scientific intelligence of the Chief Directorate of the NKGB. The information was placed in the file on *Enormoz*, the code name for atomic research. Before Kurchatov received anything, even if he was waiting for specific answers to some questions, a special department under the direction of General Sudoplatov edited the material to remove any trace of its origins.

Six weeks after the information had first reached Moscow the centre would write up an evaluation of it and send this report to the London resident, who passed it to Feklisov. Fuchs's information was described as being "extremely valuable". According to Feklisov, the evaluation even made an estimate of the amount of money—250 million roubles, or around £4 million in 1947—that the material had saved the Soviet Union. The total value of all the information received so far from Fuchs is unimaginable.

SEVENTEEN

The Next Big Thing

In November 1947 Fuchs went to the declassification conference in Washington in the company of Herbert Skinner, deputy director of Harwell. The conference was organized to coordinate the declassification of scientific papers produced for the Manhattan Project, so that information could be released to the scientific community and to industry. It was an attempt to avoid the strict limitations on the exchange of nuclear information imposed by the McMahon Act, and agreement by both British and US delegations was required to remove the security classification.

There was a feeling amongst the scientists who had worked at Los Alamos that the US representative, Victor Weisskopf, took a very restrictive view of the material and that this was aimed at limiting British use of the information. The US team took the position of General Groves, the Atomic Energy Commission and the Truman administration that the atomic bomb gave a significant advantage to the country that possessed it, and that everything should be done to prevent other countries from developing nuclear weapons. The conference had been established with the ground rules that nothing would be discussed that wouldn't

Klaus Fuchs – As he appeared at the age of 33, in this photo for his Los Alamos security pass. Fuchs worked for two years in the secret atomic research laboratory in the United States, and solved some of the most fundamental problems of nuclear weapons.

The young Klaus on his mother Else's knee. She committed suicide when Klaus was twenty. His brother Gerhard, astride a toy horse, became active in the communist party, as did his sister Elisabeth. She too committed suicide in 1938. Emil, his father was a socialist and a Methodist minister, energetic and unshakeable in his beliefs.

Street Fighting in Berlin: Fuchs grew up in the Weimar republic, where the threat of revolution bubbled beneath the surface, and public meetings were likely to end in violent conflicts on the streets. Every party had its own paramilitary organisation and politics was deadly serious.

The elections of 1932 were a turning point for Klaus Fuchs. The Nazi party had grown, and Fuchs thought that only the Communists were prepared to stop Hitler gaining power. He joined the party, and became a respected activist.

On 27 February 1933 the Reichstag, Germany's parliament building, was set on fire. Hitler seized the opportunity to order a state of emergency and banned the Communist party, ordering the arrest of thousands of its members. The next morning Fuchs went underground.

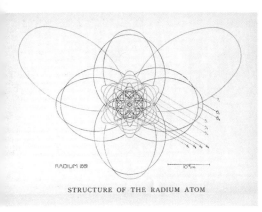

STRUCTURE OF THE RADIUM ATOM

Radium Atom: atomic physics was in its infancy, and it was attempts to understand how the smaller particles that made up an atom behaved that allowed mathematicians like Fuchs to move into the realm of science.

James Chadwick won a Nobel Prize for his discovery in 1932 of the neutron, a particle in the nucleus of the atom. Chadwick later became head of the British scientific mission to the United States.

Rudolf Peierls (*above*) along with Otto Frisch wrote a memorandum that kick-started research on atomic weapons in Britain and the United States. He recruited Fuchs to the project in 1941, and they became close collaborators and friends for the next nine years.

Max Born was a brilliant scientist forced to flee from Germany by the Nazis. He took up a post at Edinburgh and was an important influence in Fuchs' development as an outstanding theoretical physicist.

Robert Oppenheimer became the leading scientist on the United States' Manhattan project, organising thousands of scientists at Los Alamos towards a single goal: building an atomic bomb.

The first atomic weapon was ready to be tested in July 1945. The spherical device was hoisted to the top of a tower in the New Mexico desert. The resulting explosion (*below*) stunned everyone who saw it. Fuchs remembered the unearthly play of blue and green light that crackled around the expanding fire ball.

Meanwhile the war in Europe was over. Nazi Germany had been crushed, and Hitler committed suicide in April of 1945. The Red Army had reached Berlin, and controlled half of Europe. The war time alliance between the Soviet Union, Britain and the United States was already falling apart.

"Sonya" – Ursula Kuczynski, or Ruth Werner, or Ursula Hamburger, or Ruth Buerton, otherwise known to Fuchs as "Sonya" was an extremely experienced agent of Soviet Military Intelligence. She was Fuchs' contact in Britain for over a year before he went to the United States.

Harry Gold, here being led under arrest by a cigar-chomping Federal Marshall, was Fuchs' NKGB contact in the United States. He handled some of the most earth shattering secrets of the century.

Bearded and bemedalled, Igor Kurchatov was the principle scientist on the Soviet atomic project. He quickly understood that Fuchs' information provided a direct path to success. Georgi Flerov (*above right*) wrote a letter urging Stalin to begin work on nuclear weapons. He joined Kurchatov, and supervised the final assembly of the first Soviet device.

The first Soviet Nuclear bomb exploded in August 1949. Four years after the Trinity test the Soviet Union had become the world's second nuclear power, and the nuclear arms race began in earnest.

Fuchs' exposure as a spy was a serious embarrassment for the British government and the Security Service.

"Jim" Skardon, (*left*) MI5's senior interrogator was credited with clever psychological insight to break Fuchs' resolve. In fact the promise of immunity was more important. After serving 9 years of a 14 year sentence Fuchs left prison, and flew to East Germany. He went home, to his country, his political beliefs and a woman he had met underground 26 years earlier.

already be known by both sides, but the interpretation of this caused some friction. Later Fuchs wrote to Peierls saying that it would teach the Americans a lesson if the results of their work at Birmingham University for the MAUD Committee on the size and calculation of a critical mass were declassified by the British government. It would demonstrate that the British had a considerable body of knowledge that they did not owe to their presence on the Manhattan Project.

The conference lasted for two days, and after it Fuchs took the opportunity to visit Cambridge, Massachusetts, where he naturally spent some time with his sister Kristel and also paid a visit to Professor Robert Marshak and his wife, whom he had met at Los Alamos. He went as well to the Argonne Laboratories at Chicago University, where Fermi had built the first atomic pile in 1942 and where work on the fast-breeder and heavy-water reactors was continuing. His visit lasted for a few hours and he discussed the work of the laboratory on measuring the movements and electrical charges of neutrons and molecules. Officially at least, he was kept away from any current work on nuclear weapons.

Fuchs left New York on 30 November to fly back to London. He had a planned rendezvous with his Soviet contact just after Christmas, but he didn't go to the meeting; instead he allowed Feklisov to sweat it out before finally revealing why he had not shown up. Feklisov later reported to Moscow that Fuchs had not made the appointment because there was too little time between his arrival back in the United Kingdom and the day that he had to be in London. He was probably very busy following the conference, but ever since his move from New York to Los Alamos he had been the one who decided where and when he would meet his handler. He was, after all, playing a very dangerous game. Ordinary people in Britain had been very sympathetic to the Soviet Union during the war, even if at an official level that alliance had been merely one of convenience. The mood had shifted now, and tensions between the allies of the West and the Soviet Union were now acute.

Promised elections in the Eastern European countries occupied by the Soviet Union had been postponed or cancelled. The Nunn May arrest and trial had raised alarm about Soviet spies and there was talk of the British government banning members of the Communist Party from jobs involving defence or official secrets. The sea in which Fuchs was swimming was now very different from that of 1941, and the stakes were very much higher.

The third meeting in the sequence that began in September 1947 was scheduled for Saturday, 6 March 1948. The first question that Feklisov had put to Fuchs at their initial meeting was a request for more information about the hydrogen bomb, the "super". Fuchs had promised to provide an answer, but putting it together needed work. As that weekend in March approached, he was very busy. He had arranged to go to Fort Halstead on the Monday, where he was going to talk about implosion and aspects of various designs of the plutonium bomb developed at Los Alamos. Over the course of the three days he would reveal to his British colleagues all that he knew about the fission bomb used at Nagasaki, and to his Soviet comrades he would reveal his theories of a potentially far more destructive weapon that had yet to be built.

The busy weekend was not a coincidence. He had suggested speaking to Penney's team in a letter written on 2 December, and it may have been that his legitimate absence from Harwell on Monday would give him some cover for his trip to London on Saturday. Even so, the mental pressure must have been intense. Over three days he was going to supply highly sensitive information to two different sets of scientists. The information he was going to give to the scientists at Fort Halstead was from his work at Los Alamos on the plutonium bomb. The material was still secret, and he was certainly breaching the spirit if not the letter of the McMahon Act. Most of this information, however, he had already passed on to the Soviet Union by the end of 1945.

The information he was now about to give to the Soviet scientists via his NKGB contact was of a vastly different order. It was still speculative, and still unproven, the subject of sometimes rancorous debate amongst Fuchs's former colleagues at Los Alamos. They were extremely secret calculations that, if they proved correct, would lead to weapons of awesomely destructive power.

On that Saturday both Fuchs and Feklisov left their homes early. Fuchs drove once more to a railway station where he could catch a train to London. Feklisov had been given the embassy chauffeur for these meetings, and he was driven around London, heading in a direction away from the location of the planned covert meeting. Feklisov had taught the driver, Volodya, who was not a member of the NKGB, how to escape any possible followers from the British Security Service. They would drive around apparently aimlessly, but their route was planned beforehand. They avoided crossroads where there might be police officers who would report the presence of their car, and would select a straight piece of road where Volodya could put his foot down, forcing any other vehicle that was trying to follow them to speed up and give themselves away. If their back was safe they would slow down again and merge with the traffic.

After driving for an hour, Volodya would halt at the kerb. Feklisov would put his hat on the back seat in the rear window as if he were still in the car, then quickly leap out and duck into a shop or a pub. Volodya would drive away, leaving Feklisov to make his way slowly to the underground, where he would travel, using both buses and tube, to the rendezvous. These manoeuvres might take up to three hours, but by the time Feklisov got to the meeting place he could be certain that he was not being followed.

On 6 March 1948, both Fuchs and Feklisov were heading for a pub in Golders Green, the Bull and Bush. Feklisov waited at a bus stop until he saw Fuchs arrive and go into the pub, then, after checking that Fuchs also had no tail, he went in. There are some reports that Fuchs was anxious at this meeting, unwilling to go into the pub and looking behind him to see if he was followed. This seems extremely unlikely. Fuchs never took risks. If he felt there was any danger he would have abandoned the meeting. He never looked behind him to see if he was being followed, knowing that this would immediately draw attention to himself. He had criticized Harry Gold for this very failing. Feklisov has said that Fuchs always remained calm and collected.

Feklisov never described in any detail this meeting with Fuchs, but it is the most significant meeting in the history of the Cold War, of nuclear espionage, and possibly in the history of spying itself. It is equalled in importance only by the meeting with Harry Gold in September 1945 when Fuchs handed over to the Soviet Union the secrets of the plutonium bomb.

The documents that Fuchs passed to Feklisov remained secret for over forty years, but some of them surfaced in Moscow in the interregnum following the break-up of the Soviet Union. One of them consists of just seven pages, a typical scientific paper of tables and equations, accompanied by a diagram. The diagram shows the construction, in simplified form, of a bomb that would cause the fusion of atoms of deuterium (that is, hydrogen with a neutron in the nucleus) and a tritium atom (hydrogen with two neutrons in the nucleus). The initial charge would be a Hiroshima gun-type weapon of uranium 235, which would explode in a tamper of beryllium. This tamper would also contain a mixture of deuterium and tritium. This would begin the fusion reaction which would in turn ignite another charge of deuterium and tritium.

The document made an assessment of the power of the weapon. One cubic metre of deuterium—and the document did not specify the pressure at which this would be contained—would cause blast damage for a radius of 5 miles from the point of explosion and create burn damage to a radius of 10 miles. Other figures were given for different amounts of deuterium, with ranges of damage extending out to over 20 miles from the point of detonation. This was a staggering calculation. It described a weapon that was truly a city smasher, one that was so devastating that it could hardly be described as a weapon at all. The calculations of the power of a hydrogen bomb are the same figures that Fuchs included in his notes that he gave to Chadwick when he returned from Los Alamos, and were his record of the conference about the super in April 1946. In fact, everything that Fuchs retrieved from his work at Los Alamos and had given to Chadwick was now also in the hands of the Soviet Union.

Feklisov likely knew how important this material was, and he returned to the embassy with the document, copied it on microfilm and sent the film to Moscow via the diplomatic pouch. He would, as usual, wait for confirmation that the microfilm had been processed successfully before sending on the original documents. The arrival of the material in the NKGB centre sparked great interest, and also concern that the Soviet Union was trailing even further in the nuclear arms race. Terletsky, the NKGB's physicist, summarized the report, then wrote a briefing document that compared the information in the new material to the material that Fuchs had handed over in 1945. It was, he claimed, a significant advance, showing concrete designs for a super-bomb concept. The paper was forwarded to Beria, Molotov and Stalin.

A few days later, Beria wrote a memo that instructed Kurchatov and Vannikov to analyse the information and inform Khariton about its contents. Kurchatov found the original paper very interesting and understood that part of the technique of igniting the fusion process was to use the radiation from the uranium explosion. This idea was certainly an advance on the original 1945 material.

This was not the first intelligence that the Ministry of State Security had about the H-bomb, of course. There was Fuchs's original material from June and September 1945. This had triggered some work by Khariton, Isai Gurevich and Yakov Zeldovich on "The Utilization of the Nuclear Energy of the Light Elements". Zeldovich had been instructed to continue theoretical work on this new form of atomic weapon, an instruction that had been confirmed in February 1948, just a month before Fuchs's meeting with Feklisov in the Bull and Bush pub. The arrival of new information was not unexpected, then, and, taken together, the two sets of intelligence documents appeared to show that in the United States work on the super-bomb was making significant progress. To Kurchatov this was cause for alarm. From his perspective, the new diagram, description and calculations handed over by Fuchs had to be taken extremely seriously. He had, after all, supplied information including a diagram of the weapon that had been tested and used to end the war against Japan. Now he had provided a diagram and detailed calculations of another weapon that was far more powerful. It could, Kurchatov calculated, only be a matter of time before this new weapon was tested by the Americans. Kurchatov and Vannikov were clear what their next course of action should be. The USSR must start a programme to create a super-bomb along the lines described in Fuchs's papers.

On 23 April Beria issued a decree authorizing work on the H-bomb, with a target of delivering a weapon in just one year's time, in June 1949. This order was given to the Academy of Sciences, who in turn instructed the Physics Institute to set up a working group. Kurchatov was overwhelmed with work on the plutonium bomb, so Khariton and Zeldovich were drafted in under the eminent physicist Igor Tamm. At first, of course, the small team had almost nothing to go on other than Zeldovich's existing work. Now they were faced with a deadline just one year away. It required a special dispensation from Beria before the intelligence from Fuchs was sanitized and passed to Zeldovich so that he might have some idea of the reason this sudden urgent task had been thrust upon him.

It took considerably more work for the Soviet team even to get close to a viable H-bomb. Crucially, however, they had got started, and had been shown an idea that suggested that the relatively long-lived theory of nuclear fusion might actually be turned into a useable weapon. Whether the diagram handed over by Fuchs would have produced a workable H-bomb has been argued about by scientists and historians for many years. German Goncharov, the Soviet physicist who had access to much of the NKGB archives in the 1990s and who found the document supplied by Fuchs, has said that it was a vital step forwards because it isolated for the first time the principle of using radiation from a fission device to compress the deuterium and tritium fuel of the H-bomb itself. It is also assumed that the diagram and the complete document that Fuchs handed over are a copy of the patent that he filed at Los Alamos in 1946, but the complete patent has still never been released for any comparison to be made. It was almost two years since Fuchs had supplied details of the research into the H-bomb at Los Alamos to the British. It may be that what he handed over to Feklisov was exactly the same material, but it seems strange that he had not taken his ideas any further, and there is evidence that in fact he had done so.

Since the start of the British nuclear weapons programme, Fuchs had been giving seminars to the staff at Fort Halstead, where the work to design the British bomb was being carried out. The lectures were based on everything that Fuchs knew about the bomb—knowledge acquired from his work on it at Los Alamos. None of the historians who have written about the British H-bomb programme suggest that Fuchs provided any information at all. Yet documents in the British National Archives, which subsequently have been removed, show that he continued to look at the problem of igniting a hydrogen bomb. Sitting in the Archives at Kew is a slim, buff-coloured folder that contains just twelve photocopied pages. They are notes in handwriting that looks similar to that of Klaus Fuchs, in his black fountain-pen ink with a characteristic wavy bar to the figure seven. The document is titled "Miscellaneous Super Bomb Notes by Klaus Fuchs" and is a library copy of the note for the Theoretical Physics Branch of the Atomic Weapons Research Establishment at Aldermaston. Once stamped "Top Secret", how and when the pages of notes arrived at Aldermaston is a mystery. The figures, however, are an almost exact copy of the figures and tables contained in the document found by Goncharov in the archives of the NKGB. They are calculations of the energy produced when neutrons collide with the nucleus of deuterium and tritium. They take into account the work Bretscher and Frisch carried out while they were all part of the British Mission at Los Alamos. Did these notes form part of a lecture given by Fuchs to the scientists at Fort Halstead? Was the document that Fuchs handed over to Feklisov the product of work for the British on a super-bomb project? It's impossible to tell, but the two separate documents—one typed and kept in an archive in Moscow, one handwritten and kept in London citing experiments done at Los Alamos— perfectly represent the role that Fuchs played in the atomic weapons development of the three powers, Britain, the United States and the Soviet Union. The documents suggest also that the information that the Soviet Union received in March 1948 was more advanced than Fuchs's original report to Chadwick, and that they, and Britain, had the benefit of further work done by Fuchs on the ultimate nuclear weapon.

This was not the end of Fuchs's work for the NKGB. Feklisov describes meeting him in the Odeon Cinema in the Haymarket in central London, at a time when Feklisov had a broken leg because of a car accident, and again at the Nags Head pub in Wood Green. Fuchs once more failed to show up at the next meeting, arranged for May. Every time this happened his contact was left in limbo, and so too were the men in Moscow, all of them in the dark about the fate of their irreplaceable secret agent. This time a memorandum about Fuchs's failure to appear was sent to Molotov and Beria, with a request that the Committee for State Security consider the question of removing him to the Soviet Union.

Then in July, at the next meeting, Fuchs turned up, as cool as ever, explaining that he missed his last rendez-vous because a new experimental reactor had gone on line at Harwell and it had been impossible for him to leave the research establishment. At this meeting in July 1948 he passed over a large amount of material, including descriptions of the air-cooled reactors to be built at Windscale, descriptions of US designs for reactors and more details of the process to recover plutonium from spent uranium fuel rods.

In November 1948 Fuchs responded to questions from Kurchatov and his team by supplying detailed information about the manufacture of the fuel rods for reactors, the height of the cooling flanges on them and the thickness of aluminium shielding used in the core of the reactor. Feklisov could remember a list of about five questions for every meeting. Sometimes Fuchs could answer him straightaway, but other, more technically sophisticated information he supplied by handing over the relevant documents, or writing up an answer.

Fuchs, of course, could tell from the questions that were put to him how far the Soviet programme was advancing, and in one meeting he told Feklisov that he thought that their weapon would be ready within the year. The amount of information that he passed on to Soviet intelligence at his meetings with Feklisov was vast. Even the product of just one single contact would have been almost priceless. In February 1949, for example, he handed over his calculations about the two devices used in the US test explosions at the Bikini Atoll. Feklisov estimated that Fuchs gave him more than ninety documents covering the whole gamut of weapons research, from the construction of the bomb, the design of isotope-separation plants and nuclear reactors, to the recovery of plutonium. He also passed over information about production rates from which the NKGB could calculate the size of the nuclear arsenal of the United States.

Various NKGB officers have sometimes referred to other nuclear spies, like Allan Nunn May and one or two others in the UK and the United States, such as Theodore Hall. None of them delivered the same quantity of information as Fuchs; none of them possessed the theoretical depth combined with the knowledge of an integrated nuclear weapons programme that he did.

Not all of the meetings between Fuchs and Feklisov were taken up with answering questions and passing over secret papers. An incident in September 1947 caused alarm in the NKGB, and they became extremely concerned about the safety of their most important spy.

Sonya, or Ruth Werner, or Ursula Kuczynski, the GRU radio operator and agent-runner, had not seen Fuchs since he left the United Kingdom in 1943 to work in New York. Since the end of the war Sonya had been living quietly in the remote village of Great Rollright in the Cotswolds. As we have seen, her brother Jürgen had split from the German Communist Party in the UK and had returned to Berlin. Sonya herself had had no communication with Moscow for over a year. One morning, 13 September 1947, three men visited her. Two were smartly dressed and the other was a constable from Oxfordshire police. After the policeman had vouched for the others, he left and Sonya let the two men in. They did not give their names but almost before they had entered the living room one of them said, "You were a Russian agent for a long time, until the Finnish war disillusioned you. We know that you haven't been active in England and we haven't come to arrest you but to ask for your cooperation."

Sonya writes that she almost burst out laughing, and then offered them a cup of tea. They identified themselves as men from the Security Service and talked about the work that she had done in Switzerland. One of her agents there, the Englishman Alexander Foote, had defected in 1947, told everything to MI5 and was about to publish a book about the crimes of the NKGB. Sonia kept them talking and realized that they knew nothing about her work after she left Switzerland. She admitted that she and her husband were members of the Communist Party and subscribed to the *Daily Worker*, but revealed nothing about her work as an agent.

With little to go on except the gossip of a defector, the two men from MI5 were at a dead end. Their attempt to bluff Sonya had failed. They spoke to her husband Len, who adopted the same approach to the questions. Finally, they left.

The two men were Jim Skardon, MI5's chief interrogator, and Michael Serpell from B Branch, the counter-subversion division, the same man who had issued several futile warnings about Klaus Fuchs. They returned to London and nothing more was done about Sonya, who was too experienced an agent to make any sudden attempt to contact Moscow or to flee the country.

If MI5 could not make the connection between Fuchs and Sonya, the NKGB could. When they finally received news about her questioning, Feklisov in London received a handwritten note. In code it informed him that "the athlete [agent] who had recruited Charles [Fuchs] had been questioned by the opposition [British intelligence]". In response to this and to some other messages from Moscow suggesting that Fuchs might soon be placed under investigation, Feklisov persuaded him that it might be better to exchange information using a dead letter drop—a mechanism where documents could be left by Fuchs to be later retrieved by another agent and passed on to Feklisov. This way Fuchs would never be seen in the presence of anyone from Soviet intelligence.

Feklisov arranged a meeting in Kew, where he took Fuchs to a house that had a high hedge and a fence with a 10-inch gap between the wooden palings. A member of the British Communist Party who was already acting as a courier for another network of spies lived there. The plan was for Fuchs to throw a package of documents through the fence on to the front lawn. The occupant of the house would retrieve them and deliver them to the NKGB "workshop" in the embassy. A fortnight later Fuchs carried out a trial run, using, instead of highly secret and compromising documents, a copy of *Men Only*. Feklisov reported that the drop was successful, but they never used this method of communication again. It breached a cardinal rule of espionage never to mix up two networks. Fuchs was also offered another method of contact if he felt that the situation was becoming too dangerous, or if he wanted to speak directly to someone who was aware of the state of the Soviet project. He was told that he could go to an address in Paris and meet a Soviet scientist,

Sukholmin, who would have a good knowledge of nuclear physics. He didn't take up the offer.

Michael Serpell and Jim Skardon didn't connect Sonya with Fuchs, but other investigations were coming closer to home, although neither Fuchs nor Feklisov were aware of them.

Fuchs's contact in the United States, Raymond, or Harry Gold, had been questioned by FBI agents, mainly because of information given to them by Elizabeth Bentley in her confession. Gold had been put on ice after Bentley's defection, but her interrogation by the FBI soon brought him to their attention. He was interviewed by them in 1946, and by 1947 was giving evidence to a Grand Jury. The hearing did not, fortunately for him and also for Fuchs, proceed to an indictment because the jury concluded that there was insufficient evidence against Gold. His importance as a courier for Fuchs remained undiscovered. The NKGB, however, was extremely alarmed, fearing that sooner or later Gold would be arrested and Fuchs would eventually be exposed. Plans were discussed to get Gold to Mexico and eventually to the Soviet Union in order to keep Fuchs's spying secret.

Elsewhere, other material was surfacing. Gouzenko, the Soviet Embassy cipher clerk in Ottawa who had sought political asylum, had revealed details of several GRU and NKGB agents in Canada. One of these, the mathematics professor Israel Halperin, was, according to Gouzenko and the documents he had provided, a GRU agent between 1942 and 1945. A special commission set up by the Canadian government to investigate Soviet spying in Canada questioned Halperin. He was charged and tried for espionage but acquitted because most of the evidence against him was not admissible in court. Among Halperin's possessions detectives found a diary that contained around two hundred names and addresses. One of them was Klaus Fuchs, with his old address in Edinburgh and his connection to Professor Born, as well as his address in the internment camp in Canada. Another was Kristel, Fuchs's sister, with her old address in Boston before she moved to Cambridge on the other side of the Charles River. Halperin's explanation for this was that he had been asked to send Fuchs magazines and scientific literature while he was in the internment camp. Details of the addresses were forwarded to MI5, but this information did not lead to any action.

Fuchs was unaware that his name and some of his contacts had become part of various intelligence agencies' investigations. He was instead concerned by the possibility of exposure from a completely different direction. He reported to Feklisov a conversation that he had had with his immediate boss at Harwell, Herbert Skinner. Skinner and his Russian wife, Erna, had of course first made Fuchs's acquaintance in 1933 when both men were doing post-graduate research at Bristol University. They had not been particularly friendly at the time and in the intervening years had not seen much of each other. Skinner had worked on the Manhattan Project but not at Los Alamos; he had instead gone to California to work at the Caltech Laboratory. The two men had, however, become friendlier once they met up again at Harwell. Skinner now respected Fuchs. Both had been delegates to the declassification conference in Washington, and on their return Fuchs started to spend his spare time with Skinner and his wife. Skinner had mentioned to him that he had seen a report from the Secret Intelligence Service (SIS), otherwise known as MI6. It described how a group of German scientists who had worked on nuclear physics in Germany during the war were now established at Sukhumi on the Black Sea coast and were apparently carrying out nuclear research for the Soviet Union. When this conversation was reported to him, Feklisov was naturally concerned and wanted Fuchs to find out more, and if possible to discover the source of the information. Fuchs, however, thought this was a very bad idea. It would look suspicious if he started to question Skinner, and it was unlikely that Skinner would know anything anyway.

The issue resurfaced in February 1949. Skinner again told Fuchs that SIS had established contact with a Soviet scientist who had some information about work on the atomic bomb in the Soviet Union. The impression that Fuchs came away with was that this informant was not the same person who had been the original source about the Germans at Sukhumi.

Fuchs was worried. He asked Feklisov to make sure that the information he had handed over was kept very secure and could not be traced back to him. Feklisov assured him that the NKGB sanitized his material before they passed it on to the scientific group and that access to it was severely limited. Fuchs also wanted a Communist Party member to go to Bristol to remove any trace of his connection with the Committee for the Support of Republican Spain during the Spanish Civil War. This time it was Feklisov who thought that taking any action was a bad idea. Asking a member of the British CP to rummage around in old documents looking for anything that mentioned Klaus Fuchs would certainly raise his profile, particularly as Fuchs had contacted a member of the British CP in 1947 when he was trying once more to get in touch with Soviet intelligence.

It was at this meeting that Feklisov gave Fuchs the address of the contact in Paris, if he ever felt that meeting in London was getting too dangerous. He also came up with other suggestions to make the contacts less conspicuous. Had Fuchs thought of getting a girlfriend in London? This would give him an excuse for travelling there and her flat would be a convenient place for a clandestine meeting. This brought Feklisov to ask if Fuchs ever felt that he should settle down and marry. Fuchs replied that he lived in a minefield and could not ask anyone to share that risk with him. He would settle down when the time came and he could go back to East Germany, a country just recently set up by the Soviet Union, with a German communist government. Feklisov asked him whether he had any female companions and Fuchs implied that he had no regular relationship. He didn't mention that in the last few months he had started an affair with Erna Skinner, his boss's wife.

EIGHTEEN

A Family Affair

Klaus Fuchs had his last meeting with Alexander Feklisov at the beginning of April 1949. The NKGB archives suggest that it was on 1 April, but that was a Friday and the meetings were always on a Saturday, because it was easier for Fuchs to disappear on a clandestine journey to London. Feklisov believed it was the 2nd. At this meeting, Fuchs handed over a large envelope of documents, which Feklisov quickly passed on to an accomplice and then he and Fuchs talked for about forty minutes, which was the usual length of time they would devote to their meetings. Fuchs didn't say anything about his future plans, nor did he mention any problems that might prevent him meeting Feklisov in the future. Fuchs, however, had a habit of never revealing too much to his contacts, particularly about anything that might jeopardize his security. He had, after all, left Gold in the lurch twice, once when he went to Los Alamos and then when he returned to the UK.

There were in fact several potential changes in Fuchs's life that meant it might be harder to continue regular meetings with Feklisov. The first was that Fuchs had moved out of his guest house in Abingdon and was living in one of the mass-produced, single-storey prefabricated bungalows of which scores had been built for staff accommodation inside Harwell. He no longer had the convenient excuse that he was working at home if he was questioned about carrying secret papers past the guards at the security gates. As the number of people living at Harwell increased, it became like a small, socially incestuous village and it was harder for Fuchs to avoid social gatherings at the weekends now that he was a resident. The head of Harwell security, Wing Commander Arnold, was his next-door neighbour, and Fuchs was well aware that he paid close attention to the movements of the senior staff. It was now well established as part of the conventional wisdom that there was a communist threat—not only a military one from the Soviet Union in Europe, but a threat to security from members of the Communist Party in Great Britain. Whereas during the war there had been great admiration for the Soviet Union, the exploits of the Red Army and Uncle Joe Stalin, people were now extremely cautious about saying anything positive about communism, or expressing ideas to the left of the Labour Party. In this type of social climate, suspicion was easily generated.

Fuchs was also spending a great deal of his spare time with Erna and Herbert Skinner. Whether this close social proximity pre-dated his affair with Erna or was a product of it is hard to judge. Fuchs would often stay overnight at the Skinners' home, and would visit for lunch or an evening meal. The affair was carried on openly, and whatever Herbert Skinner's private thoughts, he appeared to accept it, remaining for the most part friends with Fuchs. He was, however, planning to leave Harwell. He had applied for an academic post at Liverpool University, perhaps to put some distance between his wife and Fuchs. The move was not popular with Erna, and there was some tension between them about where they would live.

Herbert was often away in Liverpool, leaving his wife at Harwell. Fuchs and Erna would spend time together at the weekends, driving to Abingdon or Oxford to visit the theatre or the cinema, or just to go on shopping expeditions. Erna was Russian, and partly because of this she was good friends with Genia Peierls, who was living once more in Birmingham with Rudolf. Erna would occasionally stay for the weekend with them and they too must have known of the affair with Fuchs. Genia remarked once that the claustrophobic atmosphere of Harwell must have driven Erna to distraction. Erna was attractive, of medium height, with dark hair and expensively but slightly untidily dressed. What she saw in Fuchs she never said publicly, although perhaps he brought out her maternal instinct, as he was apt to do in many of his relationships with women even in his late thirties. Although he could be aloof and quiet, he could also be charming, sympathetic, intelligent and entertaining.

These changes in circumstance might have been sufficient for Fuchs to be increasingly cautious and circumspect about meeting Feklisov, but something else was on the horizon that was also of some concern. He had once mentioned to Harry Gold that he was worried that his father, Emil, might inadvertently reveal his son's German Communist Party background. Now his father was coming to stay with him in the summer. Emil Fuchs had survived the war and had, if anything, thrived in the years after it. He had passed through the UK a year ago, and briefly seen his son, on his way to the United States where he was carrying out a speaking tour sponsored by the American Friends Service Committee. Travelling with him was his twelve-year-old grandson, Klaus Kittowski, the son of Fuchs's sister Elisabeth, who had killed herself in Prague in 1939. While Emil made his way around various US cities, the boy spent the time at a modern, unconventional boarding school in New England.

Emil was still a socialist and a Quaker. He had remained

in southern Germany during the war, doing his best to continue the Quaker ministry. Before his US speaking tour he had been in negotiations with Leipzig University about taking up a post as a professor of theology. Leipzig was in the Soviet occupation zone of Germany, which was soon to become a separate state, but the challenge of working with communists in a dialogue about faith and community was attractive to Emil. Grandfather and grandson visited Kristel in Cambridge, Massachusetts, and it was here, according to Klaus Kittowski, that Emil received a letter offering him the post at Leipzig.

During their return journey to Germany their plan was to stay with Fuchs for a month and they duly arrived in July. Here was another obstacle preventing Fuchs from disappearing to meet his Soviet contact on a Saturday. If the reported remarks to Harry Gold about his anxiety that his father might inadvertently reveal his KPD background to Allied intelligence officers are true, then the month of the visit must have been particularly tense for Klaus Fuchs. Unlike his son, Emil Fuchs was garrulous and sociable, outspoken even. He was entertained by Fuchs's friends at Harwell and by the Peierls in Birmingham, as well as by the Society of Friends in the United Kingdom. Erna Skinner took him under her wing, and even on his return to Germany continued to write to him, saying that Klaus was well, but like most men was no good at correspondence.

Klaus Kittowski was included in the parties and outings and remembers the friends around Fuchs as lively people, animated and intellectually stimulating. There were picnics to the woods and day trips to the banks of the Thames. There was constant conversation, much of it about physics, and the boy was certain that hardly any of them paid attention to the beauty of the river and the surrounding countryside, so engrossed were they in their talk and their ideas.

They all drank, Fuchs particularly heavily, and Klaus

Kittowski remembers one evening in particular when his uncle could be seen standing by the mantelpiece during a party, a large tumbler of whisky in his hand while Herbert Skinner and Rudolf Peierls argued about the new National Health Service and its chances of success.

Kittowski says that the likelihood of Emil going to Leipzig was discussed during their visit. Emil was concerned that this might be a problem for Fuchs, given the antagonism between the West and the Soviet Union over Berlin and East Germany. The Soviet Union had only just ended a blockade on Berlin, which was deep in the Soviet zone, as a response to the British, French and US occupying forces creating a single zone of West Germany and introducing a new common currency. Aircraft flew in supplies to the beleaguered city, while Red Army soldiers blocked access via the road corridors. Tensions were very high and Europe seemed close to another war. The blockade had finally finished in April, just a few months before Emil's arrival in Britain. It was not a good time to be talking about going to live in the Soviet zone of Germany and Fuchs must have been in despair about the foolishness of his father. However, he said that he would find out what impact this might have on his own position at Harwell, and according to Klaus Kittowski he went next door to see Arnold. He came back saying that it would not be a problem.

Arnold never wrote or talked about this particular conversation, but the possibility of Emil moving to Leipzig was undoubtedly discussed during this visit in July. It had to be, because the question of where Klaus Kittowski would live and go to school if Emil did take up the offer of a professorship was a pressing one. Emil raised the possibility of Fuchs's nephew remaining in England with him, and going perhaps to an English boarding school. As part of this plan Emil and his grandson went to see some possible schools during their stay. Klaus Fuchs would of course have to take on some responsibility for his nephew if he remained in the UK, but he said nothing to influence his father's plans, aware, as he said later, that Emil would not be influenced by anybody.

Klaus Kittowski has a distinct memory of sitting in the back of his uncle's car during a discussion with Emil about the future. Emil said that all the schools that they had seen were far too formal for young Klaus, who had got used to the relaxed atmosphere of the experimental school he had stayed at in the United States. He would just have to find a place for him in a similar school, of which there were a few in Germany. Hearing the news that he would not be burdened with the responsibility of his nephew, Fuchs said nothing. Sitting behind him, however, Klaus Kittowski saw his uncle's shoulders suddenly relax, as though a great weight had literally been removed from them.

So the summer of 1949 progressed, with Fuchs spending more time with his father than he had since 1933. He heard news about his brother Gerhard, still suffering grievously from tuberculosis, and about the drugs he was taking to hold the disease at bay. Emil also brought him news of Kristel, who was now suffering a mental illness and receiving treatment in a sanatorium in Boston. Fuchs, of course, had seen his sister more often than his father had. He knew that she was emotionally vulnerable and that her marriage was unhappy, but this news of her deterioration must have depressed him. Fuchs's father was a strong, dominant personality; his letters show him to be ambitious and pleased at the success of his lectures, and sad that his children could not be there to see him at his moment of triumph. He is proud of his son Klaus's achievement, and sad about Gerhard, but unpleasantly critical of his daughter Kristel's "unconsidered life", as he describes it, which has been a constant source of pain to him. Fuchs said very little about his father, other than that he was a strong and determined man who would not be influenced by anything that his son said.

Either by luck or because of a discreet conversation that he might have had with Kristel's husband, or indeed with Klaus Fuchs himself, Emil never publicly discussed the Communist Party affiliations of his sons and daughters, something that Klaus must have been thankful for. Far away, however, various groups of people were working on super-secret projects that made a possible slip of the tongue by Emil Fuchs seem an unimportant trifle. Klaus Fuchs's past actions were about to catch up with him.

NINETEEN

The Hunt

A threat to Fuchs's safety had arisen of which he was completely unaware. Early in the war, back in 1942, the United States Army's Signals Intelligence Service was ordered to crack all foreign codes used for military and diplomatic communications. The code breakers had been moved in 1943 to an old college building west of the Pentagon, called Arlington Hall, and this name became synonymous with the Signals Intelligence Service, much like Bletchley Park became the popular name for Britain's wartime Government Code and Cipher School.

Shortly after this move, a Russian section of about two dozen cryptanalysts was created with the specific task of breaking into Soviet diplomatic codes. The project eventually became known as "Venona". The ostensible reason for mounting this effort against the diplomatic signals of an ally was that it was important to discover if there were any moves by Stalin to negotiate a separate peace with Hitler. While this might just have been conceivable in 1943, the code-breaking effort continued even when Red Army artillery was smashing the suburbs of Berlin in 1945.

Code breaking relies on three things: an enormous

amount of hard work, some intelligent and creative people, and a great deal of luck. So it proved with the Signals Intelligence Service and the Soviet diplomatic cipher. Soviet intelligence used a system that was based on "one-time pads". Messages are turned into code from a code book that assigns a set of four numbers to a word or syllable. The resulting string of sets of numbers is then matched to sets of numbers that are printed on pages of the one-time pad. As its name implies, these pages are meant to be used only once. When all the sets of numbers on a page are correlated to the message, then the page is discarded. If used properly the method was practically unbreakable, especially before the invention of super-computers. At some time in 1943, however, the printing plant that produced the one-time pads for the NKGB in Moscow manufactured some with duplicate pages. The mistake wasn't noticed and the pads were distributed to the various embassies and consulates around the world. This meant that some of the code breakers in Arlington Hall saw repetitions in the coded messages and so were able to start interpreting some of the words.

Meredith Gardner was an intelligent Russian linguist who started work on the Soviet cable traffic in 1946. Even by then not much had been achieved. What little work had been done relied on the cooperation of the FBI, and also on the fact that many of the messages were mainly to do with trade and cargo manifests, which themselves contained very repetitive words, and where samples of the signals could be checked against, say, English versions of shipping lists.

In August 1949, however, Gardner saw a message from New York to Moscow, sent in 1944, that referred to a document with an MSN prefix. It did not take him long to discover that this was the prefix to documents from the British Scientific Mission in New York. It was a document that just four British scientists had produced, and only a handful of other people had received copies of it. More intensive work on the New York cables from the autumn and winter of 1944, and a search in the files of the Kellex Corporation and the Atomic Energy Commission for the numbered copies of the report, threw up the name of just one man whose movements tallied with those described in the encrypted signals. It was Dr. Klaus Fuchs.

The work of the Signals Intelligence Service was closely followed in the UK by the Government Communications Headquarters (GCHQ), and MI5 held its first recorded meeting about targeting Klaus Fuchs on 7 September 1949, more than two weeks before the FBI says it officially notified the British security liaison officer in Washington. The information that the intercepted Soviet signals had identified an agent who was most probably Fuchs was taken to Michael Perrin and Lord Portal by Dick White, head of B Branch (counter-espionage) at MI5.

The two men in charge of Britain's nuclear programme were stunned, but had no arguments when faced with what they were told was compelling evidence that must be investigated. They knew immediately how serious this was. It was not just possibly losing the services of one of their most important scientists; it was the effect that Fuchs's guilt might have on Britain's relationship with the United States. There were now signs that the dogmatic refusal of the US administration to share nuclear information with its wartime ally might be beginning to change. In fact, Lord Portal and Sir John Cockcroft, head of the Atomic Energy Research Establishment at Harwell, were about to go to Washington to discuss new proposals about sharing nuclear weapons technology. The news brought by Dick White could not really have come at a worse time.

Perrin went to see Cockcroft to tell him that Fuchs was going to be the subject of an MI5 investigation. Cockcroft had worked with Fuchs for some years and was sceptical. He told Perrin that Fuchs was the most security-minded of all the scientists at Harwell and, unlike most of his colleagues, "never pushes himself forward to attend or speak at conferences". Also, he pointed out that Fuchs was overworked and had recently been treated for suspected tuberculosis. Robert Oppenheimer, the former chief scientist at Los Alamos, had visited Cockcroft recently and had offered to give Fuchs a six-month sabbatical at Princeton. He had passed this on to Fuchs and the offer still stood. Clearly Cockcroft hoped that it could all be made to go away. His defence of Fuchs was genuine. He respected him and knew how valuable his abilities were. Cockcroft had recently written a paper on the construction of a new nuclear reactor, which he was to speak on at a forthcoming conference. The document included estimates of the annual yield of plutonium and the amount of enriched uranium the reactor would need as a fuel. He had sent the paper to Fuchs asking him to check the calculations. Fuchs had done so and returned it with a memo pointing out that Sir John had forgotten to take account of several things, including losses of material during enrichment and reprocessing. Fuchs had completely reworked the figures for him.

Perrin reported Cockcroft's remarks back to MI5, but they were waved away by Dick White. Enthusiasm and a concern for security were what one could expect from a spy, he declared.

The day-to-day details of the investigation were put in the hands of one of White's officers, James Robertson. By 7 September he had submitted a plan of action and he arranged to meet Perrin to sound him out about using Wing Commander Arnold, head of security at Harwell, as part of their team. White agreed the plan. He wrote back, however, that while speed was necessary, so too was caution: it was vital not to reveal to Fuchs that MI5 were watching him.

Robertson wanted permission to listen in and record Fuchs's telephones at his office and his home, and to intercept his mail. This needed a warrant from the Home Office. Robertson also wanted to place a microphone in Fuchs's home to overhear any conversations with visitors. The requests were given to Guy Liddell, the deputy director general, who then passed the requests on to a senior civil servant in the Home Office. After the warrants were granted the Post Office Special Investigations Unit, based in the City of London near St. Paul's, was called in. This unit provided the technicians to install the wire-tapping equipment in the telephone exchange and also to modify the telephone to turn it into an open microphone. The microphone in the handset wasn't good enough to pick up conversation more than a few feet away with any clarity, but the tap on the phone picked up every word spoken. The output from the bugs was recorded on to Dictaphone cylinders or acetate records, and it was only at this stage that the material was passed to MI5 for the recordings to be transcribed. Similarly, intercepted mail was opened, checked for secret writing, then photographed by Post Office staff, and only then was the material given to MI5. Some major telephone exchanges and sorting offices had a Special Investigations Unit room, but Harwell's exchange, Newbury, didn't, so a special room for the monitoring equipment and staff had to be set up. The cover story to explain all this activity was that a survey on telephone traffic in the area was being carried out.

Another officer in B Branch, W. B. Hanley, had looked through the existing files and come to the conclusion that the speculative early intelligence about Fuchs was not impressive. He disagreed with the assessment Serpell had written in 1946. There was no clear evidence to suggest that Fuchs was a communist penetration agent of the Nazi Party. But there were other problems. Nothing in the files gave any clue about how Fuchs might operate. It was possible that he had a "cut-out"—a go-between in the Soviet Embassy in London. Here Hanley revealed his ignorance of precisely what was being handed over when he suggested that Fuchs used photography to copy blueprints or diagrams. He also pointed out that Wing Commander Arnold had once suggested, without any proof, that Fuchs was running a network of other agents in Harwell. Arnold was clearly not the most reliable source. Nevertheless, he would need to be coopted, if only to provide some insight into what sort of work Fuchs did, what his daily routine was and whom he saw and met regularly. Robertson also needed to know if it was possible to insert any MI5 agents into Harwell to maintain surveillance on Fuchs.

The task of discovering evidence of Fuchs's spying was a difficult one. The first problem was that the source of the intelligence pointing to Fuchs was extremely secret—too secret to be revealed. The second major difficulty was that the information related to a period in 1944, five years earlier and a very different time from the present. Fuchs may have felt justified in handing some material to the Soviet Union then, but may no longer be doing so. MI5 may not be able to prove that he was a spy in 1944 and may not be able to prove that he was not a spy any longer. The task might be like looking in a haystack for a needle that had ceased to exist. In this circumstance, it was vital that MI5 was in a position to account for Fuchs's movements for twenty-four hours of the day. Only then would it be possible to make any firm statements about his current activities.

Wing Commander Arnold was asked to come and talk to MI5 at the Ministry of Supply building in Shell Mex House in the Strand. The cover story for Arnold was that MI5 had received some information about a possible leak of classified material and one of the people being investigated was at Harwell.

When he arrived he was introduced to Jim Skardon, who, as we have seen, was a senior officer in the surveillance branch, referred to by many in the service as "the Watchers".

Skardon was going to be responsible for the Harwell end of the operation and would be Arnold's immediate contact with the Security Service.

What Arnold had to say about Fuchs added to James Robertson's concerns about the complexity of the operation. Up until recently Fuchs had lived in Lacies Court, a guest house in Abingdon, but had recently moved to a new bungalow, in reality a "prefab", on site at Harwell. Fuchs had taken one of these, at 16 Hillside, because of the visit of his father and nephew in July. He tended, however, to spend a lot of time at the Skinners' house. Fuchs had been ill recently and had been nursed by Erna Skinner at their home, and he appeared to be on more than usually friendly terms with her. Herbert Skinner, who was Fuchs's boss and de facto deputy of Harwell, was going to take up a job at Liverpool University, made vacant by Professor Chadwick's retirement, so was spending several days a month there. Other than the Skinners, Fuchs's closest friends were the Peierls from Birmingham University, who often visited, and Otto Frisch at Cambridge.

Fuchs was fond of women and was a heavy drinker, reported Arnold; he could take a lot of whisky without being affected by it. He drove an old 8 h.p. Morris but had recently bought an MG sports car from the Skinners. This was in good condition and much more powerful. Petrol was still rationed, so when Fuchs made any journeys to Shell Mex House, which he did quite often for his work, then he would normally go by train, getting a travel warrant from the admin officer at Harwell.

It seemed to Robertson that if he wanted to subject Fuchs to twenty-four-hour surveillance he would need to seek a warrant to tap the phone at the Skinner house as well, and also put phone taps on the Peierls. The task of transcribing the daily take of information seemed to be growing to large proportions. MI5 did not have unlimited resources. The room in the Newbury telephone exchange where the listeners could work was now ready and they would stay at a nearby hotel. Keeping a tail on Fuchs as he travelled would, however, require considerably more staff, and to work out how this could be done Skardon made a visit to Harwell to observe the lie of the land.

He arrived on 14 September. The laboratories, workshops and offices were all contained within a perimeter fence with two main exits, which were guarded night and day. Outside the fence were the residential quarters and the club house. The main entrance to the establishment was directly on the Newbury—Oxford road. It was a place where any strangers or unfamiliar visitors would be immediately noticed. Neither was there anywhere that offered a site for a covert observation post. Skardon discussed the problem with Arnold. Fuchs's next-door neighbour was likely to react very badly if asked to report on Fuchs's movements. His secretary, Miss Holloway, was also fiercely loyal and it would be foolish to ask her to spy on her boss. Arnold, always happy to help, suggested that it might be possible to replace Miss Holloway at a later date and give Fuchs a secretary more amenable to snooping. For the moment, however, his movements at Harwell would be monitored by Arnold himself, along with two of his deputies whom he trusted. There was some discussion about recruiting the War Department constables who were responsible for watch-keeping and guard duty, but Arnold didn't know any whom he would trust with anything really confidential.

On Skardon's return to London a plan of operations was worked out. Arnold would get at least a day's notice of Fuchs's travel plans. He would phone them in to MI5 and then a team of watchers, on foot and in cars, would be ready in London to follow Fuchs wherever he went. Meanwhile the GPO technicians had installed the bugs and were intercepting his mail, and the whole intake of information was arriving in MI5's headquarters at Leconfield House in Curzon Street, Mayfair. As well as asking for telephone intercepts on calls to and from the Skinners and the Peierls, Robertson, eager to cover every possibility, had also set up a mail watch for anything going to Fuchs's sister Kristel in the United States. A test of these far-reaching arrangements for tailing Fuchs came on the 22nd.

The staff at Newbury told David Storrier, the MI5 officer in charge of the surveillance, that at 09.40 Fuchs had left his bungalow. The microphone was not picking up any movements. Two hours later Storrier was told that intercepted conversations between Fuchs's and Skinner's secretaries suggested that they were both about to leave, with two other people, and that all four of them would be travelling in Skinner's car. This information was passed once more to Storrier and to the physical surveillance team's HQ, which was a shabby four-storey Georgian building in Regent's Park. Ten minutes later Wing Commander Arnold phoned in with the information that both Skinner's and Fuchs's cars had left and that Fuchs was alone in his MG. Their destination was the GEC factory in Wembley, where they had a meeting at 2.30.

An hour later Arnold telephoned again to say that in fact only Skinner's car had been used and that Fuchs was probably in Skinner's Riley. Once again, this was passed on to the watchers' headquarters and to Storrier, who was now at Leconfield House. Skinner's car was picked up by the surveillance team in Wembley, where it was followed to the GEC factory. The watchers waited, then followed the car back to Harwell, peeling off before they arrived there.

Looking at the log of the day's activities, nothing had been revealed about Fuchs, but what was glaringly obvious was that the live monitoring of Fuchs's telephone and bungalow provided more precise information about his movements than Arnold's observation, which inevitably had to be carried out at some distance. As a result, the plans to involve more of Arnold's staff, perhaps boosted with some temporary War Department constabulary, were quietly shelved.

The next big test of MI5's operation was coming up on 27 and 28 September. The Royal Institution in Albemarle Street, off Piccadilly, a venerable scientific association set up in 1799, was the location for a secret symposium on the atom bomb. It seemed to MI5 that this would be an ideal opportunity for Fuchs to meet his Soviet contact, so anticipation was high. On the 26th the listeners in Newbury heard a telephone conversation between Fuchs and a member of the staff at the Weapons Research Establishment at Fort Halstead. The caller wanted to know if Fuchs was going to take part in the discussion. Fuchs replied that he had already written to Penney and told him of some points where he disagreed. These differences of opinion were about the comparison that Penney had made between the size of the explosion at Nagasaki and the test at Trinity. Fuchs also disagreed with a paper written by another of the scientists at Fort Halstead, John Corner. Fuchs, always alert to the niceties of departmental politics, didn't know if Penney wanted him to put these differences forward at the conference. Evidently this wasn't a problem and the conversation ended with an agreement that Fuchs would take part in the discussions. A few hours later, another phone call was logged, this time from Miss Holloway in Fuchs's office asking for two first-class return rail warrants from Didcot to Paddington for the next day.

This last conversation confirmed what Arnold had told Robertson and Skardon earlier that day at his weekly briefing meeting in Leconfield House. He said that in his view Fuchs would almost certainly travel by train. Robertson thought that Fuchs might make a contact during his train journey, at Reading station for example, so the surveillance should start at Didcot station. At first Storrier didn't think it was possible, but later said that he would provide the men to do it.

Before Arnold left he was shown some logs of the telephone and microphone intercepts and asked to help identify why there were some gaps. Fuchs had disappeared between Sunday afternoon and early Monday morning. What had happened? Herbert Skinner had left on the Sunday to take the sleeper train to Liverpool, explained Arnold. It was likely that Fuchs had spent the afternoon and night with Mrs. Skinner. He could not, of course, confirm this, but would at least be able to confirm Professor Skinner's absence in Liverpool when he, Arnold, got back to Harwell. On that note he left.

The listeners in Newbury had perhaps already realized that Fuchs's affair with Erna Skinner took up a lot of his time, but it hadn't yet sunk in with Robertson or Skardon. For many weeks Robertson doubted that the affair existed, bred perhaps out of an old-fashioned sense of morality, or a belief that such an openly acknowledged liaison could not exist without explosive repercussions.

The fact that the day before the trip Fuchs's secretary had requested two rail warrants for a journey to Paddington escaped everyone's attention. Arnold didn't report it on his return to Harwell, and if Storrier or Skardon had been aware they would have realized that if Fuchs was travelling with a companion he would not have made any contact with a Soviet agent during the journey. However, the watchers swung into operation, sending surveillance teams to cover Didcot, Paddington and Albemarle Street from 4.30 in the morning of the 27th.

On the evening of the 26th Fuchs and Erna Skinner again spent time together. At some point they decided it would be fun, now that Fuchs had his new MG, to drive down to London. The next day, the surveillance teams posted at the railway stations were kicking their heels and the first trace that MI5 had of Fuchs was when he was seen walking down Albemarle Street towards the Royal Institution with another man. One of them rang the doorbell and they went in.

Fuchs came out of the building at lunchtime and went to a post office across the road to make some phone calls. The MI5 agent trailing him got close enough to see that the first phone call was to the Great Western Hotel at Paddington station. He didn't manage to see the other number that Fuchs dialled. Then Fuchs hailed a taxi and went to an address in Knightsbridge—Herbert Crescent, just off Hans Place behind Harrods department store. He was let in to the house by a woman. An hour later he left and made his way by bus to Albemarle Street, where he stayed for the afternoon. Meanwhile, the team of watchers had split up, some to follow Fuchs, others to maintain a watch on the house near Hans Place. Sure enough, an hour later a man left the building; he was followed to the Physics and Chemistry Department of Imperial College in Exhibition Road, where he went into the laboratories and was heard by one of the surveillance team to ask if there were any messages for him.

Fuchs left the symposium at five o'clock, with a colleague, and walked around the corner into the courtyard of Burlington House. He picked up his MG, where it had obviously been parked all day, and drove on his own back to Herbert Crescent, where he parked and went in. His colleague made his way to the Great Western Hotel. None of the watchers could identify the woman who had let Fuchs into the house in Herbert Crescent, but it was Erna Skinner, who was staying there with some friends, a Professor Harper and his wife. It was Harper, of course, who had been followed to Imperial College.

Later that evening Fuchs, Erna Skinner and the Harpers all went in Fuchs's MG to the Blue Cockatoo on Cheyne Walk, a long-established restaurant that had been popular with Chelsea's artistic circle in the 1930s. They left at around 9.00 p.m. and all drove back to Herbert Crescent, where they dropped the ladies. Fuchs and Professor Harper then drove the MG to a garage in the Brompton Road and got a taxi back to the house.

Fuchs had been accustomed to clandestine activity for eighteen years and he was confident, as we have seen in his dealings with Gold and Feklisov, in his own ability to avoid detection. Throughout the day, a team of watchers on foot and in cars had followed him. One of the surveillance teams on foot had got close enough to record the telephone number he dialled from the post office public call box. One or two MI5 cars had tailed him from Piccadilly to Knightsbridge, to the Blue Cockatoo and back to Knightsbridge, then on to the Brompton Road. They were ordinary saloon cars, Hillmans, with non-standard, more powerful engines. MI5 took care to keep them discreet. The MI5 mechanics in the transport department garage in Battersea resprayed the vehicles a different colour every three months and their number plates were changed frequently. There was one thing that gave them away, however. They always had three men in them. It was an inflexible rule that they went on operations with a driver, a map-reader and a radio operator. To any observant person who had an inkling that he might be under surveillance, they would be very noticeable. By the end of the day, Fuchs had become aware that he was being followed.

The driver of one of the Security Service cars reported that Fuchs was "a very nervous driver, and it is quite obvious that following him in a car anywhere in the vicinity of Harwell will be even more dangerous than we anticipated."

Why would Fuchs be a nervous driver? He had owned a car in Los Alamos and driven on a motoring holiday across the border and through Mexico. He owned a car in England and took a motoring holiday through France and the Swiss Alps with the Skinners. Far from being a nervous driver, he was applying the Feklisov method of shaking a tail: driving erratically, changing speed and making last-minute manoeuvres, all designed to reveal if a vehicle was intent on following him. Just three weeks into the investigation, Fuchs surely knew that he was being watched.

The surveillance continued on the morning of the 28th, with Fuchs followed going to the second day of the symposium. He was observed walking with someone whose description fitted that of Sir William Penney, and they went to the Piccadilly Hotel for lunch in the Buttery. At five o'clock Fuchs went to get his MG out of the garage and then picked up Erna. He drove to Peterborough Place, to the flat of Eliezer Yapou, a press attaché for the Israeli government. The MI5 agent following them believed that this was a friend of Erna's, by the way that she led Fuchs into the flat.

After a couple of hours they both left and headed in Fuchs's MG to the A40 towards Oxford. Fuchs was not kept under constant observation, but was seen to stop for petrol, and then to stop again for twenty minutes on a quiet stretch of road near Medmenham, and finally they ended up at the Bull Hotel, Henley, where they stayed drinking double gins until 10.15. Fuchs then drove to Harwell and parked outside the Skinners' house. He certainly did have a high tolerance of alcohol.

So the first three weeks of surveillance ended. MI5 had learned very little about Fuchs's espionage, if indeed he was a spy, but the intense trailing of their suspect in London had revealed a few things. Arnold's information was not as reliable as he promised and it would be necessary to keep a car stationed at the Rowstock crossroads near Harwell, as well as making arrangements for Fuchs to be intercepted at Didcot station whenever he went to London. Storrier baulked slightly at this extra demand, but finally agreed to it.

Investigations were started, and files were opened on the Harpers and on Erna's friend Mr. Yapou. Their mail was intercepted under the original Fuchs warrant. As the investigation continued, the number of files opened by MI5 would grow, with the revelation of more acquaintances of Fuchs or Erna Skinner. The number of phone taps was also growing—on Fuchs's office and home, on the Skinners' home, on the Peierls' home in Birmingham, while a temporary tap was placed on Herbert Skinner's hotel phone in Liverpool. As well as this, of course, Fuchs's mail was being intercepted and there was a watch on any mail going to his sister from the UK. So far, however, there was no sign of any contact with the Russian intelligence services.

Robertson and John Marriott had considered that Fuchs might be on his guard and realize that he was being investigated. They argued that this would prompt him to do one of three things. He might cease all contact with the Russians and lie low until he felt that he was safe; he might report to Cockcroft or some other senior authority his suspicion that he was under observation; or he might decide to continue with his contacts but take precautions to evade detection.

Robertson thought that the first course of action was least desirable, from MI5's point of view, but probably the most likely. The second possibility could be countered by telling Fuchs that arrangements would be made to keep him under observation to see if he was being followed, and then tell him that there was no evidence that he was. The third option would, of course, play into MI5's hands because it would provide the greatest chance to prove his guilt. It was useful up to a point, they concluded, to take some risks in order to get the evidence they needed. They needed to shake the tree.

TWENTY

Hey Joe

W hile the FBI and MI5 were searching for evidence that Klaus Fuchs was indeed spying for the Soviet Union, they were of course completely ignorant of the work that had been going on in Russia since the Potsdam Conference in 1945, and we need now to go back four years to see what effect Truman's remark to Stalin had had. The first results of Stalin's directive to speed up the work on the Soviet bomb was the construction of a nuclear reactor in Laboratory No. 2, the site established by Kurchatov in Moscow in 1943.

The reactor, called F-1, was a small experimental pile of natural uranium and graphite. It went critical—started a chain reaction—in December 1946, producing the first small samples of plutonium for the laboratory. It was the first reactor to go online in Europe. Kurchatov knew that the small experimental pile would not be big enough to produce the plutonium needed for a weapon and a full-scale production reactor was planned in an isolated location in the Urals. Close to a town called Kyshtym, the site was named after Chelyabinsk, some 70 kilometres away, and given the postal code of 40 to disguise its true location. Construction of the reactor started in March 1948 and it went critical in June, but the Soviet scientists met some unexpected problems and the reactor had to be shut down.

As work on the bomb progressed, Laboratory No. 2 became too small and a new site was chosen for a facility specifically for experiments and production of a weapon. The location of this Soviet equivalent of Los Alamos was a small village, Sarov, which in pre-revolutionary days had housed a monastery, but was now the site of a factory manufacturing Katyusha rockets. A nearby labour camp provided prisoners to build the first new houses and laboratories. It was here, in a zone called Arzamas-16, that all the design, testing and assembly work of the Soviet bomb was carried out.

Fuchs had handed over a detailed design for the plutonium bomb, but the physical ability to produce enriched uranium, plutonium, and indeed to check the calculations that Fuchs had provided, was vital. Kurchatov took the view that the project would not succeed if everyone working on it did not have the most profound understanding of the science and technology behind the weapon.

The difficulties that the Soviet team encountered with their large-scale reactor, and later on in the process of separating out plutonium, proved that this view was correct. Kurchatov had other sources of help. In 1945 a team of NKGB officers, led by Georgi Flerov, went to Germany and rounded up many German scientists and engineers who had worked on various aspects of nuclear physics during the war. Some of them, particularly metallurgists and chemists, proved extremely useful with some of the problems. Also, of course, Fuchs was still on hand, albeit at the end of a fragile and dangerous line of communication, providing copious amounts of research material.

When Fuchs met Feklisov in April 1949, the Soviet reactor built at Chelyabinsk-40 was running properly. After its start-up in June the year before, the fuel rods had been affected by corrosion. The aluminium casing had swollen and the uranium slugs inside them had become distorted so that they could not be removed from the pile. The reactor was shut down while new fuel rods with different casings were made, after which it worked perfectly.

The next task was to extract plutonium from the irradiated uranium in the fuel rods. The Smyth Report—the official US report on the Manhattan Project—described the process used at Hanford in Washington state as a precipitation method. This required a large facility where the aluminium case was stripped off and the uranium fuel was then immersed in nitric acid, which dissolved everything and allowed the various metals to be separated. It was an intensely poisonous process, directed by remote control, which vented toxic fumes into the atmosphere via tall chimneys. Not only the process but the physical shape of the building at Chelyabinsk had been copied from that at Hanford. Finally, in another building of the complex the plutonium was refined. By June, enough plutonium for the core of a bomb existed and it was machined into shape. The two hemispheres, which were only about 8 centimetres in diameter, were coated in nickel and taken to Arzamas-16, where Flerov carried out a version of the experiment known as "tickling the dragon's tail". Frisch had done this at Los Alamos using uranium, bringing two pieces closer and closer until a reaction started. Frisch almost had an accident when he dislodged a piece of shielding, and later a physicist at Los Alamos, Louis Slotin, died when two pieces of uranium he was working with stuck together, releasing a burst of radiation.

Flerov was performing this risky experiment to assess if the two pieces of plutonium were of sufficient mass that they would become super-critical in an implosion. He carried out the test in a small hut with an armed guard well away from the other buildings, and afterwards he reported that the two pieces of plutonium would do the trick.

A testing range for the first nuclear explosion had been selected in 1947, at a site about 140 kilometres north-west of Semipalatinsk, in Kazakhstan. A 30-metre-high tower was built to support the bomb, and beneath it was a large set of workshops where the final assembly would be carried out. Inside, a crane on rails would carry the assembled bomb out of the assembly hall to the lift at the base of the tower. With Flerov's approval of the plutonium core, the bomb was ready to be tested, but first Stalin had to be consulted and give permission.

Kurchatov asked Khariton and the other heads of the various divisions if they were sure that the bomb was ready and, with their agreement, he went to Moscow. They reported to Stalin and Beria, and Stalin asked very little other than whether the plutonium could be divided to make two bombs. Khariton said no, that wasn't possible. With that the test was given the go-ahead.

Kurchatov went to Semipalatinsk in May. Thousands of workers were mobilized for the test, because Kurchatov wanted it to be far more comprehensive than the Trinity test. He wanted instruments to measure the radiation, the shock wave, and high-speed cameras to photograph the explosion. The United States had the benefit of information from Hiroshima and Nagasaki about the physical effects of a nuclear weapon. Fuchs had provided details from all three explosions, but Kurchatov wanted their own comprehensive data. To get this a variety of buildings were erected in the test area, ranging from wooden huts to four-storcy brick buildings. Water towers, bridges, locomotives, tanks and artillery pieces were also placed at various distances from the tower, and live animals were put in different types of pens to observe the effects of the initial burst of radiation.

All this took time and the work of thousands of people,

many of them slave labourers from the prison camps that were set up near all the nuclear facilities. One scientist, Lev Al'tshuler, wrote about arriving in Arzamas-16 and observing the small village with its workshops surrounded by work camps. Columns of prisoners passed through the settlement in the morning on their way to work, and marched through it again in the evening back to their prison barracks. These men were doubly unfortunate. Because they were witnesses to the atomic bomb programme, they were never allowed home at the end of their sentence. Instead, they were deported far into eastern Siberia.

In comparison to the prisoners, the scientists were treated extremely well, with plenty of food and accommodation and good pay. There were no problems to distract them from their work. There was, of course, very tight security. The most secret documents were written by hand. If anything did need typing then the key words were left blank, to be filled in by hand when the document was finished. Code words were also used as a security measure, similar to the British use of "tube alloy" for uranium and then as a metaphor for the nuclear bomb.

The senior figures, Kurchatov, Khariton and Zeldovich, all had bodyguards, who also doubled as spies of course. In fact, there were spies everywhere. At Los Alamos, the US Army Intelligence Corps had spies and informers working in the hotels and bars in Albuquerque and Santa Fe, and it was no different at Arzamas, or at Laboratory No. 2 in Moscow. Suspicion was all-pervasive, but the political climate in the Soviet Union was poisonous. Failure could lead to denunciation for sabotage or for being a Western agent. Khariton was especially vulnerable if things did not work as they should. He had studied in Cambridge at the Caversham Laboratory under Professor Chadwick, head of the British Mission to the Manhattan Project, and his father had been arrested by the NKGB in 1940 and had disappeared. Khariton's personal history was like a time bomb waiting to explode.

All the scientists were under suspicion, merely because quantum mechanics, the basis of much of their science, was considered to be opposed to dialectical materialism, the dogma of Stalinist communism. This was a time when the Soviet Central Committee supported Trofim Lysenko, the Soviet biologist who claimed that genetic information could be changed through experience. Kurchatov asked Beria to cancel a large scientific congress in Moscow because he realized that it would cause problems for himself and his fellow physicists, who would be vilified for their scientific methods. Beria said that he could not make that decision alone, so he took the problem to Stalin, who agreed to cancel the congress. One account has Stalin saying of the physicists, "Leave them in peace. We can always shoot them later."

Most of the scientists who worked on the Soviet nuclear weapon were afraid of the NKGB, and feared and hated Beria. Flerov later described him as a brute who understood nothing but believed that threats were an adequate substitute. On one occasion Avraami Zavenyagin, the deputy people's commissar of internal affairs and armaments minister, was shown a sphere of plutonium and asked the scientist holding it how he could be sure that it was plutonium and not some other metal? Such ignorance was a product of the terror induced by Stalin and Beria. People like Kurchatov, Flerov and the others lived in a bizarre universe where they loathed these people but at the same time worked as hard as they could to build the bomb. They did so because they believed not in Beria but in Russia, the revolution and the Russian people.

The scientists in Moscow, Arzamas and Chelyabinsk had all experienced the dreadful slaughter and hardships that Russia had suffered in the Second World War. Victims of an unprovoked attack, the Russian people had lost millions of men, women and children to an invading army that was barbaric in its behaviour. They had also seen the massively destructive carpet-bombing that the Allies had launched on German cities—a demonstration of indiscriminate killing from the air that had finally ended with the two atomic bombs that had destroyed the Japanese cities of Hiroshima and Nagasaki. They were in no doubt that Russia could not exist in the world without their own nuclear weapon.

So in 1949 they were all gathering at Semipalatinsk on the steppes of Kazakhstan. Kurchatov arrived in May and was in overall charge of the test. Beria arrived in the middle of August with Zavenyagin, the armaments minister. He looked at everything and made his presence felt. Kurchatov had ordered two rehearsals before the head of the NKGB's arrival, to make sure that everything had been checked and that the test itself would proceed as faultlessly as possible. Nobody had any illusions about their fate if the project failed. It would be a bullet in the back of the head, or a lifetime in the gulag.

The bomb was assembled in the hall, the components of the tamper and one half of the plutonium core lowered into place with a crane on to one half of the explosive lenses, which had been assembled on a railway truck. The final half of the core and tamper was then lowered down with the initiator in place and the rest of the explosives were assembled around it and a final casing fitted over it. The device was pushed out to the base of the tower, from where it was hoisted in a lift to the top. Here, the detonators and wiring were connected up to the explosive lenses. Flerov and two others completed the final checks, then came down in the lift.

There were two separate observation posts 15 kilometres from the tower, with the military and party officials in the southern one and the scientists to the north. A command post where the countdown would be started was 10 kilometres away, and Kurchatov, Khariton, Flerov and Zavenyagin, along with Beria and his aides and bodyguards, assembled here. The blast was scheduled for 6 a.m. on 29 August.

Kurchatov gave the order to start the countdown, and the fate of all of them was in the balance. The process of initiation and detonation was automatic; there was nothing to do but monitor the instruments, watch the clock and hope that nothing would go wrong. The implosion weapon is enormously complex, relying on thirty-two detonators to be triggered instantaneously. A break in a circuit here, or a miscalculation of the timing, would destroy months of work and ruin the test. So too would an undetected fault in the explosives. Any error in the manufacture of the tamper or the plutonium core or the initiator could mean that the bomb would not explode as it should. With Beria standing at his shoulder, Kurchatov must have had cast-iron faith in Flerov, Khariton and the rest of his fellow workers; he must have believed that nothing had affected their judgement, that no detail had escaped their attention.

A siren and loudspeaker system announced the countdown with the start at thirty minutes and then further announcements. At ten minutes the scientists knew that everything—the instruments, the power to the detonators—was working and they went outside their observation post. There were low-lying clouds, broken up with the sky appearing between them, and a pale morning sun. It had rained in the night and the air felt fresh. The tower was visible in the distance across the tall grass of the steppe.

The countdown continued: five minutes, three, one minute, then thirty seconds, ten, two, and at zero the sun was extinguished by an unbearably bright light that came from the top of the tower, and a white fireball expanded, changing colour, orange and red, as it grew and grew. The buildings and machines that had been placed close to the tower became part of the fireball, and the observers could see bricks, roofs, railway carriages engulfed in the mushrooming column of debris that rose in the sky for around 6,000 metres.

The scientists in the control room had remained calm during the countdown, but after the explosion they rushed to congratulate Kurchatov, and Beria hugged and kissed him. Some restraint was necessary in the presence of the NKGB chief, but one scientist, whose job it was to drive towards ground zero in a specially modified tank to test the radiation levels, met Kurchatov at the head of a small convoy racing towards the spot. The leader of the Soviet team was determined to go and see for himself what was left of the tower and the buildings near to it. After he had seen enough, he returned to his quarters. News of the test was telephoned by Beria to Stalin, but Kurchatov's report was handwritten and flown to the Kremlin.

Everyone who had seen this massive fireball and the resulting mushroom cloud would have felt amazed at what they had achieved, but also an almost overwhelming relief that it had succeeded and that their personal future was no longer in doubt. No one who worked towards this nuclear explosion expressed concerns about the consequences. The Soviet Union was the second country in the world to have detonated an atomic weapon, and even though the word was not in current usage, they knew that now the Soviet Union was a "superpower", that it had taken its place in the world as the equal of the United States. This was, after all, the purpose of their work, and this is what they had succeeded in doing. If there were any doubts, those having them kept them very closely confined in their own minds.

The Soviet government did not announce that it had become a nuclear power. The first public declaration was made almost a month later, on 23 September, jointly by the governments of the United States, Britain and Canada:

"We have evidence that within the recent weeks an atomic explosion has occurred in the USSR." US Secretary of State Dean Acheson confirmed the statement at a press conference in New York, where he was attending a plenary session of the United Nations. The announcement reached the ears and eyes of people in Britain the next day, on BBC radio and in the press. The headline across the top of the *Daily Express* ran "Russia Has The Bomb".

In fact, evidence of the bomb's explosion was picked up three days after it had occurred. A secret unit of the US Air Force had converted a squadron of B-29 bombers into atmospheric-sampling aircraft. They were fitted with filters and sensors that could detect the chemical and radiation residue that remained in the atmosphere after a nuclear explosion. One of these aircraft, flying from Japan to Alaska on 1 September, detected particles from the detonation at Semipalatinsk. More sampling flights confirmed these initial results, and analysis of the samples at Los Alamos showed, moreover, that the core was plutonium, not uranium 235.

It had always been assumed that the Soviet Union could build an atomic weapon of its own if it wanted to. There had, however, been some complacency in the West's assessment of how long this might take. In July 1948 a memo to President Truman from the director of the newly formed Central Intelligence Agency had said that the earliest date by which it was remotely possible for the USSR to complete its atomic bomb would be mid-1950, but the most probable date was mid-1953. This view was widely shared amongst the other intelligence organizations. The Soviet test exposed these assessments, and caused some serious questioning of the intelligence agencies' knowledge of what was happening in Russia. It also caused the US government to have second thoughts about its policy of seeking a nuclear monopoly. That had clearly ended. Was it better now to seek closer ties with their allies?

Before any public announcement of the test, the United States called for the resumption of the tripartite talks between the UK, Canada and the US about the reactivation of nuclear cooperation. Talks took place between 20 and 30 September, with a proposal that in return for starting up a new joint programme, which would be carried out in the US and perhaps Canada, Britain would be supplied with atomic weapons by the US, but would of course see its own atomic programme wound down. It was a crude attempt to maintain tight control of the technology. Not surprisingly, the members of the British delegation at the talks, which included Sir John Cockcroft, did not welcome this proposal and they were also met with scepticism in the Cabinet.

Politically, the public announcement that the Soviet Union had managed to build a nuclear weapon was a devastating blow in the United States. Another atomic power in the world, whose troops were solidly ensconced in the middle of Germany and had recently tried to take over Berlin, meant that the world had shifted on its axis. The immediate effect of this sudden change was to add more fuel to the Cold War. President Truman had been struggling to get a Bill through Congress for a Military Assistance Program for Europe. After the announcement of the Soviet test the Bill passed and was signed into law on 6 October. It allocated £1 billion to NATO for the purchase of military equipment and training for military personnel.

The Soviet test also reignited interest in the hydrogen bomb.

Edward Teller and two other scientists at Berkeley in California, Edward Lawrence and Luis Alvarez, urged the Atomic Energy Commission to build a reactor specifically to produce tritium, the isotope of hydrogen used as a fusion-bomb fuel. The scientific community, however, was split about whether the hydrogen bomb was worth pursuing, and the divisions represented to some extent the same differences of opinion that had existed at Los Alamos when Teller had persisted on working on the "super" rather than on the fission bomb. Oppenheimer still opposed work on the H-bomb, as did Bethe. Bethe said that he doubted its technical feasibility; Oppenheimer called it a weapon of genocide—a statement that would be used against him later, when he would be accused of communist sympathies and removed from the Atomic Energy Commission.

However, the situation in 1949 was not as it was in 1944. Everyone knew the atomic bomb worked. After all, even the Soviets knew how it worked. Work on the "super" would not be taking resources away from that vital question, which was the argument that Teller had faced five years earlier. He was in a much stronger position now, and he and Alvarez had a much more direct route to the decision-makers. They went to Washington and lobbied Senator Brien McMahon, chairman of the Joint Congressional Committee on Atomic Energy.

A delegation from this committee had recently made a visit to Los Alamos and had come back full of enthusiasm for the H-bomb. Teller was cutting with the grain. In November, McMahon wrote a letter to President Truman putting the views of the committee; "If we let the Russians get the Super first, catastrophe becomes all but certain." This was an opinion that was widely supported in Congress and in the press. Russia was now the great adversary, and very few people were willing publicly to question either the morality or the military usefulness of the H-bomb. Truman still had to make the final decision to spend the money on a brand-new atomic weapons programme, but the explosion of the Soviet bomb had generated a climate of fear in the United States that no president could ignore for long.

Because of the various questions that were put to him by Feklisov, Fuchs had understood the speed of the Soviet bomb project more than anyone else in the UK. On its explosion, he must have felt a great sense of satisfaction. He had run so many risks and played a major role in its success. He was, however, a past master at concealing his thoughts, and none of his friends or colleagues noticed any change in him when news of the Soviet bomb became public.

Fuchs would also have thought that the revelation of the Russians' nuclear success would increase security concerns at both Harwell and Fort Halstead. But he was well placed to spot any danger from that side. He was friendly with Arnold, head of security at Harwell, and of course with Herbert Skinner, who had told Fuchs before that he was aware of some MI6 intelligence about Soviet research. There was some other activity, though, that Fuchs had recently noticed and it must have caused some doubts in his mind. It was six months since his last contact with the NKGB, but the surveillance, if surveillance it was, had only recently started. Who was behind it and, more urgently, what could he, Fuchs, do about it?

TWENTY-ONE

Trailing Mr. Fuchs

The secret policemen charged with outing Fuchs as a Soviet spy were like blind boxers thrust into a prize fight. Bereft of information, they lashed out at anything. Their ever-increasing surveillance of more and more contacts must have consumed the time of scores of employees, from typists to senior officers. While they knew from experience that much intelligence work never produced results, there must have been some growing suspicion that the close surveillance operation was not the right approach. They needed something, some hook, another piece of evidence. Where it would come from they didn't know. In short, they needed some luck.

On 13 October Fuchs again paid a visit to London with Erna Skinner, this time to visit a doctor, Ludwig Frank, whose consulting rooms were at 10 Devonshire Place. On the way, Fuchs and Erna stopped off at 10 Wigmore Street, where a friend of Erna's, Tatiana Malleson, lived with her husband, Miles Malleson, a fairly well-known actor and director. Investigations by MI5 revealed that Tatiana had been born in St. Petersburg, then settled in Germany where she studied drama. She was Jewish, so left Germany in 1936, arriving in the UK as a refugee. She had married in Germany but divorced in 1944, then married Miles in 1946, and she continued to work as an actress. Also at the address in Wigmore Street was a woman named Vera Pohle, another German Jewish refugee, who lived in Kennington. MI5 opened files on all three people, the Mallesons and Pohle. Vera Pohle was followed back to her address and her movements monitored for several days, until she arrived at Harwell, where Wing Commander Arnold confirmed, a bit late in the day, that Erna had taken her on as housekeeper and companion.

In September Fuchs had received a letter from his cousin, Giselle Wagner, his mother's niece. Giselle had studied mathematics in Germany and planned to take up a place on a teacher training course in Cambridge. Robertson asked the Intelligence Department of the British Army of the Rhine to make inquiries about her, and they confirmed that she was planning to travel to the UK on 16 October. A warrant to intercept her mail was requested because she was "suspected of acting as an intermediary for communications between the Soviet zone of Germany and an individual employed in top secret defence work who is suspected of espionage on behalf of a foreign power". From then on her correspondence with anyone else was opened and read, and letters from the principal of her teacher training college were photographed and placed in an MI5 file. So the suspicions of the Security Service spread far and wide, dragging in innocent people so remote from the case as never to have heard of Klaus Fuchs.

Robertson believed, however, that no stone should be unturned. Fuchs's father and nephew had stayed with him in July on their way home from Emil's speaking tour in the United States. They had been away from home for some time and young Klaus had boarded at a school in the US, so they had a large amount of luggage. It was summer when they arrived, so their winter clothes were kept in a trunk and never unpacked, and it seems that Fuchs had promised to forward it to Germany as freight. It might be an indication of his subconscious attitude towards his father, but he never got around to making the arrangements. With winter approaching in Germany, Emil wrote to him on 12 October asking what had happened to the trunk and if it was time to ask for compensation from the freight forwarder. He also confirmed to his son that he was taking up the offer of the teaching post in Leipzig and would be moving there shortly.

His father's letter forced Fuchs into action and he was chivvied along by Erna to make an effort and get the trunk sent off. The telephone tap on his phone revealed to MI5 that he was going to take the trunk to freight forwarders in Oxford who could complete all the required Customs forms. They would then send it on to Germany via the mail. Robertson pulled out all stops to get the trunk searched, believing it vital that it was intercepted and opened, and he asked Skardon to get on to the Post Office immediately and hold it up at a sorting office. The result was disappointing. There was no general clearing house for parcels for the continent. The only hope of interception would be to contact the Customs Investigation Branch. If they were asked, they would send a circular to all the Customs offices at British ports and hope that a vigilant Customs officer would spot the trunk and take it aside. This would publicize the investigation to a large number of people, but with no guarantee of success. Skardon abandoned the effort.

Meanwhile, Fuchs was closely followed whenever he went into London for his regular meetings at the Ministry of Supply at Shell Mex House. There were a lot of decisions to be made about Britain's nuclear programme, and a lot of work to be done. Cockcroft had produced a report suggesting that an experimental fast-breeder reactor—one that used plutonium as fuel rather than enriched uranium—should be built at Dounreay, a remote location on the northern Scottish coast. Skinner asked Fuchs to rewrite the report because he didn't believe that the ministry would accept the decision as it stood. The meetings to discuss these thorny issues could go on all day and at lunch many of the scientists would go to the Queen's Head in the Strand for a meal. The MI5 agent would try to get as close to Fuchs as possible in order to overhear their conversation. At one of these lunchtime sessions, when Peierls, who was a consultant to the ministry, had travelled down from Birmingham, there were two tables of scientists in the Queen's Head, one table with Fuchs, Peierls and two other physicists from the meeting, and another with Skinner and some others. The surveillance report suggested that two agents had got close enough to Fuchs's table to be able to hear some snatches of conversation.

After this meeting Fuchs started taking long, meandering routes back to Paddington station, clearly in an effort to confirm whether he was being followed. There were other tactics that he used to catch out any watchers. On one occasion he strolled around Soho looking at bookshops, then made his way along Oxford Street to Marble Arch, walking into every department store, apparently inquiring about a particular brand of crockery. When he finally reached Marble Arch he delayed further by turning into the Edgware Road as if heading towards Paddington, but then ducking into an amusement arcade. He waited just a few minutes to see if anyone followed him, then quickly left the arcade and continued on his way and boarded the train to Didcot. It was a classic manoeuvre, criss-crossing a busy street, entering and leaving crowded stores, finally making an unexpected move, all designed to reveal if someone was tailing him.

On another visit, he again walked around Soho, going in and out of bookshops. He bought two magazines, one called *Paris* and the other *Health and Strength*, a male nudist magazine, which he carried out of the bookshop in the normal plain brown paper bag supplied for this sort of material. He then walked up Wardour Street to Oxford Street to wait at a bus stop. As he was boarding a bus he appeared accidentally to drop the bag containing *Health and Strength*. Fuchs did not turn to retrieve it and one of the MI5 watchers picked it up. Instead of trying to hand it back to Fuchs, the MI5 man hung on to it, thinking that it might hold some clue to a contact with Fuchs and his Soviet agent, but of course that was another indication to Fuchs that he was under surveillance.

It is certain that Fuchs was aware that he was being watched. Perhaps Robertson also realized that the constant surveillance might become obvious. Fuchs had plans to attend conferences in Cambridge and Edinburgh in November, and Robertson decided that trailing him to these cities for several days and reporting on his contacts was taking on too much. The watchers would not be familiar with the cities; the cost of mounting the surveillance operation would be too much. The trailing was to be confined to London.

It was a strange judgement. The conferences were a perfect opportunity for Fuchs to meet any contacts and to hand over material. MI5 had no evidence whatsoever that he met his Soviet intelligence handler in London rather than elsewhere, but the decision to limit the surveillance was taken without any serious discussion. It was almost as though Robertson had realized that Fuchs was not going to be caught by this type of operation. The limitations of it had to be obvious to anyone. The day that Fuchs and Erna came to London to visit their doctor in Devonshire Place, agents had been waiting at Didcot station and there were also MI5 cars on the main road. Despite these precautions, the first time that any agent made a sighting of Fuchs was when his MG drew up outside the doctor's surgery. The electronic surveillance of Fuchs's home and those of his friends and colleagues also revealed nothing other than the mundane and intimate secrets of their lives, and the fluctuating moods that affected Fuchs, Erna Skinner and her husband, Herbert.

The women who transcribed the tapes for the officers in Leconfield House became intimately connected to the people whose lives they were spying on. The microphone picked up a visit by Erna to Fuchs's bungalow at 15.20 on a Saturday, and the transcript recorded that for the next forty minutes Fuchs was vigorously clattering fire irons and stoking up the coal fire—something he did, so the transcriber reported, with monotonous regularity—and he was "tramping back and forth with fuel".

"Afterwards they were both very quiet indeed, and only an occasional murmur from Mrs. Skinner was heard." At 17.20, it was quiet. "They had gone—or Erna had gone alone??" queried the transcriber, then reported at "18.06 someone was walking about in the prefab. 18.40 Movements were heard in the distance, and the sound of a door closing."

After a while the listeners began to colour their reports with their own attitudes towards the people they were spying on. Erna Skinner was a woman who demanded attention from the men in her life and could be overly self-dramatizing. One of the transcribers took a dislike to her. The telephone tap on the Skinners' phone recorded a call from Erna to Eleanor Scott, the wife of a scientist working at Harwell. Mrs. Scott was surprised that Erna hadn't gone to London. "Erna explained that she had worn herself out on the Birmingham expedition and had not been able to go to London, with the result that Klaus was treating her like a criminal. Eleanor asked, 'You were going to London to stay were you?' Erna said yes. Eleanor made the mistake of asking Erna how she felt now. Erna launched into a description of her symptoms."

So week after week the surveillance logs accumulated. The secret listeners recorded for the umpteenth time that Fuchs stoked his fire, spoke to an irritable Erna about lunch, or heard Herbert Skinner apologetically explain that he was once more delayed by a housing committee meeting in Liverpool. Yet there was no sign of Fuchs meeting an agent of the NKGB, or leaving documents in a dead letter box, or being any sort of security risk at all.

Finally, however, Wing Commander Arnold made one of his weekly visits to Leconfield House with a piece of information. He told Robertson that Fuchs had visited him on 13 October and told him that his father, Emil, was going to accept a chair of theology at Leipzig University. According to Arnold, Fuchs wanted his advice on this: should he discourage his father from accepting the offer, having regard to his own position as a nuclear physicist in this country?

Arnold said that he did not answer straight away, telling Fuchs that he would like to consider the matter carefully. As we saw before, Klaus Kittowski remembered that Fuchs had raised the issue with Arnold at the time of their visit in July, but Arnold made no mention of this.

Arnold remained with Robertson while Skardon and Dick White joined them to discuss the question. White said that Fuchs should not allow his father to move to the Russian zone of Germany, for the very reason that Fuchs had already shown himself aware: once his father came under the influence of the Russians he might become a hostage against Fuchs. There the discussion ended, but Arnold came back to MI5 later and reported on a subsequent meeting where Fuchs had asked him if he had any further thoughts about the problem of his father. Arnold passed on the message that the Security Service—he used the word "authorities"—regarded it as highly important that those who were engaged in places and on work covered by the Official Secrets Act should have no close ties in those countries dominated by Russia. Arnold thought it was unusual for a man of seventy-three suddenly to be offered a chair and Fuchs appeared to agree.

Arnold suggested that his father might be induced to turn down the position if he could be offered a similar type of chair in the British or American zones. Fuchs thought that this was unlikely, because his father had become disillusioned as far as the Western zones were concerned. Fuchs knew, as Arnold didn't, that his father had decided that his Quaker beliefs would find a welcome home in the Soviet zone and that he believed that only in the communist East were there real efforts under way to construct a new Germany, free of materialist concerns. He also knew that his father was extremely stubborn and would never take advice from his son.

Arnold asked Fuchs if he did not fear that pressure might be brought to bear on him if his father were arrested, or through any other actions by the Soviet authorities, and what would be his reaction if that happened. Fuchs replied, according to the memo Arnold wrote for Robertson, that he didn't feel he would be induced to cooperate, but it was impossible to say what he might feel under altered circumstances. He then went on to ask if Arnold thought he should resign, but Arnold said that it was not up to him.

Fuchs had had little choice but to tell Arnold about his father's move to Leipzig, although if Klaus Kittowski is correct when he says that Fuchs discussed this with Arnold during his father's visit in July it should have come as no surprise; Arnold, however, never mentions this earlier discussion in his conversations with MI5. Fuchs may also have thought that it was an opportunity to bring some things out into the open, for him to discover the motives for the surveillance that he had undoubtedly detected. His suggestion that he might resign from his post at Harwell was not something he would offer lightly and was surely intended to force a response, if not from MI5 then from the Department of Atomic Energy. It did, but not in the form that Fuchs had anticipated.

Arnold delivered his memorandum about this conversation on 24 October and Robertson passed it to Dick White, head of B Branch. White read it and drew a line against the paragraph where Fuchs said that he did not know how he would react to pressure against his father if his circumstances changed. He then forwarded the minute in the file to the director general of MI5, Sir Percy Sillitoe, with the remark "this suggests it might be time to interrogate Fuchs."

TWENTY-TWO

The First Encounter

Dick White's recommendation that officers should interrogate Fuchs was premature. Before MI5 took any action, they had to consult many people. Permission had to be sought from the senior civil servants at the Ministry of Supply, and Sir John Cockcroft, as director of Harwell, also had to be told. He was still in the United States, discussing the possibility of collaboration between the US and British on nuclear weapons, and would not be back at Harwell until 8 December, and it looked as though the case against Fuchs would be no better then than it was at the start of the investigation.

Two months of intensive surveillance, of Fuchs and of anyone with whom he came into contact, had produced absolutely nothing. It might be true that his father's move to East Germany was a risk to security, but he had not sought to hide it; in fact, he had personally brought it to the attention of the Ministry of Supply security staff. The case was even weaker because the evidence, such as it was, was based on a partially decrypted coded message so secret that nobody outside the Security Service could be told about it. The problem for MI5 was that the evidence had been provided by an outside source. The FBI and the officers working with the Venona decrypts were puzzled by the fact that two months after officially informing MI5 of the possible source of the leak, they had heard nothing more. Pressure for a resolution of the Fuchs case could only increase. It is little wonder that MI5 threw even more resources into trapping Fuchs. Unfortunately for Robertson and Skardon, the help that they got from Arnold at Harwell was proving inadequate.

Fuchs travelled to Edinburgh on the first-class sleeper on 13 November to attend a conference on various aspects of nuclear energy. It was an opportunity to meet his old professor, Max Born, and other friends like Rudolf Peierls. Intercepted phone calls from Peierls to his wife in Birmingham told the MI5 eavesdroppers that apart from going to the cinema one evening, they had spent the time talking shop.

Fuchs returned to Harwell via the overnight sleeper to London on the 16th. He was intercepted by a team of watchers at King's Cross, from where he was followed to Paddington station. There he made a telephone call from a public call box, but the telephone booth was in darkness and the dial was dirty, so the agent trailing Fuchs could not see what number he called. Fuchs then went to the restaurant near Platform 1, took a table and ordered breakfast. A few minutes later the waiter brought another man to the table. The stranger and Fuchs talked casually over breakfast. When they had finished eating, Fuchs was handed the bill and the stranger passed him what the agent assumed was his share of the total. Fuchs then rose, settled the bill on his way out and went to board the 9.15 train for Didcot.

The stranger also left the restaurant and went into the public toilets, coming out again fifteen minutes later. He was aged about forty, and tall, about 6 feet in height, of slim build with dark brown, bushy hair and clean-shaven. He wore a grey-green sports coat and carried an air force overcoat. He took the underground to Trafalgar Square and went into a bookshop in Grand Buildings on the Strand, where he looked through a number of scientific books, then left. For the next few hours he meandered around different bookshops in central London. He first went to one in Whitehall; leaving there, he walked to Butterworth's, the legal and technical publishers who had a shop in the Strand. From there the unknown individual, whom the watchers had christened "C", went to another branch of the publishers, which was in Bell Yard behind the Law Courts, and from there he continued his way across Ludgate Circus to St. Pauls Chambers where there was another branch of Butterworth's. He was observed talking to the inquiry desk and then being shown to the Scientific Research Department on the third floor. He stayed there for several hours.

The watchers must have believed that at last they were on to something. The apparent chance encounter was even more suspicious because of the strange itinerary followed by the contact after he left Fuchs. Fuchs had not been under observation for any of the time that he had been in Edinburgh, and no doubt his journey back to Harwell had seemed a perfect opportunity to establish contact with this man. Perhaps it had been an inspired decision to leave Fuchs free of any surveillance in Edinburgh and he had at last tipped his hand?

The team of watchers waited while "C" spent three and a quarter hours in Butterworth's. Then Fuchs's mysterious contact left the bookshop and made his way slowly westwards, retracing his steps, stopping for a meal in the Strand Corner House before making his way once more to Paddington station. He was observed retrieving a rucksack from the main-line cloakroom, then he got on to the 5.55 p.m. train for Didcot. On his arrival, he boarded a bus that took him to Harwell.

MI5 learned later the next day that a colleague of Fuchs, Mr. Scott, had also gone to the conference in Edinburgh. It would be easy to say that there was a Keystone Cops nature to MI5's efforts, but the officers were themselves aware of the fact that they were by and large wasting their time and producing not a shred of evidence against their main suspect.

On 22 November Michael Perrin from the Department of Atomic Energy, Skardon and Arthur Martin, the MI5 liaison officer with GCHQ, took the unprecedented step of interviewing Frank Kearton, who had been part of the British Mission to New York and a colleague of Peierls and Fuchs. He was still on the Scientific Advisory Committee for Atomic Energy set up by Lord Portal in 1947, but had rejected any further work for the Ministry of Supply and was heavily engaged running a chemical research division at Courtaulds. The interview was an extraordinary breach of security. Kearton was occasionally consulted on the design of the diffusion plant at Springfields and he still knew Fuchs socially, so apart from desperation there can have been no reason to reveal to him that Fuchs was under suspicion. Yet this is exactly what they did. The note of the meeting confirms it:

> Kearton was told that evidence was available which indicated that Fuchs was a Soviet spy and that, therefore, detailed inquiries were being made into the whole of Fuchs career; the period of his employment in the British Atomic Mission in New York was one about which very little information was available and it was felt that Kearton, from his personal knowledge, might be able to fill certain gaps.

Kearton had been given the OBE in 1945, and both he and Perrin had worked in ICI before the war, so it may be that he was judged to be a reliable source. Kearton was of course dumbfounded, and of course he knew nothing. He told his questioners that Fuchs had been absorbed by his work and was content to remain in the background. He lived alone in a small, furnished flat and had, as far as Kearton knew, almost no friends or social acquaintances in New York. He had been in contact with a group of students at Columbia University who were working for the Kellex Corporation. He hazarded a guess that Fuchs had gone to Los Alamos because Peierls realized how much he had come to rely on him. He clearly knew nothing about the conversations that Fuchs had had with Chadwick and others about his possible return to the United Kingdom to continue his work on the Tube Alloys project there. Neither could Kearton shed very much light on how the MSN series of papers was forwarded to their American collaborators. He wasn't sure whether they were sent to a US agency or went via the British Mission in Washington.

Towards the end of the interview Kearton suggested that, out of the four men at the mission—leaving aside the female typists and computing machine operators—he would have suggested that Tony Skyrme might be more likely to be disloyal than Fuchs. Skyrme had very strong convictions, did develop wide social contacts in New York and was generally "rather odd". He had, of course, gone back to the United States and was now working at Columbia University.

There is no record of what the three, Perrin, Martin and Skardon, said to each other after Kearton had left. None of them could have suggested that the interview provided any more information that justified the security risk of revealing details of the case to someone outside the Department of Atomic Energy or the Security Service.

The following day, Wednesday, the 23rd, Robertson wrote a nineteen-page dossier on everything that MI5 knew about Klaus Fuchs, his academic career, his work on Tube Alloys, the Manhattan Project, and his friends and contacts. It was a remarkably sparse document. It showed, as one might expect, nothing to justify the belief that Fuchs had been a spy for the Russians; neither did it cover in very much detail the work that Fuchs had done in Britain and in the US. If its purpose was to provide a comprehensive background briefing for Skardon to interview Fuchs, it was not very strong and it is likely that everyone, from Dick White down, knew it. They were certainly not in a rush to confront him.

They waited for one more opportunity to catch Fuchs red-handed, in contact with a member of the Soviet intelligence services or handing over a case or set of documents to a cut-out. This would most likely occur, they believed, when Fuchs was in London, and there was an entry in his diary for another trip on 14 December to attend a meeting at Shell Mex House the next day to discuss the siting of a nuclear reactor.

Fuchs kept his travel plans up in the air until the very last moment, and the listeners at Newbury were on the alert for any information, which they would then phone in to London straight away. Arnold called to say that he thought Fuchs was going to travel by car, but he had no idea where he was going to stay. Erna spoke to her husband and told him that she might get a lift with Fuchs. They decided against this because she was not well. Finally, Fuchs was overheard asking his secretary to get a rail warrant. It was likely that he would try to catch the 13.48 train. He continued to work in his office, and then the watchers were told that he would be getting into Paddington at 21.30. Robertson, meanwhile, was attempting to arrange for Fuchs's telephone and room at the hotel to be bugged.

MI5 had a contact in the Strand Palace Hotel and he was trying to discover what room Fuchs would be staying in. The difficulty was that, with such a late arrival, the hotel would allocate him a room only when he checked in and not before. Major Denman, in charge of the GPO Special section, was told that no risks were to be taken and that if it wasn't possible to place a microphone in the room, then a telephone tap would be enough.

When Fuchs finally arrived at Paddington, the team of

watchers got on his trail. He caught the underground to Piccadilly and went into the American bar in Odeninos Imperial Hotel at the bottom of Regent Street. It was reported that he had a large whisky, then caught a bus to the Strand Palace Hotel. The tailing agents did not see him make contact with anybody. At the hotel the desk clerk could not find his reservation, so he was given Room 657. Shortly after Fuchs caught the lift to his floor, Rudolf Peierls arrived and was given the key to Room 818. There was no trace of any contact between them and Fuchs made no phone calls from his room.

Next morning the agents were on hand to observe that Fuchs had breakfast alone, and met Peierls only when they were both settling their bills at the desk. They went separately to the Ministry of Supply building. Fuchs left the meeting at midday, walked again around Soho, then along Old Compton Street, where he had a meal in a restaurant before heading to Hamleys, the large toy store in Regent Street, where he bought several toys. He continued his shopping expedition, buying some film for Erna's camera before he went to Paddington to catch the 5.15 train to Didcot. Once again, as far as the watchers were concerned it was a completely unproductive mission. MI5 was no further forward.

While Fuchs was being tailed through Soho and along Regent Street, a major case conference was taking place half a mile away at Leconfield House in Curzon Street. From MI5 the deputy director general, Guy Liddell, along with Dick White, Marriott, Martin, Robertson and Skardon met with Michael Perrin from the Department of Atomic Energy to discuss their next move. This was three weeks after Dick White had first minuted that it might be opportune to interview Fuchs.

On the question of moving Fuchs or dismissing him, Perrin reported that this might cause problems with the trades union, or with his colleagues at Harwell, or both, and this might lead to the suspicions about Fuchs becoming public. So if there was no course of action available other than removal or dismissal, then the reason to be used in public must be that Fuchs's father had moved to the Soviet zone of Germany and that this was a threat while Fuchs remained in his present secret and responsible job. Perrin also suggested that if the outcome of the interview led to Fuchs's removal to a university post, this might be arranged through Skinner, who was moving to Liverpool University and he would welcome Fuchs there.

After these preliminary discussions, the interrogation of Fuchs was set for 21 December. Skardon would go to Harwell and meet Cockcroft, who would then introduce him to Fuchs. How Skardon handled the interrogation was up to him, but if Fuchs gave any indication of being about to make a confession, and if he sought some form of assurance about his position if he did so, then Skardon was authorized to say that his position could only be improved by complete frankness. If Fuchs wanted to discuss the interrogation with someone afterwards, it would almost certainly be with Cockcroft or Arnold, and they should be told to deny knowledge of any reason for the interrogation other than the presence of Fuchs's father in the Soviet zone of Germany. How Cockcroft or Arnold should respond if Fuchs told them that it was because of a suspected security leak wasn't discussed.

The meeting concluded that it would be impractical for Fuchs to be sent on leave or removed from Harwell immediately after the interrogation and that they had no option but to allow him to continue to live and work there for the time being. The minutes of the meeting do not reflect any discussion about the possible outcome of the interrogation beyond this. There is an unspoken assumption in the record of this meeting that Fuchs will in some way reveal that he is a spy. Despite the lack of any further evidence produced by the surveillance over the last three months, his guilt was established in the minds of all those at the meeting. The investigation had gone too far for it to be called off. Portal, Kearton and the minister and his senior advisors, as well as Cockcroft, all knew that Fuchs was under investigation and it was impossible to alter that now. Fuchs was a marked man. The question was, could an interrogation by Skardon come up with the evidence to satisfy the questions raised by the FBI and justify the removal of one of the most able scientists from Britain's atomic programme?

Fuchs knew nothing of the imminent interrogation planned by the Security Service. On 20 December he worked at his office, went home and then spent the rest of the evening at a party thrown by the Davisons in their prefab.

The next morning he arrived at his office at about 9.30 after having a brief chat with Sir John Cockcroft. Whatever he said to Fuchs, Cockcroft was clearly unhappy about Skardon's visit. He spoke to Arnold a little later and told him to go and see Fuchs and tell him that someone would be coming down this morning to talk to him about his father's presence in the Soviet zone.

Arnold was panicked by this instruction. He telephoned Fuchs asking if he could come to see him, then phoned Robertson at Leconfield House to ask if MI5 approved of forewarning Fuchs. Robertson told him that they most certainly did not. Arnold said that he would tell Cockcroft this, but according to the transcript from the eavesdroppers, at eleven o'clock there was a knock on the door of Fuchs's office and he was told that someone was here to speak to him about his father. Fuchs went along to Arnold's office, where he was introduced to Skardon.

The two men faced each other. Jim Skardon was a tall, well-dressed man, a pipe smoker with a full moustache, exuding reliability, like a firm but friendly policeman; he was the embodiment of a popular image of the British state. Klaus Fuchs was shorter, thinner, with rimless spectacles and a slightly pedantic air about him, the classic foreign boffin. Fuchs at last could see a representative of the intelligence agency that, despite his long efforts, had finally been paying close attention to him for the past few weeks. Exactly why he was being followed, why his secretary was being questioned about his movements, why it was suddenly easier to get his phones repaired, he didn't know, but he knew that it pre-dated the move by his father to Leipzig. This was an interview that he had expected for some time, and now at last he might be able to discover what exactly had triggered the Security Service's interest. But he knew that he would have to be extremely careful and that he might soon be in serious jeopardy.

Skardon, for his part, was an intelligent man. He knew everything about Fuchs's activities over the past months, knew of his affairs, his disagreements, his habits while he was alone, and he might even suspect that Fuchs had spotted his tail, but he also knew that none of this was enough. Everything boiled down to one piece of evidence: a decoded Soviet signal from New York in 1944 that appeared to implicate Fuchs, from a source that was too secret to reveal. He must have known that his hand was very poor.

The MI5 officer broke the ice by saying that the presence of his father in the Soviet zone was a severe security risk and that he wanted to ask him a series of questions, which needed to be answered in order to assess the risk fairly.

Skardon reported later that Fuchs spent seventy-five minutes going over his family background and his life history, confirming the facts that Skardon knew already. He also added extra details that appeared to be truthful, but opened the way for Skardon to question him further if he suspected that Fuchs was concealing the truth. So he did not say that he was an activist in the KPD, merely that he was in a student organization affiliated to the communists. He volunteered the fact that after he had arrived in the UK he had travelled to Switzerland to visit his brother, in 1934 or 1935. This was the second reference Fuchs made to his brother, and when Skardon made no mention of the trip, Fuchs never referred to it again.

Fuchs was also candid about his associations with Hans Kahle in the Canadian internment camp and the fact that on their release he had paid a visit to him in London. Again, Skardon failed to respond to this bait. Fuchs continued his story, taking it up to 1943, where he was in New York and might have visited his sister.

It was at this point that Skardon played his only card. He told Fuchs that he had been in touch with a Soviet official or a Soviet agent and had passed on information about his work. Fuchs opened his mouth, then smiled and said, "I don't think so." He went on with his denials, saying that it did not make sense and could not think it likely that sundry pieces of information could help Russia. He had done all he could to help win the war, he said.

Skardon then questioned him about the entry in the Halperin diary, and Fuchs said he had never heard the name. Later, when Skardon mentioned that the diary also contained his sister's address, Fuchs remembered that Kristel had asked Halperin to send him scientific journals when he was in the internment camp.

Fuchs counter-attacked at this point by asking Skardon if all his information was like this.

Skardon now focused on the British Mission in New York, asking Fuchs about other people who worked there, who the non-scientific staff were, and what arrangements were made to reproduce and distribute the reports. Fuchs had a much better recall of this than Kearton had demonstrated to Perrin, and even had copies of most of the reports in the filing cabinet in his office. He went to get them.

They broke for lunch and on their return Skardon said

that he did not know what view the ministry would take about Fuchs's father, or whether Fuchs would be asked to leave, but a favourable response from the Security Service might enable Fuchs to remain in his post. Fuchs responded to this by saying that he did not know how to respond to such flimsy evidence. It was only the knowledge that Skardon could produce nothing else that had stopped him from becoming angry.

Fuchs now tried to raise the stakes slightly, by saying that if he was under this sort of suspicion he would find it impossible to keep working at Harwell and might resign, whatever the decision of the ministry. Skardon brought the conversation back to the question of Fuchs's father, asking him why he had raised the matter with Arnold? Fuchs replied that the Russians might seek to make some political capital out of his father's presence.

As the two rose and prepared to end the interrogation, Fuchs again raised the issue of resignation. Skardon replied with the clear threat that whatever the ministry decided to do about Fuchs, he would continue his investigation.

Fuchs remembered the interrogation differently. He said that Skardon told him there was circumstantial evidence that he, Fuchs, had given secret information to the Russians. He could not say what it was, nor could it be used in a court of law. Fuchs also claimed that Skardon told him he was authorized to say that if he admitted the charge, he would not be prosecuted but would be allowed to retain his position at Harwell. If he denied the charge he could not be prosecuted, but Skardon would advise the Ministry of Supply that Emil Fuchs's residence in East Germany was considered a threat to security and Fuchs might be asked to resign. Fuchs went on to allege that Skardon said he did not want this to seem like a threat, but that he would try to help him find another post in another government department.

These are two very different versions of the same

meeting, and if Fuchs is correct, then Skardon was offering him a substantial inducement. There is nothing in the files of the MI5 case to show that an offer of immunity was ever discussed, although that doesn't mean that it wasn't. Later, as we shall see, there is a clear admission by the head of B Branch, Dick White, that some offer was made to Fuchs. So Fuchs's account is probably correct.

On 21 December, however, Skardon returned to London empty-handed. He did not know what to do. In the report he wrote afterwards, he said he found it very difficult to give a conclusive view on whether Fuchs was innocent or guilty. If there was anything conclusive in his judgement, it was that no other candidate fitted the information that they had.

Fuchs returned to his office. Robertson had warned everybody listening to the telephone taps and bugs in Harwell to be on their guard for any immediate response by Fuchs. The listeners were once again disappointed. He didn't seek a meeting with Cockcroft, or with Arnold. He telephoned his dentist and spoke to the receptionist, asking for an appointment. His plate was broken and was causing him pain.

Fuchs had come out of the meeting in better shape than he went in and, whichever account of the meeting is true, he had discovered that if the Security Service had any evidence, then it was focused on what he had done in New York and it involved either his sister or Raymond. He had gained a lot more than Skardon had.

TWENTY-THREE

One Step Forward, Two Steps Back

O nly Klaus Fuchs knows what his thoughts were over Christmas 1949. For eighteen years he had been a member of the German Communist Party, and an active spy for Soviet intelligence agencies for nine of them. However much he had tried to prepare, mentally, for questioning by British or United States security agents, the first direct experience of interrogation and the knowledge that somewhere, somehow, his activities had been uncovered must have been deeply alarming. Nothing of this could be allowed to show, however. There is no record that he discussed Skardon's visit with anyone. Both Erna and Herbert Skinner came to his prefab on Christmas Eve for dinner, and he ate with them on Christmas Day. Rudolf and Genia Peierls came to visit over the holiday period, and there were social gatherings at the Skinners' and other couples' prefabs.

On 29 December it was Fuchs's birthday, and on the following day, the 30th, Skardon paid him another visit. He drove to Newbury in the van that collected the previous day's "take" from telephone taps and hidden microphones in Harwell, then he was picked up by Arnold in his car at the Rowstock roundabout, the place where one of the surveillance teams lurked in their Hillman saloon when Fuchs was expected to drive to London.

Fuchs was told by Arnold about the visit, so he was waiting for him. Skardon found him calm and self-possessed. He immediately asked Fuchs if there was anything he could say which might be of assistance to the Security Service, or if he had decided to make a clean breast of his spying for the Russians. Fuchs of course said no, he had nothing to say. He had given a lot of thought to what Skardon had told him on his first visit, but could not account for any of his allegations.

Skardon then asked what Fuchs could tell him about his sister, Kristel Heinemann. Fuchs said that his sister had gone to the United States in 1936, travelling there from Switzerland via England, where he had seen her. He had not seen her again until the Christmas of 1943, and then another time before he had gone to Los Alamos, perhaps in June or July 1944. They wrote to each other about twice a year. Beyond that he could say very little about her. He certainly knew no one in New York who could be said to be a mutual friend, and he had no idea of how his sister had made contact with Halperin to arrange scientific journals reaching him in the internment camp in Canada.

Failing to draw blood there, Skardon changed his line of questioning to Fuchs's finances, about which he had absolutely no information but was no doubt hoping that Fuchs might trip himself up. Fuchs had received only token payments from the Russians, of course, and answered honestly that he had been paid by the Department of Scientific and Industrial Research and hadn't done anything for which he might have been paid by anyone else.

Shifting his ground again, Skardon asked about Fuchs's work for Kellex Corporation at Columbia University and if he had made friends with any students. The only person he had any social contact with, replied Fuchs, was Dr. Karl Cohen at the laboratory there; apart from that, he had almost no friends in New York. Certainly no one from his past life in the United Kingdom, or from the German exile community, such as Hans Kahle, had pursued him and tried to re-establish contact. He had kept his departure for Los Alamos a secret from everybody, although Dr. Cohen might have guessed because he, Fuchs, had dissembled a bit. But he had never told anyone where he was moving to.

Skardon was getting nowhere. He was an old enough hand to know that pressing the matter any further would merely reveal his desperation. He told Fuchs that the ministry would undoubtedly, although with reluctance (these were Skardon's words), decide to dispense with his services, because his father's presence in Leipzig did form a substantial security risk. This would be the reason for his dismissal, and he should keep any other issues to himself. He said that he was sure Fuchs would find himself settled in the atmosphere of a university, but, he warned, "it was quite certain that I should desire to question him again." Fuchs replied that he was willing to see Skardon at any time, and Skardon told him that he could always be contacted through Arnold. Fuchs thanked him.

So another interrogation ended, and once more Skardon left empty-handed. Fuchs, on the other hand, had learned that Skardon wanted to talk only about his work in New York. The questioning about his sister was sensitive, but Skardon had not pursued it, and the other questions about Dr. Cohen, Kellex Corporation and any other friends in New York were clearly nothing but a fishing expedition. Fuchs knew how wide of the mark any of that was. The second interview might have been expected to cover ground that had not been covered before, but Skardon had still concentrated on New York. No accusations had been levelled about leaks of information from his work in Birmingham for Tube Alloys, Harwell or Los Alamos. The belief was growing in Fuchs's mind that any knowledge that MI5 had was solely confined to some reports he had handed over in New York, and he had already been told that what evidence they had could not be used in a court of law. The threat of an ongoing investigation was extremely serious, but Fuchs must have now thought that he would be able to survive it.

The British government now had to decide what to do. MI5 had reported back that their suspected spy had not cracked. There was no confession, and the utmost secrecy about the decrypted Soviet signals meant that nothing more could be done. But Fuchs posed far too much of a risk to allow him to remain at Harwell, and the FBI would soon be asking what the British were up to if Fuchs remained in his post. Lord Portal and Michael Perrin at the Department of Atomic Energy met the deputy director general of MI5 on 5 January, when they decided that Fuchs should be asked to resign on the grounds that his father was too great a security risk.

Later that day an internal MI5 meeting took place. Here it was agreed that once Fuchs had been told that he was to resign, the surveillance operation could be scaled down. The followers would be assigned to other targets, the electronic surveillance of his prefab would be ended, and there would no longer be live monitoring of his telephone calls. These would still be intercepted, as would his mail, but his conversations would be recorded and transcribed twenty-four hours later in London.

It fell to Cockcroft, as director of Harwell, to deal with Fuchs face to face. It was not a task that he wanted. He never claimed any great friendship with Fuchs, but they had both worked on the Tube Alloys project, he had met him when Fuchs visited Montreal in 1945, and during his work at Harwell he had come to believe that he was a great asset to Britain's nuclear programme. Now here he was, a brilliant physicist in his own right, telling Fuchs he had to go, repeating some shabby half-truth at the behest of some senior bureaucrats. He delayed meeting Fuchs for some days, and when he did so he was far too much of a gentleman to wield the knife very effectively.

Cockcroft asked Fuchs to come to his office on 10 January and told him that he must leave Harwell and transfer himself somewhere else. The Department of Atomic Energy had taken the advice of MI5 that the presence of Fuchs's father in the Russian zone presented too great a security risk. Cockcroft said that he would help him find an alternative job, and suggested that perhaps Skinner would be able to take him on at Liverpool University, or there was a vacant post in theoretical physics at Adelaide University and Professor Oliphant might be able to help out in getting it for Fuchs. Fuchs said that he had been thinking of moving to a university, but had hoped to stay on until the fast reactor had produced results. Cockcroft told him that the only other people to know about this decision were Portal, Perrin and Arnold. He then went on to say that the only chance of the Security Service changing its advice was that Fuchs should give every assistance in providing full information about himself, his life and his background.

Fuchs had heard this argument from Skardon already and had not reacted to it then. He didn't react to it now when he heard it repeated by Cockcroft, who knew less about the issue than Skardon did. Cockcroft was merely saying what he had been told to say. It doesn't seem that he was overly impressed with the concerns of MI5 and Perrin at the Department of Energy, or that he took them very seriously.

Perrin had earlier spoken to Cockcroft about a conference that was being organized in February to discuss the available information about the Russian nuclear explosion and he warned him that Fuchs would not be able to attend. He urged Cockcroft to find a successor for Fuchs as quickly as he could. Cockcroft did not take this advice. He wasn't prepared to push Fuchs, and told him that there was nothing very urgent about his departure. His idea was that Fuchs should take six months' leave of absence, starting around Easter time, which meant that he would be in Harwell at least until the first week of April. So the meeting ended, leaving Fuchs with the clear impression that the matter was not particularly urgent.

MI5, however, were appalled at the outcome of the meeting, which they had believed would lead to Fuchs's rapid dismissal. Marriott went to a meeting at the Department of Energy three days later and told both Perrin and Cockcroft that the idea of Fuchs remaining at Harwell for another three months was disturbing; so too was the added complication of the suggestion that Fuchs might go to Australia. Cockcroft replied that when news of Fuchs's departure from Harwell got round, he wanted to be able to say that there were serious security reasons for it. He expected that he would be criticized by both Professor Chadwick and Lord Cherwell for letting Fuchs go, and possibly by some others, and he didn't want them to start agitating against the Department of Energy about it. Marriott responded that that wouldn't be necessary if Fuchs's departure was on the basis of his own resignation. He didn't say so, but the implication was that Cockcroft had fudged the whole issue.

MI5's operation against Fuchs had become a complete dog's breakfast. They had discovered no more evidence than they possessed at the start of their investigation in September. Fuchs had been warned that he was under suspicion, and so would stop any further contact with Russian intelligence. Word of his departure from Harwell and the alleged reason for it would inevitably become a topic of gossip and rumour amongst the nuclear establishment, and it would surely reach the press, which meant MI5 would have the British government and the FBI breathing down their necks, while at the same time Fuchs would still be on the payroll at Harwell. The director general, Percy Sillitoe, was anxious to get MI5 out of the firing line as much as possible and wrote a letter to Sir Archibald Rowlands, permanent secretary at the Ministry of Supply, which was in overall charge of the Department of Atomic Energy. He pointed out that if Fuchs remained at Harwell for any length of time, "it was a very heavy burden on our resources of investigation which frankly I can well do without." He went on to express the frustration that was felt at every level in MI5:

> We have used in this case every kind of resource available to us for the purpose of investigation . . . Since it has been generally agreed that Fuchs continued employment is a constant threat to security, and since our own investigation has produced no dividends I should be grateful if you would arrange for Fuchs departure from Harwell as soon as is decently possible.

A few days before Sillitoe wrote this letter, and after Fuchs and Cockcroft had met to discuss his future, Skardon had paid another visit, his third, to speak to Fuchs. The FBI had been pressing MI5 for Fuchs's address in New York, because one of the Venona decrypts appeared to refer to an agent visiting an apartment. There was the chance, however slim, that somebody there, a resident or a doorman, might be able to give a description.

Skardon came straight to the point and asked Fuchs for his address in New York. Fuchs immediately told him that he had stayed at the Barbizon Plaza. Skardon said he was grateful for that information, but he knew that it was the second hotel that he had stayed in; he was more interested in the address of the private residence that he moved to after that. Fuchs said he might need a map, and Skardon of course had brought one with him. Fuchs scrutinized it and decided that the apartment building was on West 77th Street, between Columbus and Amsterdam Avenues. He said that when he left New York he probably gave as his forwarding address the Washington office of the British Mission.

Skardon then asked Fuchs more questions about his contacts with people at Columbia University, in particular Dr. Karl Cohen, head of the laboratory that was working on the diffusion plant for the Kellex Corporation. Fuchs said that he had become friends with him and had visited his home, and that Dr. Cohen had been to his apartment. No one else outside the British Mission would have known anything about his private life in New York. When he made the move to Los Alamos he went to say goodbye to Dr. Cohen and the other people in the laboratory.

Then Fuchs reiterated that he had never passed information on to the Soviets or their representatives. If he was speaking the truth, replied Skardon, then he would make inquiries to clear him. Asked about what his present situation was, Fuchs said that he had been told that he must go, but that he had not yet made any effort to find another job. He might take some leave, but had made no plans for the moment.

Before leaving, Skardon told Fuchs that MI5 had information that a representative of the Russians had called at his apartment after he had left for Los Alamos. This was the reason he was asking for the address, so that direct inquiries could be made there. Fuchs showed no alarm at this. It was extremely unlikely, he responded, that such a visit had taken place.

So for the third time Skardon retreated from Harwell with nothing. The consensus amongst the Security Service officers who had handled the investigation was that they would not be able to gain any evidence of his espionage.

They were alarmed at the cavalier way that Cockcroft had handled the question of Fuchs's resignation but, looking at the results of a three-month investigation, it was without doubt time to wind down their surveillance operation. It was a miscalculation, but an understandable one.

Fuchs surely gained the impression from Skardon's third visit that he was almost home and dry. Three times he had been questioned by the man from MI5, and everything had focused on his time in New York. The inability of Skardon, in the face of Fuchs's blanket denials, to come up with any further evidence suggested that they had very little to go on at all. Furthermore, the lack of any urgency from Cockcroft could be an indication that the case MI5 had against Fuchs was not that compelling. He surely felt safer now than he had at any time since becoming aware that he was being followed.

He hadn't told Skardon that he was thinking of taking a few days' leave, but he was, and he probably looked forward to it now with some sense of relief that the threat from MI5 had eased. There were other problems, however, that he would have to confront in the next few days. One of these was his relationship with Erna Skinner.

Fuchs could have done several things for a brief holiday, and at one time thought that he might go abroad with Mr. and Mrs. Rennie, neighbours of his in Harwell. Arnold had reported this and MI5 had discussed the possibility that Fuchs might use the trip as an opportunity to seek asylum in Russia, but had come to the conclusion that they had no grounds for taking his passport away. They were saved the complications of a foreign trip, however, because Fuchs decided to take a holiday at a more prosaic destination. On 16 January he went to the Palm Court Hotel in Richmond, south-west London, where he checked in for three nights.

He was with a lady companion, it was later reported, and the person who observed them subsequently gave an accurate description of her to MI5. But MI5 knew about this. They decided that, as the operation was running down, there was no need to follow Fuchs to the hotel, nor any need to make the effort to place a phone tap or microphone in his room. They were helped to this decision by the knowledge that Fuchs's mysterious companion was none other than Erna Skinner, his mistress from Harwell. MI5 did not refrain from eavesdropping on the couple's stay out of any sense of delicacy. Their judgement of Mrs. Skinner was harsh: "She is a Jewess of Central European origin, married to Professor Skinner since 10.1.31, whose reputation and reliability leave something to be desired." No, their decision not to concern themselves about this brief encounter in Richmond was because "There is however no evidence that she has been in any way involved in Fuchs espionage activities."

This was true, but MI5 once more missed a trick.

TWENTY-FOUR

Confession

The events of the next few days are obscure. Fuchs and Erna Skinner stayed together at the hotel in Richmond for two days. They dined in the hotel's restaurant and were open about where they were. Erna left a message for Herbert, who was in Liverpool, explaining when she would be back at Harwell, and Fuchs left his telephone number at the hotel in case he was needed for any emergencies.

Both of their lives were in flux. Herbert Skinner was moving to Liverpool in a few months' time and Erna was going with him. It was obvious from the tone of her conversations on the telephone that she was not happy about this, and it was probably because she did not relish the thought of seeing less of Fuchs. Liverpool may not have been especially vibrant and cosmopolitan, but it was surely better than the isolated, claustrophobic life of Harwell. Fuchs might have been trying to console Erna, or he may have broached the subject directly, but he told her that he too would be leaving Harwell soon. It is pointless to speculate any further about the way that their conversation developed over those two days, but what is certain is that by the end of their stay together Fuchs had told Erna the whole background to the meeting with Cockcroft and the reasons why he was being asked to resign from Harwell and seek another post. He had also gone a lot farther. He admitted to her that he had passed to the Soviet Union information about the diffusion project while he was in New York. It may be that he volunteered this information to Erna and that they discussed the possibility of his admitting it to Cockcroft, relying on the assurance that if he helped the Security Service he could stay at Harwell. We don't know if their discussions went this far, but what we do know, from a letter written by Herbert Skinner to Arnold in 1952, is that Erna knew about some of Fuchs's activities.

They checked out of the hotel and returned to Harwell. There, Erna told Herbert Skinner everything. She didn't tell him about her affair with Fuchs, or that she had stayed at the hotel with him; he knew that anyway. She told him what he didn't know, which was that Fuchs had been instructed to leave Harwell unless he admitted to his contacts with Soviet intelligence in New York. Herbert said in the same letter to Arnold that Erna was told this around 18 January when his wife and Fuchs were staying at the hotel. He also said that he believed that Fuchs had also told Cockcroft. It is clear that at that point Fuchs had admitted only to handing over some papers from his New York diffusion work. In the letter, Skinner makes the distinction very clearly. "I know K confessed to Erna about the Diff. plant a day or two prior to Jan 19th (the date he was considered for election to the Royal Society. This is confidential but did you know it?) . . . Cockcroft also told me about the Diff. plant disclosure about Jan 21st."

Arnold didn't know anything about these conversations. He had been on leave from Harwell because his mother had died. MI5 knew nothing of this because they had only kept up the monitoring of Fuchs's and the Skinners' telephones, and knew nothing of any other conversations that Fuchs might have had. The first indication that Arnold and Robertson at MI5 had that the Fuchs affair had spread its ripples out into Harwell was when Skinner told Arnold that he wanted to discuss the Fuchs question with him, and also wanted to see Sir John Cockcroft to discuss the same issue. Arnold was certain that Fuchs had discussed the matter with Skinner and thought that Cockcroft had let slip something because of a remark that "he wished Fuchs had been more cooperative". Skinner spoke to Arnold and wanted to see him on the morning of the 20th, but Arnold delayed until five that evening. At 3.30 Arnold telephoned his contact, Robertson at Leconfield House, seeking advice about what to do. At that point, Arnold believed Skinner wanted to talk about Fuchs leaving Harwell, nothing more.

Robertson rushed to consult Dick White and Marriott. They agreed a line, and at four Robertson was on the phone again to Arnold. It was vital that Arnold admit to nothing more than the official position that they had already agreed: that there had been a meeting with a security official; it was in connection with Fuchs's father; and that because of the presence of his father in the Soviet zone, the authorities believed Fuchs should resign. In reply, Arnold said that he was unwilling to admit to Skinner that he even knew about the resignation unless it was clear that Skinner was already aware that he had knowledge of it.

Robertson told Arnold he must also go to see Cockcroft and ensure that he took the same line, and they must certainly not admit to Skinner that there might be any other reasons for Fuchs leaving. After telling Arnold what to do, Robertson then got on the phone to Perrin to ask if he thought it advisable for Perrin himself to speak to Cockcroft to emphasize what Arnold would also tell him. Perrin replied that talking to Cockcroft would achieve nothing. He had, he said, already underlined that he must not mention anything of the matter to Skinner. Perrin's injunctions were clearly falling on deaf ears, and he perhaps suspected as much.

The situation with Fuchs, and the failure of the investigation into his spying, was threatening to spin out of control. If Skinner knew that Fuchs was resigning and wanted to beard Arnold and Cockcroft about it, then it could not be long before others in Harwell, and close friends of Fuchs like Peierls, would also become aware of what was happening. The lid would blow off another damaging spy scandal in Britain's highly secret nuclear programme. MI5 had very few ways to stop that happening, however. Cockcroft seemed incapable of understanding the seriousness of the situation, and Perrin thought that any efforts on his part to talk to Cockcroft would be a waste of time. The case officers at MI5 appear to have done nothing but rely on reports from Arnold about how the crisis was developing. On the 20th, which was a Friday, instructions had already been given to end the microphone surveillance on Fuchs and withdraw the watchers. They couldn't quickly be reactivated over the weekend.

MI5 heard nothing further until the Monday, when Arnold telephoned again. Fuchs had spoken to him on Sunday and asked to have a long, quiet talk. They had arranged to have lunch and were due to meet in two hours' time. He was phoning Robertson to ask for guidance. Robertson phoned back at 12.15, a quarter of an hour before Arnold and Fuchs were to meet. The advice that Robertson gave him was that Arnold should do his best to say as little as possible. He should try to lead Fuchs on and get him to reveal as much as he could before pointing out that what he had said would have to be repeated to Skardon. If Fuchs asked for any guarantee of immunity in the event of frankness, Arnold must point out that he had no power to offer it.

During the conversation Arnold told Robertson more about some possible background to the meeting. Mary Buneman, the wife of Oscar Buneman, a scientist working in Fuchs's division, had recently had an affair with another scientist and consequently, according to Arnold, had "become temporarily deranged". She was living for the moment with the Skinners. Fuchs, as a friend of the Bunemans' and as head of the Theoretical Division, was worried about the situation and had spoken to Arnold about it. So too had Erna Skinner, who had asked Arnold to call in on her to talk about it. It was a delicate situation and he did not want to discuss it over the phone.

Robertson was taken aback at this. It was utterly beyond him why Arnold should be involved in the personal affairs of the Bunemans at all. How could the urgent issue of a Soviet spy be mixed up with the problems of two people of whom he had never heard? Arnold told him that he was friends with the people involved, but there was another point to his account of extra-marital affairs at Harwell, which is that when Erna Skinner had asked to see him she had also said that she wanted to talk to him about Klaus Fuchs and had made a reference to his integrity. Robertson told him that he must say that he could not discuss the matter at all with Mrs. Skinner. Arnold agreed, but pointed out that the news of Fuchs's resignation and the purported reason behind it was beginning to spread in Harwell.

Later that afternoon, after Fuchs and Arnold had met for lunch, Arnold telephoned MI5 and spoke to Robertson yet again. Fuchs wanted to have another meeting with Skardon and Arnold said that although he did not want to be too optimistic, he thought that Fuchs wanted to talk, and talk a lot. Arnold believed—and these words must have come like a startling bombshell to the ears of Robertson—"that Fuchs might be ready to make a confession".

After rapid and urgent consultation between Arnold,

Skardon and Robertson, it was agreed that the interview should take place in Fuchs's house at Harwell at eleven o'clock on Tuesday, 24 January, the next day. Skardon would take a train to Didcot, where Arnold would meet him in a car.

Only Skardon's account of his next meeting with Fuchs exists. It cannot have been an easy morning for either of them. Skardon really had nothing more with which to confront Fuchs and could not have been expecting a great deal out of the confrontation. For his part, Fuchs must have been trying to work out what exactly he had to say to Skardon, and Skardon's account suggests that he was regretting his decision to meet the man from MI5 once more.

Skardon started the conversation. "You asked to see me," he said "and here I am."

"Yes, it is rather up to me now," was Fuchs's reply.

Then he once more launched into an account of his life, along the lines of the very first interview. He made one change, however. For the first time he talked about his underground work in the KPD in Germany. However, he didn't confess to any espionage. Skardon does not go into any detail about what Fuchs actually said, but he wrote that he believed that Fuchs was under some stress.

Skardon then said to Fuchs that he had told a long story that suggested a motive for various acts; he had not said anything about the acts themselves. Why didn't Fuchs unburden his mind, clear his conscience by telling the full story? At this remark, Fuchs reacted, saying, "I will never be persuaded by you to talk." It seemed to Skardon then that it was going to be another abortive meeting.

They went off to lunch at this stage; again, there is no account of their conversation, although Skardon says that Fuchs appeared abstracted, as though he were resolving things in his own mind. Towards the end of the meal, Fuchs said that he wanted to go back to his prefab and when they arrived he announced that he believed it would be in his best interests to answer Skardon's questions. He said that he had a clear conscience but that he was very worried about the effect of his behaviour on the friendships he had formed at Harwell.

Skardon said that he then put certain questions to Fuchs. There is no trace in his report of what he thought as he listened to Fuchs's replies, but he must have been utterly astounded. He had approached Fuchs in the beginning with the scanty and vague evidence that a British scientist had contact with Soviet intelligence in New York in 1944. Fuchs now proceeded to describe his history of passing atomic research to the Soviet Union over a period of seven years. It was the equivalent for Skardon of breaking open a child's piggy bank to discover a hoard of gold sovereigns. He had no time to be surprised or to reflect on the stunning information that Fuchs was now revealing. He was struggling to keep up with the flow and scribble down legible notes to take back to his colleagues at MI5.

Fuchs could have limited his confession to the specific time and place for which Skardon had shown he had some evidence—some meetings with Harry Gold in New York. He chose, however, to outline the full details of his spying, from the time when he handed over information about his work on the MAUD Committee Report, through his work for the British Mission in New York, and at Los Alamos, and then again in London. The worst thing he had done, he said, was hand over complete details of the atom bomb—as though there was anything more important he could have revealed to the NKGB.

There were some details that he left out. He claimed that his spying started in 1942, and he was at pains to stress that his sister, Kristel, knew nothing of his illegal association with the Russians. She may have seen something in Boston, he said, but would have believed that to be merely a continuation of his underground activity, in which she had also taken part in Germany. However, he gave details about several of the locations where he had met agents from the NKGB.

At about four o'clock in the afternoon they parted after agreeing to meet again.

Skardon knew that he must immediately tell his superiors at MI5 about this extraordinary change in their fortunes. He telephoned from an office in Harwell and spoke to Marriott, who immediately passed on the news to Dick White. Skardon was ordered to come back to London to make a full report at a meeting in Leconfield House in the morning. He was also told to tell Sir John Cockcroft briefly what had happened, although Skardon delegated this task to Arnold.

While Skardon was travelling back from Didcot to Paddington, the men at Leconfield House were congratulating themselves on their success. Marriott telephoned Perrin and told him that Fuchs had confessed. Then the group of four—Dick White, Marriott, Storrier and Robertson—laid their plans for the next stage of their pursuit. They ordered that the telephone taps and the microphone facility should be operating by the time that Skardon was due to meet Fuchs again, which was Thursday the 26th; that the twenty-four-hour watch on the electronic surveillance was to be reinstated; and the question of physical surveillance should be considered at the meeting in the morning.

The big question on their minds was what to do if Fuchs decided to make a run for it? Could he be prevented from leaving the country? This of course brought out into the open what they all understood. It was now possible to charge Fuchs, and to obtain a warrant for his arrest if he did decide to flee.

The next morning at 10.30 a meeting assembled at MI5

in the office of director general Sir Percy Sillitoe. Skardon made his report and Dick White outlined their discussions of the previous evening. The issue of electronic surveillance was brought up. The technical staff had advised against trying to set up the monitoring staff at Newbury again, and Skardon said that he found it an embarrassment. Why he should isn't mentioned, but clearly he did not want what he was saying to Fuchs to be recorded.

Sillitoe then said that the most important objective of the continuing conduct of the case was gaining further information about Fuchs and his contacts. He would tell Sir Archibald Rowlands, permanent secretary at the Ministry of Supply, what they had decided and ask that he take no further action in the case.

Later that same day, at half past four, Michael Perrin arrived at Leconfield House and joined a meeting with White, Marriott, Skardon and Robertson. White brought him up to date, then explained that MI5 was intent on finding out as much as possible about Fuchs's spying and who his accomplices were. This was as much in the interests of the Department of Atomic Energy as the Security Service. Perrin accepted the argument, but was anxious about what that meant for Fuchs's continued presence at Harwell. He wanted him out as soon as possible. He would think about sending Fuchs on indefinite sick leave as soon as MI5 had what they wanted. He then raised the possibility that he should interrogate Fuchs as well so that he could find out precise particulars of the scientific intelligence that he had handed over and details of any questions that the Russians had asked.

What, Perrin wanted to know, was the possibility of prosecuting Fuchs? White pointed out that there were problems with that. The statement Fuchs had given to Skardon was not given under a caution and would not be admissible as evidence. There was also the problem that Fuchs had been led to believe that if he told the Security Service the truth he might be able to stay at Harwell. So it might be argued legally that the statement was obtained by an inducement.

Skardon, however, thought that it might be possible to get Fuchs to make another formal statement, so a prosecution deserved serious consideration. He believed that Fuchs still had confidence that he would be able to remain at Harwell; he considered himself the "lynchpin" of the organization and in his present frame of mind it was inconceivable to him that he might be removed.

So Perrin left, making his way from Curzon Street to the Strand to report to Lord Portal, and the MI5 officers went to prepare for another, the fifth, encounter between Fuchs and Skardon the next day at Harwell.

The next morning, Thursday, 26 January, Fuchs went to talk to Arnold in his office. He wanted to know if Skardon really understood his position at Harwell and his importance in the declassification conference that was scheduled for later in the year. Arnold said that he was certain Skardon understood this, and then he asked whether Fuchs had disclosed important information to the Russians.

Fuchs now told Arnold everything. He had given information to the Soviet Union about initiators, the new super-bomb, and much of his work on the problems of diffusion barriers. It's unlikely that Arnold understood what this really meant in all its technical detail; he did know, however, that what he had heard was extremely serious. In a statement that he made later, Arnold says, "I told him that this was a dreadful blow to me and that it hurt me deeply. He seemed much affected."

When Skardon arrived, Fuchs seemed to confirm the interrogator's previous assessment that he believed he would be able to stay at Harwell. He said that he was most anxious that his position should be resolved as quickly as possible and he wondered whether the authorities would clearly understand his position. At this point, according to his own account, Skardon asked Fuchs whether he would like to make a written statement, incorporating any details he thought might be borne in mind. There were three possibilities: Fuchs could write the memorandum himself, or dictate a statement to a secretary, or he, Skardon, could write down a statement at Fuchs's dictation. Fuchs said that he would prefer it if Skardon took a statement down. They arranged to meet again, in London the next day, to do this.

Skardon then continued his written account with details of questions about Fuchs's spying. Again there is no other record of the conversation and it remains a mystery how Skardon was able to convince Fuchs that he should make a statement while at the same time allowing him to think that would be the end of it, that there would be no adverse consequences. The only indication that Skardon said anything to Fuchs about a prosecution is contained in the minutes of a telephone conversation between Dick White and Perrin the next morning. A paragraph has been removed by the Security Service, but it is a typed document written and signed by Robertson. It is clear from the tenor of the conversation that White and Skardon thought they were close to springing the trap on Fuchs. After telling Perrin that Skardon was going to continue the interview later that day in an attempt to obtain a voluntary statement, White emphasized that this was of overriding importance, bearing as it did on the possibility of a successful prosecution. He went on to say—and this was not included in Skardon's brief note of the interrogation—that Fuchs had refused to recognize the fact that espionage was an offence. Fuchs drew attention to the information that he had supplied to the British, information that he had originally obtained in the United States. Whether this was a reference to the "super" or to the other information he had given to William Penney and his group at Fort Halstead, White doesn't say. It is likely that he didn't know.

All that we can know about Fuchs's state of mind on whether he would be able to stay at Harwell is from the transcript of a tap on the Skinners' telephone. After his meeting with Skardon on the 26th was finished, Fuchs phoned Erna. She asked him how he was and he replied that he thought it was under control. Fuchs had lost control completely, of course, but his reply suggests that both he and Erna had already discussed the pros and cons of a confession—a discussion that had started during their weekend at Richmond.

As we have seen, Herbert Skinner was agitated at the thought of Fuchs resigning and he was, according to Skardon, announcing to anyone who would listen that he was taking steps to see that Fuchs remained at Harwell. White was concerned that Skinner might travel up to London to talk to Lord Portal and Sir Archibald Rowlands, who were meeting on the 27th to discuss the case. Perrin told White that he would go to see Skinner and tell him that it was in the best interests of Harwell and Fuchs that he, Skinner, should say nothing, not to Cockcroft, Fuchs or anybody else.

Fuchs took the train to Paddington the next morning, Friday, 27 January, where Skardon met him and they drove to Room 055 in the War Office building in Whitehall. Skardon wrote in his report that he cautioned Fuchs and asked him if he still wanted him to write down his statement. Fuchs said, "Yes I quite understand and I would like you to carry on."

He started once more, as he had at the first meeting where he had confessed to spying, from the beginning—that is, from the time that he was born in Rüsselsheim on 29 December 1911. For five closely typed pages, Fuchs admits to spying for the Soviet Union, but devotes much of his statement to explanations of his motives and his frame of mind at each turn of events as he changed from a student in exile to a theoretical physicist with exceptional knowledge and talent. It is less of a confession than a statement of what has driven him to where he is now, and what limits he still desires to set on that process. It is a statement made in the belief that there is still something to debate. He says that the first thing for him is to make sure that Harwell will suffer as little as possible, and that his friends retain some part of their friendship for him. He adds that he realizes that he will have to provide the extent of the information which he gave, and confesses to providing details about the design of the plutonium bomb. As for the Russian contacts, there is nobody he knows by name. "There are people whom I know by sight whom I trusted with my life, and who trusted me with theirs," he says, "and I do not know that I shall be able to do anything that might in the end give them away."

What he had said was enough to condemn him, as it did, but despite what Skardon wrote about Fuchs being cautioned, it is hard to believe that he really understood at this point what he had done. After he had gone over his statement he once more returned to the question of his future, telling Skardon he was anxious about what it was to be, and that he did not want there to be any delay in getting the matter cleared up. All that Skardon would say in reply was that the question was under active consideration. He went on to say that he was prepared to meet Fuchs over the weekend, but thought he needed a rest, and then suggested he meet Perrin to go over the technical details of his spying on Monday the 30th.

Fuchs did little over the weekend, or at least little that was picked up by the microphones and telephone taps. The listeners heard him moving about, stoking the fire, and perhaps tearing up and burning pieces of paper, although the transcriber admitted this was conjecture. There was an unbalanced sense of suspicion on the part of the listeners and also of Wing Commander Arnold, who reported to Robertson for instructions at the slightest excuse. He was, for example, alarmed to observe that Fuchs had collected three orderly stacks of documents on the desk in his office. Robertson pointed out that this was perfectly normal behaviour.

Fuchs and Perrin met on the Monday, in the same room at the War Office in Whitehall where Fuchs had confessed to Skardon on the previous Friday. This time the records contain nothing about Fuchs's motivations. The record of his confession is a detailed, blow-by-blow account of the information that he had handed over to the NKGB, and it must have made Perrin's brain reel. Although Perrin must have known something about Fuchs's work, to see it described, from the beginning of the MAUD Committee's Report in 1941 to recent theories of the hydrogen bomb, was a forceful reminder of his great depth of knowledge about nuclear weapons. To be reminded that Fuchs had worked out the physics of the initiator, the "urchin", that small, precisely engineered ball of polonium and beryllium at the heart of the atom bomb, merely emphasized the intellectual difference between Fuchs and the two men who sat opposite him. Skardon had been impressed when he discovered, the first time he interrogated Fuchs, that he had written the majority of the New York Mission's reports; yet he had recently described Fuchs as arrogant in his certainty that he was too important to Harwell to be dismissed. He now heard that Fuchs had a lot to be arrogant about.

This did not matter to Skardon and Perrin, of course. What mattered was that what he had told the engineers at Los Alamos and William Penney and his colleagues in Fort Halstead, he had also passed on to the Russians. This was the point of the exercise, as Dick White had explained to

Perrin. What Fuchs was recounting was evidence that would send him to prison.

The Soviet Union had already exploded its own atomic weapon. What Fuchs had told them was of limited intelligence value now. However, Perrin was going to attend a conference in the next few days that would discuss the available evidence about the Soviet bomb. He had told Sir John Cockcroft that Fuchs must not attend it, but he could not resist asking him his opinion now. Fuchs replied that in the light of the information he had given to the NKGB he would have expected the recent Russian blast to be a plutonium bomb. He thought this was confirmed by the measurements on the airborne fission products that had been collected. There was some doubt, however, because of the lack of chemical evidence for plutonium in the cloud. Even in the darkest moments Fuchs had a respect for scientific truth.

The meeting with Fuchs went on for four hours, with a break for lunch. When it was over Fuchs returned to Harwell, where he spoke to Erna and was told that Herbert was in bed with exhaustion.

The next day Fuchs again went to the War Office to see Skardon, who had a series of photographs of known Russian embassy staff and illegal agents to show him. Fuchs, however, identified no one. Later that day, while Fuchs returned to Harwell, Dick White, Marriott, Skardon and Robertson met Commander Leonard Burt of Special Branch to discuss Fuchs's arrest. It seems remarkable that, despite Skardon allegedly cautioning him, Fuchs did not realize that his arrest was imminent. His circumstances, however, were remarkable.

In his office at Harwell he was consulted about various secret programmes to do with the nuclear reactors under construction. Bizarrely, on 30 January, Otto Frisch telephoned him. He was about to give a talk on the BBC about the hydrogen bomb and he needed advice for security reasons about what he could and couldn't say. He had spoken to Sir John Cockcroft, and Cockcroft had told him to seek the advice of either Fuchs or Peierls. On that very same day Cockcroft was giving a formal statement to Bernard Hill, the legal advisor to MI5, to be used in the case against Fuchs. Fuchs was not aware of this but suggested anyway that Frisch speak to Peierls. He didn't explain to Frisch why he didn't have the time, but he was of course about to go and tell Perrin what he himself had told the Russians about the hydrogen bomb.

Fuchs lived now in a strange bubble, made up of Harwell, his own work and the few friends that he had, who were as separate from the world outside as he was. The fear, the sense of great danger, the awful consequences of discovery that had accompanied him when he met Harry Gold in Santa Fe, seemed to have left him. Yet just a few days ago he had told Skardon that he would not reveal the contacts whose lives he had held in his hands and who had held his life in theirs. Now he was convinced that he was in no danger. MI5 was acutely aware of this. Robertson warned Skardon on the phone that day that it was "important to keep Fuchs in his present frame of mind, in which he does not suspect any punitive action against him."

In fact, a memorandum on the case was presented to the prime minister, Clement Attlee, on 31 January. It claimed that Fuchs was in possession of considerable scientific secrets and that, as a British citizen, the only way to prevent him leaving the country was by bringing a criminal case against him. The legal advisor to MI5 believed there was a case to answer, and the Security Service asked the prime minister's permission to pass the papers to the director of public prosecutions.

But it was not such an open-and-shut case as the memo suggested. As we have seen, Dick White was very concerned about the manipulation of Fuchs, and the submission to the director of public prosecutions tried to deal with some uncomfortable facts. Skardon's caution had not been a correct legal one. He had merely warned Fuchs that he did not have to make a formal statement, and should not do so under any inducement. The problem was that Cockcroft had specifically said in his own statement that he told Fuchs, under the instructions of the Security Service, that if he cooperated he might be able to stay at Harwell. White argued that Fuchs had made his statement voluntarily and that anyway, the possible offer to Fuchs, which White does not deny, was suggested to Cockcroft at a meeting with MI5 when they believed that Fuchs might have passed a few documents to the NKGB. It could not possibly apply in the knowledge of the full extent of his activities. The director of public prosecutions bought it, and authorized the arrest of Fuchs.

On 2 February Fuchs was working in his office. He received a phone call from Peierls, who had heard that Fuchs would not be at the meeting about the Russian atomic test. Peierls was letting him know he would not be there either. Later that morning Fuchs was in a meeting with another scientist who was working on the development of the Springfields uranium refining facility when he was phoned by Perrin. He wanted to know if Fuchs could possibly manage to come up to see him by three o'clock that afternoon? Fuchs said that he supposed he could if it was really urgent. Perrin assured him it was; he should come to his room at Shell Mex House on the Strand at three. Fuchs said he would get the 1.05 train from Didcot.

It had been arranged that Commander Burt of Special Branch would use Perrin's office to arrest Fuchs and charge him. Perrin had agreed, but did not have the courage to face Fuchs and was intending to leave by a side door when Fuchs entered. However, at the last minute there was some confusion about the charges to be read out by Burt. The DPP had drafted two, both for offences under the Official Secrets Act, one for an offence in the UK, the second for an offence in the United States. This had to be agreed with the Foreign Office, who took their time responding because they wanted them to be cleared by the embassy in Washington. They were finally phoned through to Burt in Perrin's office while Fuchs waited patiently in the foyer for the summons.

Fuchs was finally told that Perrin was free and he entered. He saw Perrin with a stranger, who introduced himself as Commander Burt and told Fuchs that he was under arrest for breaches of the Official Secrets Act. As Fuchs was trying to deal with the sudden realization that he was now in the hands of the police, Perrin slipped out through the door. Fuchs shouted after him, "Do you realize what this will mean for Harwell?"

Fuchs was taken to the cells in Bow Street. Robertson had told Arnold that the arrest was imminent and that Commander Burt and other officers from Special Branch would arrive in Harwell that evening after six to search Fuchs's office and collect his papers for evidence. This they did. The transcript of the microphone records that at 22.00 "Searchers were at work."

At 22.11 an incoming telephone call is unanswered. The transcript ends with the laconic, "Nothing else to report."

TWENTY-FIVE

Trial

N ews of Klaus Fuchs's arrest was on the front pages of the daily newspapers the following day, Friday, 3 February 1950. Rudolf Peierls, attending a conference in Oxford, was shaken by the news. He phoned his wife almost immediately and the MI5 telephone tap on their home recorded their conversation. Genia spoke to him in Russian, but the MI5 listeners translated it. Peierls said that he was going to see if he could visit Fuchs in prison, and Genia replied, "But my dear, you are in the same danger yourself."

"No."

"How?"

"I don't know, but I couldn't care less now anyway."

"Admittedly, but it isn't all the same to me. Still, who could have done this dirty thing?"

Whether Peierls was in the same danger or not, he telephoned Scotland Yard and spoke directly to Commander Burt, saying that he wanted permission to pay Fuchs a visit in Brixton. Burt reported to MI5, and White and the legal officer decided that Peierls should be given permission but that the visit should be monitored in some way. When Peierls spoke to Burt again to find out if he could see Fuchs, Burt suggested that they should meet to have a discussion first.

At their meeting, Burt asked Peierls if he would explain to him, and to Marriott, the MI5 officer who was also present, how he knew Fuchs and what their relationship was. Would he mind if they took notes?

Peierls told them about his long association with Fuchs, but when asked if he would report what Fuchs said to him when they met he refused, on the grounds that he could not promise to break the confidentiality of the conversation before knowing what he might be told. Burt and Marriott accepted that his reply was the only honest response he could make.

Peierls went to Brixton Prison and saw Fuchs in the deputy governor's office on the afternoon of the 4th, a Saturday. A warder was present as well as a Special Branch sergeant, who was told to make a report of the conversation. However, Peierls and Fuchs spoke for the most part in very low tones and their conversation was inaudible. The Special Branch officer reported that the conversation was slow and difficult, and that both sounded embarrassed. Peierls tried to get Fuchs to explain why he had done what he did and told him that he should tell the authorities as much as he knew. Fuchs replied that he had said a lot already.

Fuchs was probably still in shock. He was being held in the hospital wing at Brixton because the governor thought that it was more comfortable, but the sudden incarceration and the discovery that the British state was going to seek its pound of flesh for his betrayal had been a blow that would take a lot longer than three days to get over. He believed that if he was found guilty of treason he would be sentenced to death. Peierls told him that Herbert Skinner had offered to pay for his legal defence, but apart from asking him to thank Herbert, Fuchs seemed indifferent, as he did to a question from Peierls whether it would be useful for him to meet Fuchs's solicitor. Fuchs, of course, knew exactly what the case against him was and that his defence lawyers would have almost no influence over his fate.

Peierls left, returned home and wrote a lengthy letter to Commander Burt in which he said that he would help in any way that he could. He came up with an argument that he urged might be used in Fuchs's favour, that he had been seriously overworked over the last two years, had been ill and might be suffering the effects of a mental breakdown that had led him to confess to things that he hadn't done. On the other hand, he unhelpfully wrote, Fuchs may have realized that discovery was certain and confessed in order to protect his most recent contacts.

Rudolf Peierls was astute, and questioned what would have led Fuchs to have shouted what he did to Perrin at the time of his arrest—part of the story that had been widely reported in the press the following day. He had talked on the phone to Perrin, he said, but Perrin would not discuss anything about the case.

Enclosed with the letter to Burt was one to Fuchs from Genia. It was tear-stained, but she attacked Fuchs because his actions would throw suspicion on many other scientists and because he had betrayed the friendships that he had built up with colleagues past and present: "You did not have to be on such personal relations with them to play with their children, and dance and drink and talk."

She urged Fuchs to tell everything he knew and to reveal his accomplices so that his friends would not come under suspicion. He had, it appears, told Rudolf Peierls that he was not prepared to do that because it would appear as though he were now trying to seek a better deal for himself. This was a childish attitude, wrote Genia. It was not the time to worry about appearances, but to do what was right.

Peierls sent the letter to Burt because, he wrote, he was sure that he was in a position to get it to Fuchs with the least delay. No doubt he also realized that Burt would read the letter anyway. Peierls was an energetic and resourceful man. After writing his report to Burt he telephoned him at Scotland Yard and said that if he could have an officer waiting at Euston then Peierls would personally hand the report to the guard on the next express train from Birmingham. Burt agreed.

When he first heard the news about Fuchs, Peierls had phoned the Skinners, but Herbert had already spoken to Genia and told her that he had known something about the situation for a couple of weeks.

Erna Skinner, of course, was distraught. She had asked Peierls to find out if Fuchs wanted her to visit him, and she was anxious to hear how Fuchs had responded to the suggestion. When they talked on the phone after Peierls's visit to Brixton, Peierls pulled no punches when he told her that Fuchs merely suggested that it was up to them.

The Skinners could not decide what to do. Herbert was worried about being photographed by the press if they went to Brixton and asked Arnold if it was possible to go there in the evening. In the end they went during the day, almost a week after Fuchs's arrest. By then Erna had received the news that her father in the United States was ill, possibly dying, and she was worrying about obtaining a passport, while Herbert was anxious that she should not travel alone to the US, where he thought she would be hounded by the press.

By the time that the Skinners saw Fuchs, MI5 had installed a microphone in the meeting room and recorded their conversation. Erna was upset and embarrassed, and didn't know what to say. Her very first remark to Fuchs was that her father was dying and she would have to go to visit him urgently. She then asked if it was possible to smoke, and when the warder told her that it wasn't she asked for a drink.

Fuchs had written a letter to them both shortly after his arrest, admitting that he could have walked away and left it all but had decided that he needed to clear everything up. However, "the smooth Perrin" had prevented that conclusion. It was a long letter, in which he asked them not to be too hard on him. The visit, where Erna's distress and Herbert's helplessness were all too apparent, was a great shock. He wrote to them the next day, "For a moment everything else seemed to matter nothing, except that I had hurt you both so terribly and that—through my guilt—I now failed you again."

The Skinners continued to stay in touch with Fuchs, but they could never overcome their shock that he had been working as an agent for the Soviet Union for so long. They moved to Liverpool, but Erna's emotional collapse continued and she suffered a nervous breakdown.

Fuchs had other visitors who remained loyal to their friendship. Ronald Gunn, who had helped him enrol at Bristol University in 1933, spent many long hours on the telephone seeking to arrange legal representation for his friend (all of it monitored and transcribed by the typists at MI5) and then went to Brixton to visit. Corder Catchpole, the leading Quaker and close friend of Fuchs's father, also made a prison visit, as did his cousin Giselle Wagner. Several of his colleagues from Harwell wrote letters offering help and best wishes.

Jim Skardon also paid Fuchs a visit, not out of any charitable motives but in pursuit of more information about his Soviet contacts. He took with him a pile of photographs of assorted Russian Embassy staff, prominent members of the British Communist Party and suspected illegal Soviet intelligence agents.

Fuchs looked through them, discarded most of them, looked through some others, but appeared hesitant about identifying anyone. Skardon's position was a difficult one, because as a possible witness for the prosecution he ought not to be interrogating Fuchs. He noted that he was careful to avoid a cross-examination and said that he would see Fuchs again, if he was prepared to do so after the committal proceedings, which were scheduled for two days' time on 10 February.

Fuchs was already beginning to go over in his own mind his surveillance by MI5, his confession and his arrest. The question—and it must have loomed large—was how much should he reveal about his contacts? He had made a decision to confess, based on his own self-interest, and it had backfired. Did he now have the right to implicate others, his comrades in espionage?

One vital issue was what evidence did MI5 have that had led them to start investigating him in the first place? He asked Skardon this when he visited him. Skardon noted:

> Fuchs asked me whether I could tell him if there was any evidence besides his own admission against him, and I indicated to him that I thought it was unlikely that any would be called since his confession was a complete case. He said that he had no intention of going back on his statement, but he was curious to know how much real knowledge we had. I was unable to satisfy his curiosity.

Fuchs knew that his arrest had been on the front page of every newspaper, so his contacts were aware that he had been uncovered, and he could at least give them a head start to avoid their own arrests. He knew that the first person he had handed secrets to, Kremer, or "Alexander", the Soviet military attaché, was no longer in Britain. He didn't know what had happened to the others. MI5 and the police were leaking information to the press, and the details of "the girl from Banbury' were already a major story. Fuchs hadn't seen

"Sonya' for almost seven years, and he had no idea where she was now.

Sonya had stayed in the same isolated, draughty cottage in Great Rollright, near Chipping Norton, where Skardon and Serpell had knocked on the door to question her back in 1947. Life had been harsh. Her contact with Moscow had ended, for reasons that she didn't understand, and so too had the arrangements to provide money and messages via a dead letter box near the village. Her husband, Len, was unhappy and she was tired of her inactivity. In the depths of the winter of 1949, with freezing waterpipes and one small coal fire to heat a single room, she had come to the end of her tether. She arranged a visit to Prague where she met her brother Jürgen. From there she wrote a coded letter to the Moscow centre, asking them to send some money, repeating the arrangements for the dead letter box and finally asking permission to return to Germany.

A year later, in January 1950, Sonya's situation was even worse. Len was recovering from a severe motorcycle crash and had been made unemployed as a result. They were broke and Sonya was in despair. She still made regular visits to the dead letter box and there, finally, she found a message saying that she could return to Germany. She buried her Party card and transmitter, and started to pack. Her two youngest children were able to travel on her passport, but Len and her oldest son, who was at university in Edinburgh, would have to remain.

Every day Sonya expected a knock at the door from the police or men from the Security Service. She paid even more attention to any passers-by or strange vehicles near the village. Nothing happened. No one came. On 27 February, three weeks after Fuchs was arrested, Sonya and her two younger children caught a flight from London to Hamburg and then on to West Berlin. From there they went to

Friedrichstrasse railway station in the Soviet zone and waited to be picked up by Jürgen's wife. Sonya had got away.

Alexander Feklisov, "Eugene", also heard the news about Fuchs's arrest on the morning of 3 February. His first reaction was to go over the way he had handled his meetings with Fuchs to see if there had been the chance of failure to spot a tail or anything else suspicious. He could think of nothing. The next question was how quickly could he leave Britain? Moscow centre had already ordered him to do so, but his boss at the embassy, Nikolai Rodin, thought otherwise and cabled back to Moscow arguing that MI5 surveillance on the embassy had increased, so if any of the staff left quickly then he would be identified as Fuchs's case officer. Moscow agreed, so Feklisov stayed. Rodin was correct in his assessment. MI5 were paying close attention to the movements of Soviet diplomatic staff and drew up a list of those who had left the country over the last three months. Some staff did leave in February and the MI5 registry drew their dossiers and photos so that their details might be shown to Fuchs.

Skardon met up with Fuchs after his committal proceedings at Bow Street Magistrates' Court on 10 February. Fuchs sat at the back of the court with his solicitor and a warder. Skardon showed him some more photographs, and after a few moments Fuchs identified one of them. Skardon turned it over. On the back was the name Kremer, the military attaché at the embassy in London, whom MI5 believed was almost certainly a GRU officer. He had returned to Moscow in 1943. Clearly Fuchs's cooperation was not going to be all that whole-hearted.

The committal proceedings and Fuchs's approaching trial were causing some severe headaches for MI5 and the government. The FBI had not only asked to see Fuchs's confession, but also wanted to send two of its agents to question him. The request was embarrassing, because Fuchs, as a prisoner on remand in Brixton, had certain rights and was now under the jurisdiction of the Home Office and the Prisons Department. Even Skardon had to negotiate meetings with Fuchs and the prison governor. The biggest problem, however, was that Fuchs's arrest had exploded in the American media and members of Congress were repeating some of the anti-British sentiments. They were threatening to derail negotiations that it was hoped would lead to more nuclear collaboration between the US and Britain.

The head of MI5, Sir Percy Sillitoe, wrote to the head of the FBI, J. Edgar Hoover, refusing to send copies of Fuchs's confession on the grounds that these documents were now legally privileged, and could not be released to the public without the order of the trial judge.

The most pressing issue, however, was how to handle the trial at the Old Bailey. MI5, in its submission to the prime minister about the possible arrest of Fuchs, had pointed out that there was provision for the case to be held in camera—that is, without the public or the press being allowed to witness the proceedings. Superficially attractive this might seem, but experienced heads in the government knew that it would lead to accusations of a cover-up. The attorney general, Sir Hartley Shawcross, had already received letters from two Members of Parliament asking why Fuchs had been allowed to remain at Harwell for so long, and he had suggested that the prosecuting counsel should cover this question in his opening address to the court.

MI5 were naturally appalled at this idea and wrote to him saying that they had complete answers to these questions, but that they affected other government departments and surely it was better for this whole matter to dealt with properly in Parliament?

The case was highly sensitive, and even before the committal proceedings discussion started to work out what could and could not be said in court. The first case conference was held on 8 February at the chambers of the Dickensian-sounding prosecuting counsel, Mr. Christmas Humphreys. Gathered there were the DPP, MI5's legal officer Mr. Bernard Hill and Jim Skardon, and Arnold and Perrin from the Ministry of Supply.

Christmas Humphreys had prepared his opening speech, but both Perrin and Hill wanted changes. Perrin pointed out that the government would not admit that the Russians had the bomb. The most they would admit was that the Russians had caused an atomic explosion. If it came out in open court that Fuchs had given to the Russians full details of the first plutonium bomb, this would create alarm and despondency both here and in America. The fact that the country was in the middle of a general election, with polling day just three weeks away, wasn't mentioned, and probably didn't need to be. Perrin's point was accepted and Christmas Humphreys amended his opening remarks.

The committal hearing was short and, as we have seen, Fuchs's confession, although submitted as evidence, was not made public. Counsel for Fuchs entered a plea of not guilty and the case was set down for the opening session beginning 28 February, the Tuesday following the general election.

Christmas Humphreys's efforts at limiting the information given at the Bow Street hearing caused a lot of comment in the press. Another case conference was called a few days before the trial at the Old Bailey, and this time the big guns were in evidence. The government's law officers were there en masse, with the attorney general and his two treasury counsel, Christmas Humphreys and Roger Seaton, in attendance. So too was Director of Public Prosecutions Sir Theobald Mathew; the assistant DPP; and Sir Roger Makins, deputy under-secretary of state at the Foreign Office and a former minister at the embassy in Washington. The Security Service had also risen to the occasion, with Dick White joining his colleagues Skardon and Hill. Michael Perrin was the sole representative from the Ministry of Supply, but had brought opinions from Lord Portal and Sir Archibald Rowlands, his permanent secretary.

It was their view, said Perrin, that not enough had been said at the magistrates' court about the extent of the information that Fuchs had passed to the Russians. This of course had largely been a result of Perrin's arguments before the hearing, but he had prepared a document, which he presented and which he proposed to give in evidence at the trial.

It was Sir Roger Makins's turn to shoot any more disclosure down in flames. Both he and MI5's lawyer, Mr. Hill, argued that the extent of Fuchs's spying could not be revealed in open court, and that it was undesirable for any of the proceedings to be held in camera. "The Foreign Office point of view was that they were adverse to any more sensational information being discussed at the trial, which would provide the American press with further sensational news to publish." Perrin's suggestion was not adopted.

The attorney general then turned on MI5 and said that Lord Chief Justice Lord Goddard, who would be presiding over the case at the Old Bailey, might ask how it was that Fuchs came to be employed at Harwell when he was a known communist from 1942 onwards. Dick White responded sharply: the Security Service had no knowledge that Fuchs had ever been a member of the British Communist Party. All that the Security Service knew was that there was a Gestapo report from Kiel alleging Fuchs to be a communist. This fact had never been confirmed by police reports in this country.

This tetchy meeting was brought to an end by the DPP, who said that Fuchs's barrister, Mr. Derek Curtis-Bennett, KC, had suggested that Fuchs had invented the whole story. Clearly if he took this line and continued with Fuchs's plea of not guilty, no one would be able to control the evidence that might be revealed in court. So the conference made arrangements for Perrin to meet Curtis-Bennett that evening in order to convince him that the story was genuine. This very clear breach of procedure, which was highly unethical on the part not only of the government's law officers but of Curtis-Bennett as well, demonstrates just how sensitive the Fuchs case had become.

The nuclear information that he had handed over to the Russians still had the potential to cause widespread damage to political reputations and so must remain secret— not from the Russians, who of course knew it all, but from the British public and the press.

Perrin's meeting with Fuchs's legal counsel obviously paid off. The trial opened, in front of Lord Chief Justice Lord Goddard, and no defence was offered.

Goddard had a fearsome reputation. One young barrister who appeared before him in a murder trial said later that he was as impatient of any defence as "Bloody" Judge Jeffreys. He was a firm advocate of capital punishment and also argued in the House of Lords that birching young offenders was an effective deterrent. A few years later he presided over the Bentley case, sentencing Derek Bentley, a young man with a mental age of nine years, to death by hanging for being an accomplice in the murder of a policeman.

The prosecution of Fuchs was led by the attorney general, Sir Hartley Shawcross, who reminded the court that Fuchs was charged with committing offences under the Official Secrets Act and that the country to which this information is passed need not be an enemy. In fact, he went on, "it is enough that the foreign country concerned should be a potential enemy, perhaps through some unhappy change of circumstances might become an actual enemy, although perhaps a friend at the time that information was communicated."

Here Goddard interrupted. "Or never become an enemy at all."

Shawcross continued. In fact, the information was conveyed to agents of the government of the Soviet Union. He went on to say something about Fuchs's politics. "The prisoner is a communist, and that is at once the explanation, and indeed the tragedy of this case . . . It is a tragedy that one of such high intellectual attainments as the prisoner possesses should have allowed his mental processes to have become so warped by his devotion to communism."

At this point the attorney general referred to the phrase that Fuchs himself had used in his confession, a form of "controlled schizophrenia"—a condition, Shawcross said, that was a direct result of his belief in communism. This naturally brought him to Fuchs's confession, and he read out passages from it to provide an account of Fuchs's membership of the Communist Party and his arrival in England in 1933, up to the time that he was interned in Canada. According to the transcript of the trial, Shawcross said that Fuchs returned to the UK in 1942. This may be an error in the transcript, but it is unlikely, because the attorney general then went on to describe how he quickly applied for naturalization. There is never any reference to Fuchs's activities in 1941 or 1942 and he implies that it was in 1943 that Fuchs approached agents of the Soviet Union. Of course all the charges in the indictment refer to incidents dating from 1943, the first one when Sonya met Fuchs in Snow Hill Railway Station in Birmingham, although whether this was in 1943 or earlier has never been established. Shawcross then proceeded to explain that Fuchs never had any contact with Communist Party members in Britain.

Shawcross then came to perhaps the most difficult part of his speech, which was to impress upon Goddard and the members of the press crammed into the public gallery that Fuchs's revelations had been extremely serious, but at the same time to suggest that the most important secrets were still somehow secure. It was a difficult balancing act. "My Lord, as to the value of the information he did convey it is not in the public interest to say any more than this. There were of course many fields of atomic research . . . which were unknown to him. On the other hand, he was a scientist of the highest standing in his own particular field . . . and one must regard the disclosures as very grave indeed."

Finally, Shawcross—aware that the only evidence used in the trial was Fuchs's own confession—was anxious to draw a distinction between the confessions produced in the show trials in Prague and Moscow and that of Fuchs. No pressure of any sort had been put on the prisoner, he stressed; the confession from which he had quoted extensively had been freely given, while Fuchs was still a free man. The attorney general concluded by saying that he relied on the evidence and the plea of guilty, and would call no witnesses.

Now it was the turn of Fuchs's defence, and his counsel, Mr. Curtis-Bennett, rose to his feet. He did intend to call witnesses, and Jim Skardon entered the witness box, where he was questioned to establish that the only reason Fuchs was in the dock was because of his confession, and that Fuchs was cooperating with the Security Service to the best of his ability. Skardon agreed. Faced with Fuchs's decision to plead guilty, his defence counsel's only possible course of action was to put the best light possible on his client's character and motives, in order to plead for a lenient sentence. It was a difficult brief, and with Goddard on the bench nigh on impossible.

Curtis-Bennett got what he could out of Skardon, then went on at length about Fuchs's early life in Germany, the rise of Hitler and the Nazis, and how any man, determined to fight the rise of this evil, would join the communists. He told this part of the story in great detail and Goddard began to show signs of impatience. Curtis-Bennett persisted, and then suggested that in fact Fuchs had not made any secret of his communist sympathies.

Goddard could contain himself no longer. "I don't know whether you are suggesting that was known to the authorities?" he said.

Curtis-Bennett replied that he didn't know what the authorities knew, but Fuchs had made no secret of it.

"I don't suppose he proclaimed himself as a communist when naturalized, or taken into Harwell, or when he went to the USA?" retorted Goddard.

Curtis-Bennett wasn't going to give up. "If I am wrong the Attorney General will correct me. It was on his records in this country at the Home Office that he was a member of the German Communist Party."

Shawcross was by now on his feet. He was anxious to deflect this potential criticism of the Security Service and admitted that when Fuchs was questioned by the Enemy Aliens tribunal it was recognized that he was a refugee from Nazi persecution because he was a communist. Later, however, there was no evidence of his communist associations, and in fact, said Shawcross, he considered it his duty not to take any interest in politics in this country.

Curtis-Bennett insisted that it was known here that Fuchs was a communist in Germany but didn't pursue it any more. He went on to say instead that, this being the case, when he was used by people in this country during time of war it was almost automatic that Fuchs would put his allegiance to the Communist Party first. It was this that bore on the issue of his state of mind which he, Curtis-Bennett, was trying to put before the Lord Chief Justice.

Goddard knew exactly where this was leading and he interrupted Curtis-Bennett.

"I have read this statement with very great care more than once. I cannot understand this metaphysical philosophy or whatever you like to call it. I am not concerned with it. I am concerned that this man gave away secrets of vital importance to this country. He stands before me as a sane man, and not relying on the disease of schizophrenia or anything else."

"If your Lordship does not think that the state of mind a man acts under is relative to sentence . . ." Curtis-Bennett got no further.

"A man in that state of mind is one of the most dangerous that this country could have within its shores," said Goddard.

It was a good indication that any plea of mitigation would get nowhere, but Curtis-Bennett ploughed bravely on. He had a duty to his client to put the case forward and, in an attempt to make Goddard think, said, "Knowing your Lordship is not going to visit him savagely, but justly, both in the interests of the state and the interests of this man, I can only try to explain what your Lordship has said you fail to understand. Though I fail in the end, I can do no more, but do it I must."

Goddard allowed him to proceed. Curtis-Bennett pointed out that for three of the four counts the Soviet Union was an ally of Great Britain, fighting the same enemy, and he asked a very pertinent question: what would the response be if the attorney general had tried to bring the same charges against Fuchs in 1944? He would not have done so, and this countered the argument that for the offences to be committed it didn't matter whether the country receiving information was an enemy or not. But Curtis-Bennett had to say that Fuchs had handed over the information he did not because the Soviet Union was an ally, but because he was a communist.

He then went on to stress once again that without the confession there could be no case. He asked Goddard to consider his verdict and sentence in the light of Fuchs, a human being affected by his past, and now truly contrite about his actions.

With hindsight, Curtis-Bennett seems hamstrung by the confession. There are moments in his speech when he seems to suggest that there has been some sort of inducement, but cannot get Fuchs to assist him. It probably wouldn't have made any difference. Goddard had a reputation for rejecting the idea that any evidence might be inadmissible.

Lord Chief Justice Lord Goddard found Fuchs guilty and asked him to address the court before passing sentence. Fuchs said nothing except to thank the court and the governor of Brixton Prison. Goddard then proceeded to sentence him. He said that Fuchs was extremely lucky not to be charged with treason, which would of course have carried the death penalty. It was close to it, and it clearly irked the judge that he could not don the black cap and announce a death sentence. Fuchs, he said, had betrayed the idea of political asylum. He had betrayed his own work, for which this country had paid him and kept him in comfort, and had also betrayed the work of many others and caused suspicion to fall on them. He had imperilled the good relations between the UK and the United States and had caused incalculable harm to this country and the United States merely for the purpose of furthering his political creed.

As for sentence, he went on to say that it was not so much for punishment, for punishment could mean nothing to a man of Fuchs's mentality. "My duty is to safeguard this country and how can I be sure that a man, whose mentality is shown in that statement you have made, may not at any other minute allow some curious working of your mind to lead you further to betray secrets of the greatest possible value and importance to this land? The maximum sentence which parliament has ordained for this crime is fourteen years' imprisonment, and that is the sentence I pass upon you."

Fuchs was led away to prison. He was thirty-nine years old. He might not be free again until he was fifty-three.

TWENTY-SIX

A Visit from the FBI

The investigation, trial and imprisonment of Klaus Fuchs had begun with MI5 receiving a sliver of information from the Signals Intelligence Service in the United States. The FBI was closely connected with the decoding work that produced the incriminating messages and had officially informed MI5 via the British Embassy in Washington in September 1949. Since then, the FBI had been continually frustrated in its efforts to find out how MI5's investigation was progressing. Either MI5 or the Foreign Office were always finding reasons why the FBI could not interrogate Fuchs or receive copies of the confessions he had made to Skardon or Perrin.

The Foreign Office line was that handing over the details of Fuchs's spying career would only add to the damage already caused to US and British government relations. Access to Fuchs was vital for the FBI investigation, however. J. Edgar Hoover, the bureau's director, and case officer Robert Lamphere needed to uncover Fuchs's contact in the United States and only Fuchs could positively identify him. The decoded signals that had given them a lead to Fuchs were not comprehensive enough to provide further information.

The FBI had interviewed Kristel Heinemann, Fuchs's sister, but the description that she and her husband Robert had given of the man who had come to find Fuchs could fit probably four million United States citizens. Kristel said that she couldn't remember his name either, but it might have been "Joseph". Fuchs was the key, and as far as the FBI was concerned the British were stonewalling.

After intense lobbying, assisted by the British Embassy in Washington, the Foreign Office gave way. They agreed that copies of Fuchs's confession would be provided after the trial, along with a transcript of the trial itself. By February 1950 there was such a queue of US agencies demanding this information that the Foreign Office suggested the FBI should negotiate with the State Department to get first access, or stand in line with the US Atomic Energy Commission, the Atomic Energy Section of the CIA and the State Department itself.

The FBI still demanded the right to question Fuchs directly, even though the Foreign Office explained that Fuchs could not be forced to answer questions and that as a convicted prisoner he had certain rights. He was now under the charge of the Prison Commissioners, who also had to agree to any questioning. MI5 had been exchanging some intelligence about Fuchs's contacts and his movements as he volunteered the information to Jim Skardon. Skardon also passed on the FBI's questions to Fuchs, who most of the time seemed prepared to answer them, and Skardon took photos sent to him by the FBI for Fuchs to identify.

Skardon finally persuaded Fuchs to talk to the FBI, and the FBI agreed, reluctantly, that an MI5 officer would be present during their questioning. Two agents would interrogate Fuchs. One was Special Agent Robert Lamphere, who had been working on the case since the first Soviet cables were decrypted, and the second was a senior officer, the assistant director of the FBI, Hugh Clegg, who came with the backing of Hoover himself. The visit was almost derailed because Fuchs had heard that one of his former colleagues had been refused a United States visa because he had been in contact with Fuchs while he was in prison. Fuchs told Skardon that this was typical of the overreaction of the US government and he could not see the point in talking to FBI officers if friends that he mentioned were immediately accused of being communist agents. He said that they would be suspecting Herbert Skinner next. Skardon reported that Fuchs was very angry and it took some persuading to calm him down. It was unfortunate, because Skardon had brought with him some FBI mug-shots of Harry Gold. Fuchs didn't, apparently, pay that much attention to them, saying that he did not recognize the person in the photos. Skardon did what he could to placate Fuchs, and the FBI visit went ahead.

The two FBI agents arrived in the company of Jim Skardon at Wormwood Scrubs Prison, where Fuchs was now held, on Saturday, 20 May, at ten in the morning. They were taken to an interviewing room and Fuchs was led in. They introduced themselves and said they appreciated that he was prepared to talk to them and that he was under no obligation to answer their questions.

Several accounts written later by Robert Lamphere say that they spoke to Fuchs about his sister Kristel, saying that she had been helpful—a subtle way, they suggested, of putting pressure on Fuchs, who would be aware that his sister was still vulnerable. Skardon, however, doesn't say anything about this in his contemporaneous report to MI5; instead he claims that the FBI agents asked a few basic questions that they thought might help to establish the identity of Fuchs's contact in the US. They then produced a series of photographs, some taken some time ago and some, according to Skardon, that looked as though they were frames taken from a film. Fuchs rejected most of these, but kept five on the table. Skardon thought that they were of the same man, Harry Gold, whose passport pictures Fuchs had rejected at the time of Skardon's last visit. While Fuchs didn't discard the photos, he didn't confirm that they were the likeness of his contact, merely saying that he could not rule them out. He repeated for the benefit of the FBI agents a description that he had already given earlier, saying that by his contact's reaction to technical information Fuchs assumed that he had some technical knowledge. He remembered that he had an eastern seaboard, rather than western, accent and was probably Jewish.

He then talked about his sister, denying the FBI allegations that he had ever written to her asking her to give his regards to "Joseph" and saying that, if he had warned her that the man might call on her, he might have used the name "Jack", but he would not swear to it.

After an hour and a half the visit ended, and the two agents and Skardon left.

Fuchs wasn't aware that the FBI had been questioning Harry Gold, or Raymond as he still thought of him, for the last five days. It was a peculiar arrangement, because Gold had not been arrested, or charged, and the FBI could not compel him to answer their questions. Gold could simply have declined to talk to them, or request that he be accompanied by a lawyer during the interviews, but he did neither. He went out of his way to appear cooperative, going to the FBI offices in Philadelphia at times to fit in with his work at a local hospital. The interviews went on for hours, and he was getting tired, and worn down.

In one of the first interviews, Gold was shown a photo of Fuchs and asked if he recognized him. He claimed that he did recognize the photo, but it was because he had seen it in a magazine, probably *Newsweek*. The FBI agents, Scott Miller and Richard Brennan, suggested that he had met Fuchs in Boston in 1945 and that he had been his contact in New York. Gold denied it. He was questioned about his movements, his holidays and travel arrangements. He denied everything. The agents produced photos not only of Fuchs but of other Communist Party members and suspected Soviet agents whom they were investigating, and they honed in on his whereabouts on certain dates in 1943 and 1944. Gold bent over backwards to appear cooperative, saying that he had nothing to hide. He even allowed the FBI to shoot some cine film of him walking down the street in Philadelphia.

At their last four-hour questioning session, Miller and Brennan asked Gold if he would allow them to search his room. Remarkably, he agreed, but only if the FBI carried out the search at a time when his brother and father were not at home. The visit was arranged for the morning of Monday, 22 May. Gold spent most of the weekend at the hospital laboratory where he worked, instead of scouring his room for any evidence of his clandestine travels.

In London on the morning of the 22nd, Lamphere and Clegg again met Skardon and went to Wormwood Scrubs for their second interrogation of Fuchs. They were armed this time with the short film of Harry Gold that they had collected from the FBI laboratory before they flew to London.

The meeting started with more questions about the various meetings that Fuchs had had, and Clegg and Lamphere seemed intrigued by the very long interval between the two meetings that took place when Fuchs was stationed at Los Alamos. Fuchs repeated what he had told Skardon and Perrin about his various meetings in the United States.

At about eleven o'clock, according to Skardon, the interview room was blacked out and a cine-projector and screen were set up. Fuchs was told that the film he was going to see had been shot last week, on 18 May, while Gold was under surveillance in Philadelphia. This wasn't true: Gold knew he was being filmed, but if Skardon was aware of this he didn't mention it in his report. He wrote that the film was of Gold moving about the streets, and it seemed to him that the same piece of film was the original for some of the stills that Fuchs had seen at the first meeting with Clegg and Lamphere. The film was about 60 feet in length so would have lasted for just a few minutes. The image was not, according to Skardon, crystal clear, but it was good enough for identification.

Fuchs looked at the film twice. He then said, "I cannot be absolutely positive, but I think it is very likely him." He added that the man in the film had one obvious characteristic as his contact—that he looked over his shoulder all the time to see if he was being followed. It was something that had always irritated Fuchs. He didn't say anything more positive, instead adding that he didn't know why he was uncertain about the identification; perhaps he would be more certain if he saw him in person. He finished by suggesting that the film should be shown to Robert Heinemann, Kristel's husband. It was the best that Clegg and Lamphere would get.

They broke for lunch and met again in the afternoon, where the questions from the two FBI men focused not on the film or on Harry Gold, but went over again in detail all of his contacts, starting with Kremer in London, the meetings he had with the woman in Banbury and more about his meetings in the United States. According to Skardon, very little new information emerged from this series of questions.

At half past four the interview ended, Fuchs returned to his cell and the two FBI men again went back to their hotel.

There was a six-hour time difference between the soot-covered stone cell blocks of Wormwood Scrubs in London and Harry Gold's room in Philadelphia. By the time the interview with Fuchs came to an end in the afternoon, the two other FBI agents had been rifling through Gold's books and papers for a couple of hours. They were exceptionally thorough. Gold had over three hundred books on the shelves in his room, to do with his scientific work as well as thrillers and other fiction. One of the searchers found a paperback with a label from a bookseller in Rochester, New Jersey, where Gold had been to visit another contact. He made up a story that he must have bought the book in a second-hand bookstore.

Harry had woken very early that morning and done what he should have done more thoroughly the day before: searched his papers and belongings for incriminating evidence. He had found plenty—things like ticket vouchers and receipts, which he should never have kept and now destroyed, but he was aware that he had been strangely negligent, as though he had already given up.

The slow examination of the bookshelves continued. One of the agents held something else up. "What's this, Harry?"

In Brennan's hand was a street map of Santa Fe, and marked on it was the bridge where Harry had waited for Fuchs. Harry sat down. All energy had left him. He had denied that he had ever been west of the Mississippi. Miller and Brennan waited. The pause lasted for an eternity.

The words struggled from Harry's throat. "Yes, I am the man to whom Klaus Fuchs gave the information on atomic energy." Harry Gold, the man to whom Fuchs had given the secrets of Los Alamos, had cracked.

When the two FBI men in London returned to see Fuchs in prison on Tuesday the 23rd, they didn't say anything about Gold's confession. They may not have known about it, although this seems unlikely. They did, however, press Fuchs once more on the meeting that he had had with Gold in Santa Fe and his earlier meeting in Boston. They ranged widely around the political views of his family, his father and brother, and of course Kristel, his sister. They also asked about Halperin, the Canadian professor who had Fuchs's name and address in his notebook along with an early address for Kristel. Fuchs stonewalled. He didn't know if Kristel had been asked similar questions, and if she had he didn't know what her replies had been. It was best for him to say nothing.

At the next session, following lunch, the emphasis of the questioning shifted away from his family and the details of his contacts and moved instead to the nature of the information that he had handed over to the Soviet Union, with Lamphere and Clegg trying to discover more than the details that Fuchs had already told Perrin.

On the next visit, on Wednesday morning, details of Gold's confession had been absorbed in London and Clegg opened the interrogation by going over what Fuchs had already told them. Then he announced that Gold had confessed and was under arrest. Clegg now knew more details and was in a position to try to prise open Fuchs's story. He mentioned that at their first meeting Gold was wearing gloves and carrying a spare pair, while Fuchs was holding a green book and a tennis ball. Fuchs agreed. His contact's name was Raymond, prompted Clegg, and Fuchs agreed. He had been offered $1,500 by Gold but had refused to take it, claimed Clegg. Fuchs said that he did not remember that. Neither did he remember, when Clegg talked about the enrichment plant, saying that it was going to be built in Georgia or Alabama. Fuchs didn't even know that it was going to be built in a southern state. He did not remember meeting Gold, or Raymond, twice in September 1945. In fact, Fuchs remembered nothing more, particularly when the details of Gold's contact arrangement with his sister were mentioned. He could not remember being told the name of a contact by his sister, nor did he remember her giving him a telephone number to make contact with Raymond. He was stonewalling with a vengeance now, determined to deny that his sister knew anything about Raymond, or about her brother's spying. The session ended.

That afternoon the heat was off Fuchs, because the FBI men turned their attention to his fellow scientists. It was a waste of time, a blunderbuss approach based on gossip and paranoia. They asked about his close associates at Los Alamos, men who had been vital to the project, like Hans Bethe and Richard Feynman, as well as his British colleagues in the Theoretical Division, Tony Skyrme and Frank Kearton. Fuchs said drily that none of them, as far as he knew, were spies or active communists. Towards the end of this session, which must have been a great relief to Fuchs after the earlier questions about his sister, Clegg said that he wanted to prepare a statement that he would like Fuchs to sign under caution. It would take some time to prepare and the next interrogation was arranged for the following afternoon, Thursday the 25th.

Clegg and Lamphere continued to visit Fuchs for the next six days. Most of the sessions were taken up with Fuchs reading drafts of the statement that he was being asked to sign, and detailed questions about various meeting places, clearly based on information that Gold was now providing. Fuchs was asked to confirm addresses and other details of meetings with Gold in Queens, and of his first rendezvous. He was also questioned in greater detail about the information that was handled by Gold. Skardon formed the impression that Gold knew almost nothing about what he was handling, and the two agents wanted as much detail as possible. They asked Fuchs for the titles of the papers that he handed over and for details of his superior officers in the United States.

While the final statement was being prepared, Clegg and Lamphere, along with the embassy FBI liaison officer

John Cimperman, were asked to go to Leconfield House for a meeting with Perrin. He had obviously been told about the FBI's attempt to dig deeper into the precise nature of the scientific information that Fuchs had handed over and he put it to them that some of this material should not be included in the statement. He pointed out that the Atomic Energy Commission might be unwilling for any technical details to be given. Just why the FBI and the Atomic Energy Commission needed Perrin to arbitrate between them was a question that was never asked, and Skardon wrote that Clegg seemed very happy to take Perrin's advice. Clegg wrote up a second document, with all the scientific details deleted, and it was this statement that would go to the Grand Jury as evidence against Gold.

The pair from the FBI continued to question Fuchs, returning one more time to Kristel's role in his meetings with Gold. Lamphere told him that the telephone number that Kristel was given to pass on to Fuchs was the number of Jerome Kaploun, vice-president of Amtorg, the Soviet trading organization in the United States. Fuchs once more absolutely denied any knowledge of any message from his sister, or of Kaploun, and would not budge from that position.

At last, the final draft of a document was shown to Fuchs and he was prepared to sign it; it was witnessed by all three security agents, Clegg, Lamphere and Skardon. Throughout the ten pages of the statement there is never any reference by Fuchs to Harry Gold; "Raymond" is the only name used to describe his contact. Without Gold's confession that he was Raymond, the document provides no clue to the identity of the man Fuchs dealt with while he was in the United States. But at the end of the statement Fuchs says that he has identified two photographs that he believes are of his contact, and Lamphere later wrote that Fuchs was handed two photographs of Gold and that on the back he signed a declaration that the photograph was a likeness of Raymond.

The questioning of Fuchs by the FBI ended on Friday, 2 June. At this last meeting he was asked about the editorial staff of the *Washington Post* newspaper, what he knew of their political views and if he had had any contact with any of them or believed them to be supplying information to the Soviet Union? Fuchs, of course, was mystified by this question and told them that he knew nothing at all about the newspaper or its staff and the matter seems never to have been taken further by the FBI.

Gold was arrested 24 May and his interrogation by FBI agents lasted for many weeks. He became a key witness in the cases of many other members of the large Soviet spy ring in the United States, and he did not stand trial until 7 December. Two days later, he was sentenced to prison for a maximum term of thirty years.

With the departure of the FBI agents, Fuchs had identified most of his contacts or intermediaries of Soviet intelligence. On 27 June he was transferred from Wormwood Scrubs to Stafford Prison in the Midlands; the move had been postponed to make it easier for Skardon and the FBI to question him. During the transfer he was driven by MI5 to Kew, where he pointed out to Skardon the places that had been selected for messages if at any time he was unable to make contact with his Russian agent. This was planned like a military operation and worked out with the prison authorities so that this small detour would never be noticed, either by the prison guards at Stafford or, more importantly, by the press. MI5 made a great deal of fuss about these locations, and didn't seem to realize that after the trial run both Fuchs and Feklisov decided that they wouldn't bother to use this system of communication. Nevertheless, the residents of the house where Fuchs had thrown a copy of *Men Only* through the fence were questioned. They were members of the

Communist Party, but all of them denied any knowledge of Fuchs or any connection with Soviet intelligence, and MI5 realized that they could prove nothing.

It was not only the prison move that had been delayed for the benefit of the FBI. So too was the move to deprive Fuchs of his British citizenship. The hearing was held in camera in July. Skardon felt that stripping Fuchs of his nationality was wrong. He wrote to the tribunal saying he had not told Fuchs that this would happen because he felt that it would jeopardize his cooperation. He now thought that he had perpetrated an injustice against Fuchs by hiding the truth from him, and wrote saying that loss of citizenship was unnecessary, that Fuchs had been punished for his crimes and had renounced his former allegiance to the Soviet Union. Without his confession, Fuchs would not have been prosecuted. He knew it, and so did MI5, wrote Skardon. Perhaps Skardon felt a twinge of guilt about the way that Fuchs had originally been manipulated into confessing and saw this process of denaturalization as a second double-cross. It is certainly remarkable that Fuchs's chief interrogator was prepared to intervene so strongly on his behalf.

It was to no avail. Fuchs was stripped of his citizenship. He was deeply upset by the decision. He spent the rest of his time in prison as a stateless person.

The last person he identified to Skardon was Sonya, Ursula Beurton, as the mysterious woman from Banbury. Skardon had shown Fuchs her photograph several times before, but he had never picked it out. When he did, it was several months after his arrest and trial and he was certain that she was no longer in the country. He never identified his last contact, Alexander Feklisov.

TWENTY-SEVEN

Legacy

The work in which Klaus Fuchs was engaged both at Harwell and in assisting the weapon project at Fort Halstead continued after he was jailed, of course. But his absence was noticed. A few weeks after the trial, William Penney wrote a document about the future of the British atom bomb project and his need for highly qualified personnel. He knew that the bomb design he was currently working on could be improved, but, he said, "there are only four people in this country who have the knowledge and ability to discover within three or four years what those major improvements are. One of them is myself. Two are university professors who are unwilling to do more than give advice. The fourth is in prison."

Penney and his organization came under severe scrutiny early in February 1950. The success of the Soviet Union in exploding its own weapon raised some serious questions. The First Sea Lord, Lord Fraser, summed it up when he said, "How does it come about that knowing all that we did in 1945 we are still without an atom bomb by contrast with the Russians who, starting from scratch, have apparently already passed us . . ."

Other government figures were also concerned about the success of the bomb project, but more—as they always were—with its cost. Sir Henry Tizard, who took a position that he had held consistently since 1941, put the case that with the current rate of progress Britain would never be able to achieve a stockpile that would enable her to exercise any influence over the United States. It was better then, in his view, to abandon an independent effort and concentrate on guided weapons and conventional armaments. Portal and Penney responded vigorously to these arguments, and they were helped by the impact of Fuchs's trial and imprisonment on United States and British nuclear collaboration.

Since the end of the war, British governments had been determined to restore the original collaboration with the United States that had been ended with the McMahon Act of 1946. Cooperation at economic and military level improved considerably with the growth of tension over Berlin and the fate of the governments of Poland and Czechoslovakia. Meetings between British and American representatives in Washington led to an agreement known as the Modus Vivendi, which was signed in January 1948. It reaffirmed the wartime status of the Combined Policy Committee as the place for dealing with atomic problems of common concern, such as agreement over the supplies of uranium and other topics for technical cooperation. There were disagreements in the US government, however, about how far this should go. The Congressional Joint Committee on Atomic Energy, set up by the McMahon Act, took a hard line on sharing information, while other departments differed. The Berlin crisis of 1948 exacerbated these differences. At the height of the airlift and the Soviet blockade of the western part of the city, the United States based sixty nuclear-capable B-29 bombers in the UK. They were not armed with nuclear weapons, but their existence sharply focused the question of the defence of Europe against the Soviet Union and what nuclear information might legitimately be shared with the UK.

The explosion of the Soviet atom bomb, "Joe 1", brought this question to a head and in September 1949 a new set of talks began. The US administration followed the wartime argument that all raw materials and production plans should be located in the United States or Canada because in the UK they were too vulnerable to attack. The British side obviously argued that there should be full cooperation, with an independent British programme. If the US could not support this, then the minimum requirement must be a share of the weapons stockpile and guarantees that the agreement could not be arbitrarily changed.

The decision by the Truman administration to go ahead with the H-bomb programme complicated the whole question of collaboration, strengthening the hand of those in the US who wanted to restrict the flow of information, and by the end of the year it looked as though more concessions would be needed from the British. While people like Ernest Bevin and Lord Portal argued strongly for British independence, money had always trumped strategic arguments. The arrest of Klaus Fuchs, however, hit any possibility of collaboration firmly on the head. The Combined Policy Committee did not meet for another two years.

The British bomb programme remained intact and the team continued with plans to create a new weapons laboratory at Aldermaston. They continued to come up against problems, one of which seemed very serious. Penney's team wanted the first device tested to be a working weapon, one that could be dropped from the new fleet of jet-powered V bombers destined for service in the RAF. It was to be a demonstration that the British had a useable weapon, not an experimental device. For safety, in service the bomb would be finally assembled once the jet bomber that would carry it was in the air, and this wasn't compatible with the US design of the bomb core that Penney was following. There was a danger that the plutonium would reach critical mass as it was inserted into the explosive and uranium shell.

It seemed to Penney that the design of the core had to be changed. It was a difficult and risky step to take when the programme was already under fire for taking so long, but Penney took the plunge and came up with a new design, the product of several months' hard work. However, two of his mathematical physicists, Corner and Pike, were not certain about the result. They remembered that Fuchs had given them a document that looked at various options for core design—a problem that he had worked on after the Nagasaki explosion. There were essentially three different possibilities discussed in his paper, with a range of explosive yields for each one. Corner and Pike looked at Fuchs's calculations and reworked them in the light of the new British design. They were dismayed to see that it would deliver a much weaker yield. They preferred a different design that was, they were aware, reliant on Fuchs having a good memory. They did the calculations again and presented them to Penney, who accepted that they were correct so modified his design. The new assembly would, if Fuchs's original paper was right, produce a much larger yield than the Nagasaki bomb, but it was more susceptible to variations in the compressing wave from the surrounding explosives. But that was a less important problem that had to be solved, and it was. The first British atomic bomb was detonated in a bay of the Monte Bello Islands, about 80 miles off the north-western coast of Australia, on 3 October 1952, in the hull of a frigate, HMS *Plym*. The test was designed to simulate an atomic attack on a port.

Earlier that year William Penney had asked for a meeting with Klaus Fuchs. The request was forwarded to MI5 by Lieutenant General Sir Frederick Morgan, controller of atomic energy in the Ministry of Supply in

Shell Mex House. Penney, who knew Fuchs anyway, could have arranged an ordinary prison visit when he wanted, but presumably felt that to do so might look suspicious. MI5 were not particularly enthusiastic about the idea of Penney visiting Fuchs. They saw no reason for him to do so. They wrote back saying that they thought that Fuchs had given a comprehensive account of his activities to Michael Perrin, implying that there was no reason for Penney to talk to Fuchs. Morgan thought that they were being a bit high-handed.

It's strange that Penney should want to see Fuchs at this stage. At the time he made the inquiry he was immersed in preparations for the test at the Monte Bello Islands, and in particular was grappling with a problem of the timing of the explosive detonators, something that was extra critical with the changes in design. Did he want to discuss with Fuchs something that he was concerned about that might affect the success of the British test?

We don't know, and he didn't manage to see Fuchs before the explosion on 3 October. But Penney persisted, and finally MI5 consented to a visit, with Skardon in attendance. It took place at Stafford Prison in February 1953. No record of the meeting is available, but in a later letter to Skardon it seems that Penney wanted to know the last time that Fuchs had met his NKGB contact and whether he had passed on any information about plans for Capenhurst, the location for the uranium-enrichment plant, and if he had given any figures for its capacity. If Fuchs had handed Feklisov this information it would have been almost four years old by the time Penney talked to him in prison, and it remains a puzzle why Penney needed to know this.

Less than a month after Britain had become the world's third nuclear power, the United States demonstrated its technical superiority by exploding the first thermonuclear device, a fusion or H-bomb—the "super" that Edward Teller had worked on obsessively for years. An atomic explosion based on the Fuchs—von Neumann patent had been set off in the Greenhouse series of tests in the spring of 1951. This used a fission explosion to ignite a small amount of deuterium and tritium, like using a blast furnace to light a match, as someone remarked. It boosted the fission explosive but was not a true fusion device.

Teller and his colleague Stanislaw Ulam thought about the results and realized that the fusion reaction could be ignited by the radiation from the primary fission. Ulam believed that the neutron blast would do the trick; Teller thought that electromagnetic radiation—X-rays, which were faster than neutrons—could be channelled to the fuel for the fusion weapon.

The ideas were presented to a conference at the Princeton Institute for Advanced Study. Scientists from Los Alamos, consultants Hans Bethe and John von Neumann, attended, along with members of the Atomic Energy Commission. They were convinced that it was a way forward, and the result was the "Mike" shot, on 1 November 1952—a huge piece of apparatus that weighed 62 tons and was 20 feet tall. It exploded on an atoll in the Pacific Ocean with a force of 10.4 megatons, equal, it was estimated, to twice the explosives used in the whole of the Second World War. The energy released by the fusion process, the same nuclear reaction that occurs naturally in the heart of the sun, vaporized the coral island and caused blast and burn damage to wildlife 14 miles away from ground zero. While the device, with its refrigeration equipment to keep the fusion fuel in liquid form, was too large and cumbersome to be a weapon, the test proved the concept and soon other tests took place, this time of useable H-bombs.

The Russian scientists were not far behind. The intelligence handed over by Fuchs in March 1948 was an event that "played an exceptional role in the subsequent course of the Soviet thermonuclear program", according to German Goncharov, the former head of the Theoretical Division at Arzamas-16, the Soviet nuclear weapons laboratory. Kurchatov's colleague Yulii Khariton was put in charge of a special unit to work on fusion in June 1948 and he was allowed to see the intelligence received from Fuchs, as well as the more anecdotal information he gave in 1945.

Khariton's unit worked at Arzamas, while another theoretical group under Igor Tamm worked at the Physics Institute in Moscow. This group included Andrei Sakharov, who decided to work on the project because he believed that it was vital to create a super-weapon for the country and to maintain the balance of power throughout the world. A permanent justification for nuclear physicists, it seems.

The Soviet designs for an H-bomb went through several versions. One of them was a compound bomb, which layered deuterium and tritium in between uranium around a plutonium core. It was nicknamed "the layer cake", and was similar in design to an earlier idea put forward by Edward Teller. Then another physicist in Tamm's unit, Vitalii Ginzburg, suggested that lithium deuteride might be used as a source of deuterium and tritium in the fusion layer. The great advantage was that lithium deuteride is solid at room temperature, but under the initial shock of the radiation from the primary fission bomb it will break down to produce free atoms of tritium, which will then be available as the fusion fuel.

This idea may have been a product of espionage in the United States. Goncharov claims that it was, and there have been some suggestions that it was the young Theodore Hall who was the source—he had also provided some designs for the explosive shaped charges when he was at Los Alamos—but there is no evidence for this. It may well be that US and Russian scientists arrived independently at the solution of storing tritium inside a bomb.

The Soviet government tested the layer-cake device,

with lithium deuteride as a fuel, in August 1953. It produced a blast twenty times the size of the Trinity explosion. With the announcement of this test, a scientific dispute broke out about whether the Russian bomb, "Joe 4", was a true fusion device or, as Hans Bethe claimed, was just an enhanced fission device. Khariton vigorously defended Joe 4, claiming that 20 per cent of the energy of the explosion was produced from fusion of tritium, and that unlike the US Mike device it did not need enormous refrigeration equipment to keep the deuterium and tritium liquid. Joe 4 was a deliverable weapon. In November 1955 the Soviets exploded another device—their third development on the road to the "super"—that relied primarily on the detonation of tritium from the radiation blast of a primary fission weapon. Sakharov described how, in freezing weather, tens of miles from ground zero, he felt the heat of the explosion on his face like a blast furnace. It was the equivalent of 1.6 megatons of conventional explosives.

However, in March 1954 the US had already detonated a true fusion weapon, also utilizing lithium deuteride. The test explosion, "Bravo", produced a fireball that rose to a height of 45,000 feet in one minute and created a mushroom cloud that reached to an astonishing altitude of 114,000 feet, higher than any jet could fly. The explosive power was around 15 megatons, a thousand times larger than the Nagasaki plutonium bomb.

By 1957 Britain managed to detonate a device that was based in part on a fusion explosion. How much Fuchs's early lectures at Fort Halsted contributed to this test we don't know; Penney destroyed all his papers after he retired, and the same has happened with most of the files of the Department of Atomic Energy. Fuchs, however, believed that he had supplied such information to the Soviet Union, and he surely would have passed on what he knew to William Penney and his colleagues.

These weapons were truly horrific—genuine weapons of mass destruction that would, if used, kill millions of people at a stroke. The scientific debate about which device was a true fusion weapon was macabre and surreal. The race to accumulate more and more destructive power was not only focused on the scientists' ability to create more technically advanced nuclear devices, but the tried and tested plutonium bombs were now being made in large numbers. By 1955 the United States had manufactured a remarkable 2,422 nuclear weapons, the Soviet Union had 200 and Britain had produced 14. The three governments whose former political leaders had sat around the conference table at Potsdam now had weapons of a power that was unimaginable during the Second World War.

The man who was the key vector of this nuclear proliferation sat in a cell in Stafford Prison, or for a few hours a week used an electric sewing machine making mailbags. He corresponded with a few friends and his family. His brother Gerhard had died in 1951 in East Germany. His father was still active as a professor and a pastor in Leipzig, and his nephew Klaus Kittowski was also living there.

When Klaus Kittowski was eighteen he decided that he would like to visit his uncle in prison. He had to spend some time making the arrangements, writing to his uncle asking him if he could visit and seeking permission from the East German government for a passport and a foreign-currency allocation. As the arrangements for his trip progressed, he got a message from a woman, an official in the government press office named Grete Keilson. She met Klaus and said that when he visited his uncle in prison she would be grateful if he would pass on her best wishes.

Grete, of course, had become friendly with Fuchs in Paris in 1933 when he was on his way to the United Kingdom. As a Comintern functionary she had spent the war in exile in Moscow, then had returned to Berlin and started working for Hermann Matern, head of the Party Control Commission of the Socialist Unity Party (SED), created in 1946 from the German Communist Party and the Social Democratic Party. She continued to do what she had done in Moscow—that is, maintain files on Party members to maintain Party discipline and security. She was a member of the Party's Central Committee.

The young Klaus had no difficulties leaving East Germany, although other than the personal message from Grete and, of course, from Fuchs's father his visit was motivated by nothing more than a desire to meet his uncle and a wish to go to England. He spent several weeks travelling around the country before finally making his way to Stafford Prison. His uncle had obviously been affected by prison life, but he was as polite and as intellectually sharp as ever.

Fuchs was clearly pondering what to do once he was released from prison. His British nationality had been snatched away from him. Moreover, there had been some talk about the possibility of extraditing him to the United States to stand trial, and the fate of Harry Gold, sentenced to thirty years, and the execution of the Rosenbergs—whose espionage had been far less serious than his own—were very good reasons to remain out of the clutches of the FBI.

Fuchs was uncertain about East Germany, however. He knew that returning KPD exiles, those that had not spent the war years in Moscow, were treated with suspicion, and several leading members had been expelled and accused of treason. He asked some searching questions of Klaus Kittowski about the current state of the Party in East Germany and the current leadership of the Central Committee.

The young Klaus then said that he had a message from Grete. Fuchs was completely startled by the mention of her name, reacting as though he had been stung, then he laughed, but said nothing in reply. Klaus did not know what to make of this reaction. The visit came to an end and the young Klaus left, making his way back to East Germany.

Fuchs had been sentenced to fourteen years in 1950, but became eligible for remission because of his good behaviour in 1959. His father, Emil, wrote to the home secretary and the prison governor, as well as to the British Communist Party barrister, D. N. Pritt, seeking permission for his son to fly to East Germany on his release. At the same time he approached Grete Keilson for help in getting a DDR passport for Klaus. Grete lobbied the Central Committee on Emil's behalf and a passport was rapidly authorized.

Fuchs left Stafford Prison on 23 June 1959 and was driven to the airport, where he boarded a plane, landing at Schönefeld in East Berlin. He was met at the airport by Grete Keilson and his father, in a chauffeured Party car, then was driven through Berlin to an apartment. Over the next few weeks he was taken to see old comrades from Kiel and also a nuclear research facility at Dresden. He moved to an apartment in Dresden, but wherever he was, agents of the Stasi, East Germany's security police, were watching him. Even the cleaning lady who was assigned to his flat was a Party member working for the Stasi, and so too was his driver, Lieutenant Nitschke, who filed daily reports on Fuchs's movements, although as both Fuchs and Grete Keilson were high-ranking Party members the reports are discreet. Fuchs and Grete got married on 9 September 1959, twenty-six years after they had last seen each other.

Fuchs had said to Skardon—and it was a confession repeated in court during his trial—that he had developed severe doubts about the Soviet system and that he had seen a different side of society in Britain during his time at Harwell. Now he happily embraced East German communism. He became a privileged member of the Party, with a large house, a car and a post at the East German Atomic Research Institute in Rossendorf, Dresden, where he quickly became director. He was a celebrity in East Germany, with fraternal visits organized with other East European countries, receptions and the granting of honorary degrees.

The NKGB were immediately aware of his presence in East Germany, of course. They knew the extent of his confession as soon as it was sent, in suitably packaged form, to British military attachés in foreign embassies and to NATO allies; the NKGB received it via an agent in the French Ministry of Defence. They were, however, anxious to discover why Fuchs had confessed and what role he had played in the arrest of Harry Gold.

In May 1960 the chair of the NKGB, Alexander Shelepin, an enthusiast for foreign assassinations, authorized an invitation to Fuchs and Grete to join an East German delegation attending a conference in Moscow on the peaceful uses of nuclear energy. It was proposed that at the conference the NKGB would invite Fuchs to take a twenty-day trip to visit all of the Soviet Union's peaceful nuclear laboratories and research institutes. During this trip someone would question him, "tactfully", about the circumstances of and possible reasons for his arrest.

Fuchs spent just seven days in Moscow, because he had to attend an important meeting back in Berlin, but his translator, Lieutenant Engineer Starikov, who of course was reporting back to the NKGB, said that he was greeted in a friendly fashion by all of the scientists that he met who knew something about his work for the USSR. The only fly in the ointment was Fuchs's arrival in Moscow, where there was nobody to meet them at the airport, and this produced a complaint from Grete.

He apparently spoke candidly about the fact that he had fallen behind in the whole question of nuclear research during his nine years in prison and suggested that, if it was possible, Soviet scientists specializing in nuclear reactors should be posted to the DDR for an extended period of time to help the East German training programme.

On 28 May two NKGB officers approached Fuchs and invited him to the Peking Restaurant in central Moscow. The men, Comrades Leonid Kvasnikov and D. N. Pronsky, expressed their gratitude for the work that Fuchs had done in the past and regretted that he had been taken away from his regular life and scientific work for so long. Fuchs tried to head off the discussion by saying that he had given an account of his work and time in prison to the Party in Germany on his return and had spoken to Walter Ulbricht, the first secretary, later president, of the DDR. At the present time he was most concerned about the organizational and scientific work of the Institute for Nuclear Physics where he was now deputy director.

The agents persisted, politely, and Fuchs said that during his interrogation he learned that the British had received the first indications that he was working with the NKGB from the United States. After a conversation with the MI5 officer it became obvious to him that the British suspected him of intelligence activities, but had no evidence against him. It would all have gone away if he had not confessed. In his view this had been prompted by serious political ambivalence and by doubts about the correctness of Soviet policies, which he had begun feeling due to the influence of bourgeois propaganda and his detachment from sources of truthful information. He said that he had identified Gold after being shown two film strips; in the second of these Gold looked as though he had got a load off his chest, and after watching this Fuchs identified him and testified against him.

On the question of what materials he had told MI5 he had handed over, he said that he had told them about everything, with the exception of materials on the hydrogen bomb.

It was a carefully edited account of what Fuchs had told

Skardon and Perrin, and the NKGB men did not press him about the Paris agent Sukholmin, whom Feklisov had suggested he speak to, whose name and address he had revealed; nor about the Party members in Kew whose front garden was suggested as a message drop.

A report of the interview went from Shelepin to Nikita Khrushchev, the Soviet first secretary and prime minister. Fuchs returned to Berlin. The director of the East German Central Institute for Nuclear Physics, Professor Heinz Barwich, was unhappy at government interference in the institute, and no doubt the imposition on him of Fuchs as his deputy brought matters to a head. He defected to the West and Fuchs replaced him. He was as a result the most senior nuclear physicist in the DDR, but the institute was a shadow of Harwell. Fuchs tried to organize a collaborative venture with the Soviet Union for the construction of nuclear reactors, but the contribution that East Germany could make was negligible, so any collaboration was a non-starter. The East German economy was too small to justify the costs of an independent reactor programme, and Fuchs's plans were shelved.

Fuchs had never been recognized by the Soviet Union for his espionage and his contribution to their weapons programme. At the time of his trial they officially denied all knowledge of him, alleging that the whole thing was a provocation designed to create anti-Soviet feeling. Now that he was back in the bosom of the KPD it might have seemed safe to offer him some award. Other spies, like the double agent Kim Philby, had been welcomed in Moscow, and given pensions and medals. Fuchs was ignored. One of the reasons was the desire on the part of the Soviet Union to present itself as a modern scientific society, capable of creating nuclear weapons and sending men into space without the need to copy Western methods or rely on stealing secrets; the other reason was simple antagonism between the scientists and the spies of the NKGB.

In 1965 Fuchs's last contact, Colonel Alexander Feklisov, now deputy chief of a NKGB training school, wrote to the head of the NKGB First Chief Directorate, the foreign department, Lieutenant General Alexander Sakharovsky. In his letter Feklisov described Fuchs as a progressive fighter against fascism who had been an illegal Party member in Germany and had made substantial contributions to the consolidation of the USSR's military strength. Now, in view of the twentieth anniversary of the victory over fascism, his services should be recognized by giving him an important government award or by granting him honorary membership of the Soviet Academy of Sciences.

Sakharovsky decided to find out what the scientists thought of this proposal. In the margin of the page is a handwritten note: "The President of the Academy of Sciences, Comrade Mstislav Keldysh, is opposed." So Fuchs remained without an award.

He died in January 1988, just before the final collapse of a Communist Party that had commanded his allegiance for most of his life. Fuchs, the mathematician, theoretical physicist and spy, who helped create the Cold War and the nuclear arms race, who gave vital material assistance to the nuclear programmes of the United States, the Soviet Union and Britain, received recognition from none of them.

Towards the end of his life he gave an interview to an East German film crew. Despite the fact that the interview was authorized by the Central Committee and the Stasi, he gave little away. He sits, eloquent, assured, charming, warmly engaging with the attractive female interviewer. This surely is how he captured the affections of Jessie Gunn, and broke the heart of Erna Skinner. He certainly makes no complaint about the way he has been treated.

His widow did, however. Shortly after Fuchs died, his last Russian handler, Alexander Feklisov, came to visit his grave. He had not seen Fuchs again after their final meeting in April 1949. Fuchs's widow, Grete, did not spare his feelings. "You should have come sooner," she said accusingly.

Epilogue:
Fuchs: the Final Chapter?

Considerably more information about Klaus Fuchs has now come to light since my trip to Moscow many years ago. Great political upheavals have revealed that which was once a deadly secret, although governments and security agencies are now once more trying to nail the lid back on the coffin of the past. Still, informed research by academics and scientists has provided considerably more knowledge about the amount of material delivered by Fuchs to the GRU, and then to the NKGB. It is not only the quantity and quality of the information that Fuchs provided that is important; knowledge of the way that information was passed on to and used by the Soviet scientists is crucial to understanding his importance. Much more still remains to be investigated in the archives in Moscow, but we know enough to appreciate his broad overall importance to Soviet decision-making and to the ways in which Kurchatov steered his team. A memoir by his last NKGB contact in London, Alexander Feklisov, and research in some NKGB archives, also added a great deal to our knowledge of Fuchs's technique as a spy and the ways in which he sustained his covert existence for nine years. So too did the release of the FBI files on their investigation of Fuchs, containing as they do the lengthy interrogation and confessions of Harry Gold, Fuchs's handler in New York and Los Alamos.

In Germany, the fall of the East German government revealed the existence of the filmed interview with Fuchs conducted in the last years of his life, plus some more details about his early political activity, including the background of Grete, the women he met in Paris in 1933 and married in 1959. Information about Grete and the German Communist Party milieu of the 1930s is also contained in her files in Moscow.

In addition to this, the Security Service in Britain, MI5, released the papers on their investigation of Klaus Fuchs, his associates in the German Communist Party in exile in Britain and his GRU contact "Sonya", or Ursula Beurton. Peculiarly, despite the passage of time since Fuchs was arrested, the sets of papers from both the FBI and MI5 were, and remain, heavily censored.

There is therefore a wealth of primary source material about Fuchs. It might seem that there is nothing else to be discovered. However, several huge gaps remain in our knowledge of some crucial points in his life and it is unlikely that the answers to them will ever be found.

I remain intrigued by the fact that, in his first interview with Skardon, Fuchs mentioned that he might have made a journey to Switzerland in 1934 to visit his brother Gerhard. When Skardon doesn't respond to this, Fuchs never mentions it again. It is this that makes me believe that Fuchs is, from the very first, testing Skardon, attempting to discover the limits and the source of his information. I find the mention of this visit suspicious for the following reasons. First, Fuchs had a very good memory; both Feklisov and the scientists at Fort Halstead have gone on record testifying to this. Second, if Fuchs did not see his brother in Switzerland in 1934, then the first time he saw him after leaving Berlin in 1933 was during his visit to Switzerland for a skiing holiday in 1947.

Fuchs and Gerhard were close—close enough for Fuchs's early political activities to be influenced by his older brother. I find it impossible to believe that he could not remember when he saw Gerhard, considering their contacts were so rare. So this reference to a visit in 1934 can mean several things. He was deliberately misleading Skardon. Or he had the money and false papers to travel to Europe without the entry or exit being registered on his Home Office records. If it was the latter, then perhaps he made a visit to see either Grete or his brother, and was more active on behalf of the Party or the Comintern than he, or the official record, suggests. This second possibility raises the question of whether he had already been recruited by Soviet intelligence at that time. I think it is unlikely. If he had been an agent of the Soviet intelligence agencies at that early date then the contact had lapsed long before 1940 when he was interned, because it appears that neither the GRU nor the NKGB had any information about him when he later began handing over material to them.

Another question that remains unanswered is exactly when did he become aware that work was being carried out in Britain on the possibility of a nuclear weapon, and when did he make contact with Soviet intelligence? It is clear he was aware of what he would be doing at Birmingham long before he started working there in May 1941. We know he spent some time in London before then, and presumably that was when the contact that led to his recruitment by the GRU started. But Peierls had been in correspondence with Professor Born in Edinburgh about Fuchs in November 1940, and we know that Born and Fuchs had discussed the morality of working on nuclear weapons at length. Did Fuchs know about the work that Frisch and Peierls were doing long before he received the formal invitation to work on the MAUD Report?

Then there is the greatest mystery of all. Why did

Fuchs confess? The answer to this question is more complicated than it might at first seem. Fuchs's nephew, Klaus Kittowski, believes that he did so to protect his sister Kristel, who knew far more than Fuchs was prepared to admit about his contacts with Harry Gold. She was mentally ill and Fuchs would naturally seek to protect her from questioning. In addition, if Kristel did become part of the investigation, then Fuchs would lose control of the situation. Klaus Kittowski didn't at the time I spoke to him know the details of the final stages of the MI5 investigation. The crucial period when Fuchs made the decision to confess was the two days in January 1950 that he spent with Erna in the Palm Court Hotel in Richmond. Before that time he had successfully denied all of Skardon's allegations and MI5 had decided to scale down their surveillance operation. They made no attempt to bug the hotel room that the couple stayed in, and both Fuchs and Erna Skinner are now dead, so we will never know what conversations took place. What is obvious is that whatever passed between Fuchs and Erna during that time influenced him to change his mind and make a confession. According to Herbert Skinner's account, Fuchs may have told Cockcroft about his spying in New York before then, but at the hotel in Richmond he revealed to Erna the full extent of his espionage. It must have been an intensely traumatic experience for both people involved. However, it is one thing to confess to a lover and entirely another to confess to a secret policeman. Would Fuchs have done so entirely under his own volition, or would Erna have encouraged him, or perhaps argued against this course of action? We will never know.

Two things must have influenced their discussion, however. One was the offer of immunity made by Skardon, which in essence was "Tell us everything and it might be possible for you to stay at Harwell." Did Fuchs really believe this?

It seems he did, and it seems that Skardon and everyone else in MI5 knew this. The record of the interrogations becomes somewhat sparse after Fuchs's first confession to Skardon. There is no contemporaneous note of the fourth interrogation in the file, only a brief report by Skardon written up later. Skardon is aware that Fuchs's prefab and office have been bugged, and says that he finds the prospect of his continuing conversations with Fuchs being overheard inhibiting. As a result of this, MI5 decide not to reinstate the electronic eavesdropping and so save Skardon any embarrassment. This means, of course, quite conveniently, that there is no record of the conversations that led up to Fuchs's signed confession. But why would Skardon not want his conversation overheard? Was it because he knew that he was exceeding his authority in offering immunity to Fuchs in return for a complete and detailed confession of his espionage?

Certainly, as we have seen, MI5 in the form of Dick White and their legal officers were aware that there was a danger that Fuchs might retract his confession and claim that he was induced to make it, so rendering it inadmissible evidence, and they went so far as to brief Fuchs's defence lawyers on the issue. Despite this, in fact Mr. Derek Curtis-Bennett, counsel for Fuchs, made a half-hearted attempt to raise the issue at the trial. Was Fuchs being exceptionally naïve to rely on the promises of Jim Skardon during his interrogation? Possibly so, but this brings into play other questions that as yet still have no answer.

In a document dated 27 January 1950, a record of a meeting with Dick White and Michael Perrin, which is actually a copy rather than the original, White says to Perrin that Fuchs does not consider espionage to be an offence (presumably in this particular case). Emphasizing the reasons for this, White says that Fuchs drew Skardon's attention during the confession to the information that he had supplied to the British after obtaining it in the United States. There is of course no record of this exchange in Skardon's notes. And the conversation was not covertly recorded, or if it was it is not in the MI5 files released to the public.

We have seen that Fuchs spent longer than almost any other member of the British Mission at Los Alamos after the war, and that he was uniquely placed to gather material across a broad range of the research that went on there. He worked on modifications to the Nagasaki bomb for the Bikini tests and took over editing parts of the Los Alamos "Bible", its official history. He was actively engaged with Teller and Von Neumann in research on the H-bomb, and supplied all of that information to Britain along with other highly secret information on fast reactor design, weapons stock piles and production rates of plutonium and uranium. The amount and depth of information that Fuchs supplied to the UK was extremely important. We have seen that he was in regular contact with William Penney, head of the British bomb programme, and that he made visits to the weapons establishment at Fort Halstead to give lectures to the staff. This may, in fact, be the tip of the iceberg of the extent to which Fuchs provided secret information from Los Alamos to the British bomb project. At the moment, remarkably, despite the length of time since Fuchs was arrested, it is still not possible to make a proper assessment of the assistance Fuchs provided to Penney and the team building the first British fission and fusion bombs. I think it was substantial.

Early in my research for this book I came across a file in the National Archives in Kew, which I mention in Chapter 17. It was in an old series of records of the Atomic Weapons Research Establishment and it was called "Miscellaneous Super Bomb Notes by Klaus Fuchs". It is a twelve-page document of calculations and equations concerning the fusion process that occurs in a hydrogen bomb, or super-bomb as it became known in Los Alamos. The file was dated 1954, which is absurd, because at that time Fuchs was in prison. I mentioned the existence of the file in a message I posted on a nuclear history website on 26 September 2013. When I went back to the National Archives to have another look at the document in November 2013, I was told that the file was unavailable because it had been requested by a government department. It had been requested in October, by the Ministry of Defence, and has still not been returned to the public domain at the time of writing, over six months later—a long while, one might think, to look at a file of twelve pages.

This was not the only file that might provide evidence of Fuchs's deep collaboration with the Atomic Weapons Research Establishment. Others that were quickly removed by the Ministry of Defence at the same time, all from the same series and all dated 1954, covered information from Los Alamos on nuclear weapons; information about the United States' development of a thermonuclear weapon; theories of radiation hydrodynamics, an area in which Fuchs specialized at Los Alamos; and a list of classified nuclear data.

Even more intriguing are files that the Ministry of Defence has admitted it possesses but still refuses to place in the public domain. These detail the collaboration between the Weapons Establishment and Harwell, where Fuchs of course was head of the Theoretical Physics Department, on fusion shock waves. They cover papers from 1946 to 1953 on the super-bomb, and the only possible source for material as early as 1946 was either Klaus Fuchs or Egon Bretscher, whose papers we saw were smuggled out of Los Alamos by Fuchs at the request of Bretscher's wife. In addition, there is a file containing the collected notes of super-bomb lectures by Enrico Fermi. These lectures were given by Fermi at Los Alamos and Fuchs attended them, and no doubt took copious notes. Another file contains information about the super-bomb, based on wartime Los Alamos papers. The source of those documents might prove interesting. Yet another file contains a memorandum between Robert Oppenheimer, scientific head of the Manhattan Project, and Rudolf Peierls, head of the British Mission in New York and Los Alamos. This file is also dated 1954, although by then Oppenheimer had abandoned any work on nuclear weapons and so had Peierls. The memorandum is most likely one that was written in 1942. It clearly affected the relationship between the Manhattan Project and the eventual British Scientific Mission. It was secret then, but it is hard to see why that document, which might prove historically interesting, is not now in the public domain.

It might be argued that there is a valid reason why many of these documents are not available. They contain detailed formulae and scientific information about nuclear weapons, the dissemination of which could lead to nuclear prolifera-tion and might even be used by terrorists. This argument is clearly spurious. The information in them is almost seventy years old. With states like Pakistan, North Korea and Iran either possessing or embarking on building nuclear weapons, and the former apartheid government in South Africa succeeding in testing one, the proliferation cat is well out of the bag, and potential nuclear terrorists have more welcoming sources of information than the National Archives at Kew. In any event, it is quite possible for the documents to be released with their specific sensitive scientific informa-tion, if any exists, redacted, as is already done in many security files. In this way at least more information about the early origins of Britain's nuclear programme, and its reliance on the work at Los Alamos, could be assessed. Perhaps that reliance is really what the problem is.

For the moment it is impossible to say what the files might reveal about Fuchs's role in transporting information from Los Alamos to Britain, but, as we have seen, clearly he believed it to be significant. He was spying not only for the Soviet Union, but for Britain as well. As we have also seen, he believed that this would affect the way that the authorities dealt with his case. He was wrong.

Why did he confess? Was he misled and betrayed by Skardon? Why did he have no inkling that his arrest was imminent? Did a deal between him and MI5 about his trial fall apart under the vindictiveness of Lord Chief Justice Goddard?

These are questions that still remain. Behind them is the bigger one, of the importance of Fuchs to the overall British nuclear effort. I started my search for the truth about Klaus Fuchs many years ago, believing that the answers would lie in Moscow. Some of them did and have eventually come to light. Other, equally important, answers exist, ironically not in Moscow but in files in London which at the time of writing still remain hidden. There can be no good reason why they remain so.

Books

Albrecht, Ulrich, *Die Sowjetische Rustungsindustrie*, Westdeutscher Verlag, Opladen, Germany, 1989.

Albright, Joseph, and Kunstel, Marcia, *Bombshell*, Random House, New York, 1997.

Andrew, Christopher, *The Defence of the Realm*, Allen Lane, London, 2009.

Andrew, Christopher, and Gordievsky, Oleg, *KGB: the Inside Story*, Hodder & Stoughton, London, 1990.

Andrew, Christopher, and Mitrokhin, Vasili, *The Mitrokhin Archive*, Allen Lane, London, 1999.

Arnold, Lorna, *Britain and the H-Bomb*, Palgrave Macmillan, Basingstoke, Hampshire, 2001.

Baggott, Jim, *The First War of Physics*, Pegasus Books, New York, 2010.

Baird, Kai, and Sherwin, Martin, *American Prometheus: the Triumph and Tragedy of J. Robert Oppenheimer*, Alfred A. Knopf, New York, 2005.

Bower, Tom, *The Perfect English Spy*, William Heinemann, London, 1995.

Bullock, Alan, *Ernest Bevin: Foreign Secretary*, William Heinemann, London, 1983.

Burke, David, *The Spy Who Came In From the Co-op*, The Boydell Press, Woodbridge, Suffolk, 2008.

Cathcart, Brian, *Test of Greatness*, John Murray, London, 1994.

Feklisov, Alexander, and Kostin, Sergei, *The Man Behind the Rosenbergs*, Enigma Books, New York, 2004.

Fowkes, Ben, *Communism in Germany Under the Weimar Republic*, Macmillan Press, London, 1984.

Gowing, Margaret, *Britain and Atomic Energy, 1939–1945*, Macmillan & Co., London, 1964.

Gowing, Margaret, *Independence and Deterrence: Britain and Atomic Energy, 1945–52*, Macmillan & Co., London, 1974.

Hennessy, Peter, *Never Again: Britain 1945–1951*, Jonathan Cape, London, 1992.

Herken, Gregg, *Brotherhood of the Bomb*, Henry Holt and Company, New York, 2002.

Hewlett, Richard G., and Anderson, Oscar E. Jr, *The New World, 1939/1946: A History of the United States Atomic Energy Commission*, Vol. 1, Pennsylvania State University Press, Pennsylvania, 1962.

Holloway, David, *Stalin and the Bomb: the Soviet Union and Atomic Energy 1939–1956*, Yale University Press, New Haven, 1994.

Hornblum, Allen M., *The Invisible Harry Gold*, Yale University Press, New Haven, 2010.

Kern, Gary, *A Death in Washington*, Enigma Books, New York, 2004.

Kershaw, Ian, *Hitler 1889–1936: Hubris*, Allen Lane, London, 1998.

Kramish, Arnold, *The Griffin*, Houghton Mifflin Company, Boston, 1986.

Laucht, Christoph, *Elemental Germans*, Palgrave Macmillan, Basingstoke, Hampshire, 2012.

Lota, Vladimir, *GRU i atomnaia bomba*, Olma Press, Moscow, 2002.

Moorehead, Alan, *The Traitors: the Double Life of Fuchs, Pontecorvo and Nunn May*, Hamish Hamilton, London, 1952.

Montgomery Hyde, H., *The Atom Bomb Spies*, Hamish Hamilton, London, 1980.

Montgomery Hyde, H., *George Blake: Superspy*, Constable, London, 1987.

Moss, Norman, *Klaus Fuchs: the Man Who Stole the Atom Bomb*, Grafton Books, London, 1987.

Panitz, Eberhard, *Geheimtreff Banbury*, Verlag Das Neue Berlin, Berlin, 2003.

Patterson, Walter C., *The Plutonium Business*, Paladin Press, London, 1973.

Peierls, Rudolf, *Bird of Passage*, Princeton University Press, New Jersey, 1985.

Preston, Diana, *Before the Fallout*, Transworld, London, 2005.

Rhodes, Richard, *The Making of the Atomic Bomb*, Simon & Schuster, New York, 1986.

Rhodes, Richard, *Dark Sun: the Making of the Hydrogen Bomb*, Simon & Schuster, New York, 1986.

Rosenbaum, Ron, *Explaining Hitler*, Random House, New York, 1998.

Ryabev, L. D. (ed.), *Atomnaia Bomba USSR, 1945–1954*, 2 vols, State Corporation for Atomic Energy, Moscow, 1999–2000.

Ryabev, L. D. (ed.), *Atomnaia Proekta USSR, Documents and Materials*, Vol. 3, State Corporation for Atomic Energy, Moscow, 2008.

Sillitoe, Sir Percy, KBE, *Cloak Without Dagger*, Cassell and Company, London, 1955.

Szasz Ferenc Morton, *British Scientists and the Manhattan Project: the Los Alamos Years*, Macmillan, Basingstoke, Hampshire, 1992.

Weinstein, Allen, and Vassiliev, Alexander, *The Haunted Wood*, Modern Library, New York, 2000.

Werner, Ruth, *Sonya's Report*, Chatto & Windus, London, 1991.

Williams, Robert Chadwell, *Klaus Fuchs, Atom Spy*, Harvard University Press, Cambridge, Mass., 1987.

Wolf, Markus, *Man Without a Face*, Jonathan Cape, London, 1997.

Wright, Peter, *Spycatcher*, Viking Penguin Inc., New York, 1987.

Articles and papers

Physics Today, Special Issue, November 1966:
    Holloway, David, "New Light on Early Soviet Bomb Secrets"
    Goncharov, German, "Thermonuclear Milestones: (1) The American Effort; (2) The Beginnings of the Soviet H Bomb Programme; (3) The Race Accelerates".

Bulletin of the Atomic Scientists, Vol. 94, No. 4, May 1993:
    Khariton, Yulii, and Smirnov, Yuri, "The Khariton Version".

Exploring Intelligence Archives, Routledge, 2008: Goodman, Michael, and Holloway, David, "The Interrogation of Klaus Fuchs, 1950".

Intelligence and National Security,17:4, 2002: Lee, Sabine, "The Spy That Never Was".

Der Leibniz-Sozietät der Wissenschaften zu Berlin, November 2011: Flach, Gunther, and Fuchs-Kittowski, Klaus, "Zum Gedenken Klaus Fuchs vom atomaren Patt zu einer von Atomwaffen freien Welt".

Contemporary British History, Vol. 19, No. 1, Spring 2005: Goodman and Pincher, "Clement Attlee, Percy Sillitoe and the Security Aspects of the Fuchs Case".

Los Alamos Scientific Laboratory of the University of California LAMS-2532: *Manhattan District History, Project Y: The Los Alamos Project*, Vol. 1: *Inception until August 1945*; Vol. 2: *August 1945 through December 1946*.

Prospero—The Journal of British Rocketry and Nuclear

History, No. 1:1, April 2004: Goodman, Michael, "Santa Klaus: Klaus Fuchs and the Nuclear Weapons Programmes of the UK, US and USSR".

Journal of Undergraduate Sciences, Vol. 3, Summer 1996: Schwartz, Michael, "The Russian American Bomb: the Role of Espionage in the Soviet Atomic Bomb Project".

Historical Studies in the Physical and Biological Sciences, 34:1, 2004: Goodman, Michael, "Grandfather of the Hydrogen Bomb? Klaus Fuchs and Anglo-American Intelligence".

Archive sources

The National Archives, Kew, London:

The Security Service Files on the Klaus Fuchs Investigation are contained in the KV 2 series, as are the Security Service files on his friends and colleagues:

KV 2/1245–1270 contain material on Klaus Fuchs.

KV 2/1658–1663 contain material on Rudolf and Eugenia Peierls.

KV 2/2080–82 contain material on Professor Herbert Skinner and his wife Erna.

KV 2/1871–1880 contain material on Jürgen Kuczynski.

KV 2/3223–4 contain material on Ronald Gunn.

Other files are:

KV 6/41–45 contain material on Ursula Beurton, or Ruth Werner.

The former UK Atomic Energy Files in the AB 1 series contain files of correspondence between Peierls, Fuchs, Chadwick and others. AB 3 and AB 6 contain files from the Tube Alloys Directorate with correspondence between Akers, Perrin, Peierls and Fuchs.

Atomic Weapons Research Establishment files are contained in the ES 1 and ES 10 series, the latter containing correspondence between Fuchs and Penney.

The Digital Archive of the Woodrow Wilson Center for

International Scholars, Washington, DC, contains the papers and notebooks of Alexander Vassiliev.

The Federal Bureau of Investigation files on the interrogation of Harry Gold and Kristel Heinemann are digitized and available online via the FBI website.

Other archive sources are the Bundesarchiv, Berlin, which contains material of the former KPD and in file series DY 30 information about members of the Central Committee of the Socialist Unity Party of former East Germany.

The BStU in Berlin, the "Stasi" archive, contains personal and surveillance files on Klaus Fuchs and Margarete Fuchs-Keilson.

Material on Margarete Keilson can also be found in the Comintern Papers contained in the Russian State Archives of Socio-Political History, Moscow.

INDEX

Academic Assistance Council
60–1, 62
Acheson, Dean 264
Air Defence Research Committee
80, 109
Akers, Wallace 89, 112–17, 123,
134–6, 179
Alamogordo 149
see also Trinity Test
Aldermaston *see* Atomic Weapons
Research Establishment
Al'tshuler, Lev 259
Alvarez, Luis 265
American Friends Service
Committee 23
Anderson, Sir John 113, 115, 117,
178, 193
Anglo-American atomic
collaboration 89, 96,
109–19, 264, 348–9
Combined Policy Committee
115, 348, 349
McMahon Act and 191, 193,
216, 219, 348
Modus Vivendi agreement 348

Quebec Agreement (1943)
114–15
see also Manhattan Project
anti-communist climate 184, 188,
218, 234
anti-fascism 25, 38, 39, 44, 48,
52, 59, 361
anti-semitism 61, 125
Archer, Jane 186, 187
Archer, John 94, 95
Argonne Laboratories 176, 181,
217
Arlington Hall 240, 241
Arnold, Wing Commander Henry
22–4, 29, 184–6, 234, 237,
243, 245–50, 253, 267, 269,
274–6, 278, 282, 284–5,
288–9, 290–2, 294, 298,
301–5, 307, 309, 313, 317, 321,
327
Arzamas-16 256, 257, 259, 260
atomic bomb
Frisch–Peierls Memorandum
80–1, 90, 116
MAUD Report 80–2, 86–8,

90, 93, 104–5, 109–12,
190–1 , 365
see also plutonium bomb;
uranium bomb
Atomic Energy Commission (US)
216, 242, 265–6, 344, 352
Atomic Energy Research
Establishment (UK) 21–4,
29–31, 178–9, 182–5, 187–9,
190–2, 194, 197, 199, 202–3,
207–8, 212–13,216, 218, 225,
230, 234–7, 242–8, 250,
252–3, 267, 269, 273, 275,
277–9, 283–4, 288–9, 290,
293–9, 300–9, 311–17, 322,
326, 328, 332, 347, 357, 360,
366, 369
Atomic Research Institute (East
Germany) 357–8
Atomic Weapons Research
Establishment (UK) 199, 224,
368–9
Attlee, Clement 191, 315
Auschwitz 42

B-29 bombers 17, 153, 158–60,
171, 264, 348–9
Badham, Colonel 189
Bagot, Millicent 118, 119
Bainbridge, Kenneth 110
Barbusse, Henri 25
Barwich, Heinz 360
Bentley, Derek 329
Bentley, Elizabeth 204, 209, 229
Beria, Lavrenty 8–9, 104, 126–7,
130, 151, 157, 205, 210, 221–3,
225, 258, 260–3
Berlin
airlift 348–9
Berlin Technical School 41
Berlin Wall 10
blockade of 30, 237, 348

beryllium 143, 151, 175, 176, 220,
313
Bethe, Hans 13–14, 15, 16, 17, 18,
78, 111, 116, 135–8, 140, 144,
148, 167, 168, 172, 180, 190,
266, 343, 352, 354
Beurton, Len 75, 227, 324
Beurton, Ursula *see* Kuczynski,
Ursula
Beveridge, Lord 60
Bevin, Ernest 192, 193, 349
Bikini Atoll 172, 177, 226
Birmingham University 14, 22,
63, 77, 78, 86, 87, 90, 179, 183,
188, 198, 217, 246
Bletchley Park 240
Blunt, Anthony 84
Bock's Car 160
Bohr, Niels 56, 77–8, 80–1, 210
Bolshevik revolution 33
Born, Hedi 64-5
Born, Max 55, 60, 62–5, 68–9,
73, 82, 73, 82, 93, 97, 111, 190,
230, 278, 365
Bosanquet, Daphne 99, 119
Bradbury, Norris 169, 172–3, 176,
179
Bragg, William 60 "Bravo"
354
Brennan, Richard 338–9
Bretscher, Egon 22, 87, 173, 175,
224, 369
Bridges, Lord 197
Bristol University 53–7, 62, 98,
183, 230, 322
British atomic programme 23,
111, 135, 164, 187, 192, 207,
347, 350
cost estimates 114
see also Anglo-American
atomic collaboration;
Atomic Energy Research

Establishment; MAUD
Report; Tube Alloys
Directorate
British Communist Party 58, 104,
206, 207, 228, 322, 328, 357
British Intelligence *see* MI5; MI6
British Scientific Mission 14, 25,
27, 28, 116, 117, 120, 123,
128-9, 133, 134, 164, 167, 169,
171, 175, 202-3, 224, 241, 259,
280, 281, 287, 297, 306, 368,
370
British Supply Council 120, 121
Broda, Engelbert 102, 151, 181-2
Brownshirts *see* Sturmabteilung
(SA)
Buchenwald 48
Buneman, Mary 304
Buneman, Oscar 304
Burt, Commander Leonard 314,
316-17, 318-21
Bush, Vannevar 110, 113
Byrnes, Jimmy 17, 155, 156, 192

Cairncross, John 104
Caltech Laboratory 230
Camp Y *see* Los Alamos
Canadian atomic programme 89,
90, 114, 115,169, 171, 263-4,
265, 349
Canadian group of Soviet agents
180-1, 229-30
Capenhurst 22, 192, 199, 202,
208, 351
Casablanca Conference (1943) 113
Catchpole, Corder 322
Cavendish Laboratory 55, 63, 78,
80, 86, 87, 102, 102, 151, 181,
182
Central Intelligence Agency (CIA)
336
Chadwick, James 14, 78, 80-1, 87,
89, 95, 96, 97, 110, 115, 117,
123, 129, 134, 135-6, 150,
167-73, 175-7, 178, 180, 182,
190, 195, 202, 221, 225, 246,
259, 281, 295
Chalk River reactor site 152,
180-181,182
Chamberlain, Neville 67
Chelyabinsk 255-7, 260
Cherwell, Lord 111, 295
Christie, Agatha 84
Christmas Humphreys, Travers
327
Churchill, Winston 110, 111, 113,
114, 134, 153-4
Cimperman, John 344
Clarke, David 119
Clegg, Hugh 336-7, 339-40,
342-4
Cockcroft, Sir John 30-1, 80, 96,
109, 182-3, 188-9, 190, 192,
242-3, 254, 265, 270-1, 277,
284-5, 289, 293-5, 298,
301-3, 307, 311, 314-16, 366
code breaking 240-1
Cohen, Karl 122, 292, 297
Cold War 3, 10-11, 30, 220, 265,
361
Columbia University 121-2, 123,
155, 281, 291, 297
Comintern 42, 44-8, 72, 108,
355, 365
Communist International 36
Communist Party of Austria 102
Communist Party of China 74
Communist Party of Denmark 48
Communist Party of Germany
(KPD) 32-3, 35-42, 44-6,
48-52, 58, 61, 68, 70, 72, 74,
76, 83-5, 98, 100-1, 108,
206-8, 235-6, 286, 290, 305,
332, 356, 360, 364

banned in Germany 40-1
in Britain 52, 58, 84, 206-7, 227
Communist Party of Great Britain
23-4, 234, 322
Conant, James 110, 113
Congress Against War and
Fascism 44, 48, 52
Congressional Joint Committee
on Atomic Energy (US) 348
Corner, John 200, 249, 350
Cripps, Sir Stafford 192
Curie, Irène 8
Curie, Marie 8, 15
Curtis-Bennett, Derek 328-9,
331-4, 367

Dachau 41
Dalton, Hugh 192
Darwin, Charles 110
Davis, Air Vice Marshal E.D. 199
Davison, Boris 112
dead letter drops 101, 228, 274,
324
defections 26, 181-3, 191, 204,
209, 229, 360
Denman, Major 282
Department of Scientific and
Industrial Research (UK) 89,
98, 117-18, 123-4, 185, 291
deuterium 87, 167, 174-7, 182,
220-1, 223, 224, 352-4
Deutsch, Arnold 84
dialectical materialism 260
diffusion plants 88-9, 96, 106,
117, 121-4, 131, 134-5, 192-3,
209, 280, 297
Dimitrov, Georgi 46-8, 53
Dirac, Paul 112
Dounreay 270-1

Eastman Kodak 125
Ebert, Friedrich 33-4

Edinburgh University 25, 60,
62-3, 67-8, 324
Einstein, Albert 17, 61
electromagnetic separation plants
129, 134
Enola Gay 158
equilibrium time problem 96
Ershova, Zinaida 8, 9
explosive lenses 140, 143, 147,
148, 154, 159, 172, 195-6, 198,
261

"Fat Man" 156, 157, 159, 160, 171
Feather, Norman 87
Federal Bureau of Investigation
(FBI) 26, 117, 133, 204, 209,
229, 241-2, 255, 278, 285,
293, 296, 325-6, 335-46, 356,
363-4
Feklisov, Alexander ("Eugene")
209-15, 217-26, 228-32, 233,
235, 252-3, 256, 266, 325, 345,
346, 351, 360-2, 363, 364
Fermi, Enrico 17, 78, 109, 112,
155, 168, 176, 213, 217, 369-70
Feynman, Richard 137, 140-1,
343
First World War 32, 71
Fitin, Pavel 127
Flerov, Georgi 2-4, 6-9, 103-5,
107, 256-8, 260-2
Foote, Alexander 227
Fort Halstead 22, 196, 197,
199-202, 218-19, 224, 249,
267, 311, 313, 347, 364, 368
Foulness 196
Fowler, Ralph 86
Frank, Ludwig 268
Fraser, Lord 347
"Fred" (Soviet handler) 126
Freier Deutscher Kulturbund 58,
83, 206

Freikorps 33–4
Frisch, Otto 77–81, 87–8, 94, 97, 104, 116, 138, 148, 154, 156, 159, 183, 194, 224, 246, 257, 314–15, 365
Frisch–Peierls Memorandum 80–1, 90, 116
Fröhlich, Herbert 87
Fuchs, Elisabeth (KF's sister) *see* Kittowski, Elisabeth
Fuchs, Else (KF's mother) 34–5
Fuchs, Emil (KF's father) 22–3, 24, 25, 29, 34–5, 41–2, 54, 179, 214, 235–9, 246, 269–70, 274–6, 277, 284, 285, 286, 288, 292–4, 302, 322, 341, 355, 356, 357
Fuchs, Gerhard (KF's brother) 21, 30, 32, 36, 37, 45, 56, 57, 58, 60, 87, 117, 122, 180, 181, 187, 207, 208, 249, 311, 320
Fuchs, Karin (KF's sister-in-law) 41
Fuchs, Kristel (KF's sister) *see* Heinemann, Kristel
Fuchs–von Neumann patent 177, 352
fuel rods 192, 225, 257
fusion bomb *see* hydrogen bomb

Gagarin, Yuri 5
Gardner, Meredith 241
Garrett, Major G. 118–19
Geiger, Hans 14
Germany
    Kiel mutiny (1918) 33
    Nazi-Soviet non-aggression pact 49, 68, 70, 84, 86
    post-First World War 32–3
    Reichstag fire (1933) 40, 47, 48, 53

rise of Nazi Germany 35–43, 45, 60
    Weimar Republic 33–5, 37
    see also Communist Party of Germany (KPD); Social Democratic Party of Germany (SPD)
Gestapo 42, 48, 145–6, 189, 328
Ginzburg, Vitalii 353
GKO (State Defence Committee, Soviet Union) 104–6, 126, 130, 166
GLEEP nuclear reactor 21–2
Goddard, Lord Chief Justice 287–8, 290–2, 326, 328–34, 371
Gold, Harry ("Raymond") 124–33, 134, 141–2, 144–6, 150–2, 162–7, 177, 178, 180, 182, 195, 204–5, 220, 229, 233, 235, 236, 252, 306, 315, 337–45, 356, 358, 359, 364, 366
Goncharov, German 168, 223, 224, 353
Gorbachev, Mikhail 3
Göring, Hermann 40, 47
Gouzenko, Igor 180–2, 183, 191, 209, 229
Government Communications Headquarters (GCHQ) 242
Gowing, Margaret 1
Greenglass, David 152
Groves, General Leslie 16, 17, 112, 113, 116, 117, 135–6, 139, 154–6, 160, 268, 170, 172, 216
GRU (Soviet Military Intelligence) 2n, 73–5, 84, 89, 90, 95, 99–102, 105–8, 126–7, 130, 180–1, 210, 226, 229, 325, 363–5
Gunn, Jessie 55–6, 64, 361

Gunn, Ronald 59, 281–2 55–6, 67, 322
Gurevich, Isai 222
Gurney, Ronald 57–8
Gysi, Klaus 36–7

Hahn, Otto 77
Halban, Hans von 86–7, 89, 102, 107, 182
Haldane, J.B.S. 73
Hall, Theodore 152, 226, 353
Halperin, Israel 26–7, 29, 229–30, 287, 291, 342
Hamburger, Rolf 74
Hammerstein-Equord, Helga 42
Hammerstein-Equord, General Kurt von 42
Hammerstein-Equord, Maria-Luise 42
Hanford 147, 154, 257
Hankey, Lord 88, 104, 110
Hanley, W.B. 244–5
Harben, Philip 84
Harper, Professor 251–4
Hartley Hodder, C. 61
Harwell *see* Atomic Energy Research Establishment
heavy water 86–7, 114, 115, 181
heavy-water reactors 102, 107, 115, 217
Heinemann, Kristel (KF's sister) 28–9, 34–5, 63–4, 65, 108, 122, 132, 141–2, 144, 177, 204, 217, 230, 236, 238–9, 248, 287, 291, 306–7, 336, 337, 340, 342, 344, 366
Heinemann, Robert 108, 127, 144, 336, 340
Heisenberg, Werner 55-6, 60, 153
Heisenberg's uncertainty principle 55, 56
Herweg, Carl 61

Hill, Bernard 315, 327, 328
Hindenburg, Paul von 36, 37, 39, 40
Hinton, Sir Christopher 96, 198, 199
Hirohito, Emperor 161
Hiroshima 158, 159, 160, 162, 164, 165, 167, 171, 220, 258, 261
Hitler, Adolf 17, 35–9, 40–3, 49–50, 59, 67, 70, 77, 84, 150, 240, 331
Hollis, Roger 186–8
Hoover, J. Edgar 326, 335, 337
Hotel Cosmos, Moscow 5–6
hydrodynamics 137, 144, 147, 172,198 201, 369
hydrogen bomb 11, 19, 137, 156, 167–8, 173–5, 177, 202, 213, 218, 221–4, 265–6, 313, 314–15, 349, 351–3, 368–9
"Bravo" 354
"Joe 4" 354
"Mike" 352, 354

ICI 81, 88, 89, 97, 112, 198, 280
I.G. Farben 41–2
Institute for Nuclear Physics, East Germany 359–60
International Brigades 72, 75
Ioffe, Abram 103
Isle of Man 69–70

Japanese surrender 161, 162
"Joe 1" 349
"Joe 4" 354
Joliot-Curie, Frédéric 86
Joyce, William (Lord Haw-haw) 24

Kaftanov, Sergei 91, 105–6
Kahle, Hans 25, 71–4, 76, 83–4, 185–7, 189, 287, 292

Kapitsa, Pyotr 103
Kaploun, Jerome 344
Kearton, Frank 27, 122, 280-1,
  285, 287, 343
Keilson, Margarete 45-53, 65, 68,
  355-8, 362, 364-5
Keilson, Max 45, 46, 49
Keldysh, Mstislav 361
Kell, Sir Vernon 62
Kellermann, Walter 70
Kellex Corporation 28, 121-4,
  209, 242, 281, 29, 292, 297
Kemmer, Nicholas 87
KGB 10
Khariton, Yulii 103, 222-3,
  258-60, 262, 353, 354
Khrushchev, Nikita 360
Kiel mutiny (1918) 33
Kistiakowsky, George 138, 152 ,
  168, 196
Kittowski, Elisabeth (KF's sister)
  34, 35, 36, 41-2, 64, 235
Kittowski, Gustav 41-2, 64
Kittowski, Klaus (KF's nephew)
  23, 42, 179, 235-8, 246, 269,
  274, 275, 355, 356, 366
Kline, Evelyn 140
Klopstech, Hannah 207-9
Kowarski, Lew 86-7, 107, 181
KPD *see* Communist Party of
  Germany
Kremer, Semyon 84-6, 89-90,
  95, 99, 100, 102, 104, 107,
  323, 325, 340,
Krivitsky, Walter 186
Kuczynski, Jürgen 58, 76, 84-5,
  100-11, 206-7, 227, 324-5
Kuczynski, Margaret 207
Kuczynski, Robert 74, 76, 84
Kuczynski, Ursula (Ursula
  Beurton, Ruth Werner,
  "Sonya") 74-6. 100-2, 106-8,

122, 124, 127, 130, 141, 151,
  226-9, 324-5, 330, 346, 364
Kurchatov, Igor 4, 7-9, 103, 105,
  151-3, 157, 166, 193-4, 205,
  210, 213, 215, 222-3, 225,
  255-6, 258-63, 353, 363
Kurchatov Institute 3-4, 7, 10
Kurti, Nicholas 27, 87
Kvasnikov, Leonid 359

Lamphere, Robert 335-7,
  339-40, 342-5
Lauritsen, Charles 110
Lawrence, Edward 265
Lawrence, Ernest 110, 122, 170, 183
Lend Lease Agreement 192-3
Lenin, V.I. 36
Liddell, Guy 186-8, 244, 283
Liebknecht, Karl 33-4
lithium deuteride 353-4
"Little Boy" 156-9
Los Alamos 13, 14, 20, 22, 23, 27,
  45, 112, 116, 117, 131, 135-40,
  142, 143-6, 147-53, 155-7,
  159, 162, 164-5, 167-73, 175,
  178, 179-80, 182-3, 190,
  193-202, 204, 214, 216-19,
  221, 223-4, 230, 233, 243,
  252, 256, 257, 259, 264, 266,
  281, 291-3, 297, 306, 313,
  339, 341, 343, 352, 353, 364,
  369-71
  see also Manhattan Project
Los Alamos University 172
Lotta, Vladimir 105, 106
Lubbe, Marinus van der 40, 47
Lubyanka 8, 205, 213
Luxemburg, Rosa 33
Lysenko, Trofim 260

McFadden, J. 189
McMahon, Brien 348

McMahon Act 191, 193, 219, 266, 348

mail intercepts 187–8, 243–4, 247–8, 253–4, 269, 270, 293

Maisky, Ivan 85

Makins, Sir Roger 327, 328

Malenkov, Georgi 126

Malleson, Miles 268–9

Malleson, Tatiana 268–9

Manhattan Engineering District 25, 112

see also Manhattan Project

Manhattan Project 7, 16–18, 116, 121–3, 126, 128–9, 136–40, 146, 154, 156–7, 165–6, 169, 171, 174, 179, 183, 191, 202–3, 209, 210, 214, 216–17, 230, 257, 259, 281, 370

British Scientific Mission 14, 25, 27, 28, 116, 117, 120, 123, 128–9, 133, 134, 164, 167, 169, 171, 175, 202–3, 224, 241, 259, 280, 281, 287, 297, 306, 368, 370

compartmentalization principle 117, 139

declassification of papers 214, 216–17

Smyth Report 210, 257

Soviet intelligence and 125–6

see also Gold, Harry

Trinity test 13-20, 149, 151, 154, 156, 162, 165, 171–2, 194, 201, 249, 258, 354

Marriott, John 254, 283, 295, 302, 307, 308, 314, 319

Marshak, Robert 217

Martigny, Grete 55

Martin, Arthur 280, 281, 283

Matern, Hermann 356

Mathew, Sir Theobald 327

MAUD Committee 80–2, 86, 87, 90, 110–12, 137, 217, 306, 313

MAUD Report 87, 88, 90, 93–4, 104–5, 109–12, 190–1, 306, 313, 365

Mayne, Miss 116

Meitner, Lise 77

Metropolitan-Vickers 81, 88, 106

MI5 1, 2, 10, 23–4, 29–31, 55, 58, 62, 72, 87, 92–5, 97–100, 117–19, 183–9, 206, 227–8, 230, 242–54, 255, 268–72, 274–6, 277–83, 285–6, 289, 293–9, 301–9, 315–16, 318–19, 321–3, 325–8, 335–7, 345–6, 350–1, 359, 364, 366–8, 371

B Branch 24, 184, 187, 227, 242–4, 276, 289

C Branch 184

MI6 230, 267

microphone surveillance 244, 248, 250, 273, 282, 290, 299, 303, 307, 312, 317, 321

"Mike" 352, 354

Miller, Scott 338, 339, 341

Modus Vivendi agreement 348

Molotov, Vyacheslav 106, 152–3, 157, 221, 225

Monsarrat, Nicholas 84

Monte Bello Islands 350, 351

Moon, Philip 149-50, 167

Moorehead, Alan 1

Moral Rearmament Movement 184

Morgan, Sir Frederic 350–1

Moro-Giafferi, Vincent de 53

Mott, Nevill 55–9, 63, 87, 179, 183

MSN papers 241, 281

Münzenberg, Willi 44, 52

M.W. Kellogg 28, 121

Nagasaki 160, 162, 164, 165, 167,

171, 172, 201, 218, 249, 258, 261, 350, 354, 368

NATO 265, 358

Nazi-Soviet non-aggression pact 49, 68, 70, 84

Nazis 1–3, 7, 13, 17, 22–3, 24, 25, 35–43, 45, 48, 49, 52, 58–61, 65, 67, 68, 70, 72, 77, 86, 87, 91, 92, 106, 150, 153, 185, 187, 244, 331, 332

Nitschke, Lieutenant 357

NKGB 2, n2, 7–10, 72, 102, 104, 126–7, 130, 133, 151–2, 165–6, 177, 180–1, 203, 204–10, 213, 215, 219, 221, 223–9, 231, 233, 241, 256, 259–61, 263, 267, 274, 306–7, 313–14, 316, 351, 358–61, 363, 365

   agents in the US 151–2

   see also Gold, Harry ("Raymond")

   contacts with KF *see under* Fuchs, Klaus, contacts with Soviet intelligence

   Department S 210

   suspension of New York spying operation 204–5

Noske, Gustav 34

Nova Scotia 69

nuclear fission 17, 77–8, 81, 86, 87, 96, 103, 121, 138, 143, 146, 151, 152, 160, 167, 174, 176, 199, 218, 223, 266, 314, 352–4, 368

nuclear fusion 167, 174, 175, 182, 220–1, 222, 223, 265, 351–5, 368–9

nuclear physics, development of 14, 15, 57–8, 65

nuclear proliferation 10–11, 214, 355, 370

nuclear reactors 4, 17, 21–2, 87–8, 109, 112, 135, 138, 152, 168, 180, 183, 191–2, 195–6, 202–3, 208, 213–14, 217, 225–6, 243, 255–7, 265, 282, 294, 314, 358–9, 360, 368

   fast-breeder reactors 217, 270–1

   heavy-water reactors 102, 107, 116, 217

nuclear weapons *see* atomic bomb; hydrogen bomb

Nunn May, Allan 30, 102, 152, 181–2, 183, 185, 191, 204, 206, 214, 218, 226

Oak Ridge 28, 122, 129, 147, 149, 209

Official Secrets Act 274, 317, 329

OGPU 2n, 72, 126, 185

   see also NKGB

Oliphant, Marcus 77–8, 115, 123, 170, 294

one-time pads 241

Oppenheimer, Robert 17, 112–13, 116, 136, 137, 139, 143, 147, 149, 151, 156, 167–9, 190, 243, 266, 370

Palestine protectorate 193

Panfilov, Aleksei 90

Papen, Franz von 37, 38–9

Parker, Jean 140

Party Control Commission of the Socialist Unity Party (SED) 356

Pearl Harbor 73, 96, 111

Pegram, George 110

Peierls, Genia 78, 92, 140, 187–8, 207, 235, 290, 318, 320–1

Peierls, Rudolf 14, 17, 22, 27, 31, 63, 78–82, 86–90, 92–7, 104, 109, 110, 112, 113–19, 122–4,

129, 131, 135–8, 144, 154, 156,
167, 168, 169–70, 173, 178–80,
185–8, 194, 198–9, 217, 236–7,
246, 248, 254, 271, 278, 280,
281, 283, 303, 315, 316,
318–21, 365, 370
Penney, William 20, 149, 158–9,
171, 192–201, 217, 218, 249,
253, 310–1. 313, 347–51, 354,
368,
Perrin, Michael 89, 112, 116,
118–19, 135, 242–3, 280–1,
283–4, 287, 293–5, 302–3,
307–17, 320, 322, 327–9, 335,
339, 342, 344, 351, 360, 367
Pervukhin, Mikhail 152–3
Philby, Kim 84, 360
phone-tapping 144, 244, 246,
254, 270, 272, 283, 289, 290,
299, 307, 311, 312, 318
Physics Institute, Moscow 223,
353
Pieck, Wilhelm 48, 49
Pike, Herbert 200, 350
Pilley, Angela 206
Placzek, Else 182
plane waves 198
plutonium 3, 4, 14, 16, 22, 107,
109, 112, 113, 115, 135, 138,
143–4, 146, 147–8, 151–2, 154,
160, 165, 176, 191–2, 195–6,
199, 201–3, 208, 213–14, 225,
226, 243, 255–8, 260, 270–1,
350, 353, 368
plutonium bomb 19, 22, 107,
137–8, 140, 142–3, 146, 147–9,
151–2, 154, 158–60, 165, 166,
170, 172, 176, 191–2, 195–6,
198–202, 218–20, 223, 255–8,
260–2, 264, 312, 314, 327,
350, 353, 354, 355
100 Ton Shot 149, 151

core design 142–3, 151, 154,
172, 175, 195–6, 198
explosive power 143, 152, 154,
156, 157
"Fat Man" 156, 157, 159, 160,
171
initiators 148, 151, 160, 195–6,
199, 200, 201, 261, 262,
309, 313
"Joe 1" 349
Soviet bomb 255–67
Trinty Test 13–20, 149, 151,
154, 156, 162, 165, 171–2,
194, 201, 249, 258, 354
see also Manhattan Project
Pohle, Vera 269
polonium 127, 131, 134, 135, 171,
174, 176, 273 143, 148, 151, 170,
195, 199, 202, 313
Portal, Lord 186–7, 192–4, 197,
199, 202, 242, 280, 285, 293,
294, 309, 311, 328, 348, 349
Potsdam Conference (1945) 153–7,
166, 255, 355
Pritt, D.N. 357
Pronsky, D.N. 359

Quaker movement 22–3, 34, 55,
63, 69, 92, 179, 235–6, 275, 322
quantum mechanics 55–7, 60, 62,
174, 260
Quebec Agreement (1943) 114,115,
134, 135, 153

Rabi, Isidor 155
radar 78, 104, 109, 160
Radium Institute 103
Radó, Sándor 75
RDX high explosive 126
Reichsbanner 35
Reichstag fire (1933) 40, 47, 48,
53

Ripel, Hans 99–100
Robertson, James 243–6, 248–50, 254, 269–70, 272, 274–6, 278, 281–3, 285, 289, 302–5, 307–8, 310, 313–15, 317
Robson-Scott, Mr 94
Rodin, Nikolai 325
Roosevelt, Franklin D. 15, 17, 110, 111, 113, 114, 134, 153
Rosenberg, Ethel 209, 356
Rosenberg, Julius 209, 356
Rote Hilfe (Red Aid) 42
Rowlands, Sir Archibald 296, 308, 311, 328
Royal Canadian Mounted Police 26
Royal Institution 249, 251–2
Royal Ordnance factory, Woolwich 194
Royal Society 62, 85, 184, 301
Rutherford, Ernest 14, 15, 60, 103

SA *see* Sturmabteilung
Sakharov, Andrei 353, 354
Sakharovsky, Lieutenant General Alexander 361
Sarov 256
Savchenko, Sergei 210
Schreiber, Kurt ("Kaspar") 94, 98, 99
Scientific Advisory Committee (UK) 88–9, 104, 153, 280
Scott, Eleanor 273
Seaborg, Glenn 191
Seaton, Roger 327
Second World War, outbreak of 59, 67–8
Secret Intelligence Service (SIS) *see* MI6
Semipalatinsk 258, 261, 264
Semyonov, Semyon ("Sam") 126, 129

Serpell, Michael 118, 119, 184–8, 190, 227, 229, 244, 324,
70 Club 99
Shawcross, Sir Hartley 326, 329–32
Shelepin, Alexander 358, 360
Shishkin, Mikhail 210–11
Siebert, Hans 207
Signals Intelligence Service (US) 240–2, 335
Sillitoe, Sir Percy 276, 296, 308, 326
Simon, Franz 87, 89, 95, 97, 115, 124, 135
Skardon, William "Jim" 2, 23–31, 50–1, 83, 85, 227–9, 245–7, 249–50, 270, 274, 278, 280–9, 290–4, 296–8, 303–16, 322–8, 331, 335–40, 343–6, 351, 357, 360, 364–8, 371
Skinner, Erna 57, 230, 232, 234–6, 246, 250–4, 268–70, 272–4, 282, 283, 290, 298, 299, 300–1, 304, 311, 314, 321–2, 361, 366
Skinner, Herbert 22, 57, 179, 183, 216, 230–2, 234, 236, 246, 248, 250, 252–4, 267, 271, 273–4, 284, 290, 294, 299, 300–4, 311, 319, 321–2, 337, 366
Skyrme, Tony 27, 122, 198, 281, 343
Slade, Dr 89
Slotin, Louis 257
Smyth Report 210, 257
Social Democratic Party of Germany (SPD) 23–6, 61, 187, 356
Society for the Protection of Science and Learning 60–1, 62, 63, 73, 78

Sorge, Richard 75

Soviet atomic programme 2–3, 4, 7, 105–8, 152–3, 166, 194, 210, 211, 223, 226, 255–67, 314, 327, 347, 349, 353–5,

Soviet Cultural Appreciation Society 59

Soviet Union
Berlin blockade 30, 237, 348
collapse of 10
Comintern 42, 44–8, 72, 108, 355, 365
intelligence services *see* GRU; NKGB; OGPU
Nazi-Soviet non-aggression pact 49, 68, 70, 84, 86
show trials 59
Soviet-KPD collaboration 72, 100
territorial expansion 153

Spanish Civil War 59, 72, 231

Spartacists 33

SPD *see* Social Democratic Party of Germany

Springfields 22, 192, 280, 316

Stalin, Joseph 36, 49, 59, 68, 70, 84, 85, 103, 104, 105, 106, 126, 141, 152, 153, 156–7, 166, 193–4, 205, 221, 234, 240, 255, 258, 260, 263

Starikov, Lieutenant 358

Stasi 357, 361

Stephens, W. 94–5

Stimson, Henry 155, 156

Storrier, David 248–50, 253, 307

Sturmabteilung (SA) 35, 36, 37, 39–40

Sudoplatov, Pavel 210, 215

Sukholmin (Soviet scientist) 229, 360

Sukhumi 10, 230, 231

Swan, Johnston 93

Sweeney, Major Charles 160

Szilárd, Leó 17–18

Tamm, Igor 223, 353

Taylor, Geoffrey 198

Tehran Conference (1943) 206

Teller, Edward 14, 19, 111, 137, 167, 174–5, 177, 190, 213, 265–6, 351–3, 368

Terletsky, Yakov 210–11, 221

Thälmann, Ernst 41, 46, 48

thermonuclear weapons *see* hydrogen bomb

Thompson, George 80

Tinian 158–60, 171

Tizard, Sir Henry 80, 109, 348

Trinity gadget 79, 167, 169, 172, 194, 200, 201

Trinity Test 13–20, 149, 151, 154, 156, 162, 165, 171–2, 194, 201, 249, 258, 354

tritium 175, 176, 220–1, 223, 224, 265, 352, 353–4

Truman, Harry S. 15, 153–4, 156–7, 255, 264, 265, 266

Truman administration 193, 216, 349

Tube Alloys Directorate 78, 79, 84, 85, 86, 88, 94, 97, 98–9, 101, 109, 119, 136, 153, 155, 160, 161, 177, 178, 183, 184, 185, 202, 244, 256, 281, 293–4

Tuckett, Angela 207

Ulam, Stanislaw 156, 167, 173, 177, 352

Ulbricht, Walter 48, 359

uranium 9, 65, 77–9, 81, 87–88, 96–7, 103–4, 105, 100, 112–14, 129, 135, 137–8, 143, 144, 146, 148, 151
enrichment 22, 28, 97, 104,

107–8, 135, 139, 147, 169, 192, 196, 202, 208, 243, 342, 351
  separation 78-9, 81, 89, 93, 95, 112–13, 121–3, 129, 134–5
  uranium 235 78-9, 81, 88, 95, 109, 112, 117, 123, 137–8, 147, 148, 152, 156, 165, 175, 181, 192, 220, 264
  uranium 238 81, 88, 195, 199, 203
uranium bomb 88–9, 138, 139, 147, 148, 175
  "Little Boy" 156–9
Urey, Harold 110
US atomic programme 109–13, 222, 349–50, 351–2, 354, 355, 370
  see also Anglo-American atomic collaboration; Manhattan Project

V bombers 349
Vannikov, General Boris 210, 222
Venona decrypts 240, 278, 296
Victory in Europe Day 150
Volodya (chauffeur) 219
von Neumann, John 138, 144,

174-5, 177, 352, 368
Vyshinsky, Andrei 59

Wagner, Giselle 269, 322
Weisskopf, Victor 216
Werner, Ruth *see* Kuczynski, Ursula
West, Rebecca 1
White, Dick 24, 187–8, 242–3, 262, 274–6, 277, 282–3, 289, 302, 307–8, 310–11, 313–16, 318, 327–8, 367–8
Wills, Henry Overton 62,
Wills Laboratory 55, 57
Windscale 22, 192, 199, 201, 208, 213–14, 225
Wright, Peter 24

Yakovlev, Anatoly ("John") 129–33, 141, 144–6, 165, 205
Yapou, Eliezer 253

Zabotin, Colonel Nikolai 180
Zavenyagin, General Avraami 210, 260–2
Zeldovich, Yakov 91, 194, 195, 226 103, 222–3, 259
  Zhukov, Marshal Georgi 157